PREFACE

IF any apology were needed for making a Pedigree, we have at all events Scriptural authority for doing so: "Enquire, I pray thee, of the former Age, and prepare thyself to the search of their fathers."

But in truth the apology is no more needed than for writing History, for the true Pedigree is History. It is true that there are bogus pedigrees, and a legion of people who concoct them; but they are unworthy of notice, and are only ridiculous and pale shadows of the genuine pedigree, made up as they are of generations of forefathers who never lived or, if they did, were entirely other than they are represented to be. There is, too, the pedigree written entirely from the unworthy motive of pride, with the mistaken object of enhancing the status and vainglory of the last link, who has contributed nothing to the work of former generations, and whom very possibly former generations might disown.

But what light does the historical pedigree—even if it be a short one, or one of persons generally considered to be of no account—throw on the history of a Nation? And a long one, going back to the First Crusade, is History in brief, made more interesting and more fascinating by its human and personal element. It is like a lamp which lights up dim portraits in a long corridor, and doorways which lead into long closed rooms filled with the furniture of bygone days: or it may be likened to a Rosary every bead of which is fragrant with the memory of tears and prayers.

Few pedigrees are of greater interest, from an historical point of view, than those of Huguenot families, for they touch the history of two countries, and are as a rule those of men and women who stood apart from the common herd in more or less degree, and whose lives are a record of continued struggle against the tyranny of Church and State: "That old Huguenot phalanx who, from father to son, were always ready for death."

Whether they are the histories of great families or smaller ones, of those of high rank and ancient name, or of lesser folk, honourable, steadfast, honest and of strong character, who by their numbers were the leaven which leavens the lump, and who, to a far greater extent than is supposed, helped to make England what she is.

For the Huguenot immigration was not that of a few thousand refugees who settled at Rye, Sandwich and Dover, but a swarm which commenced to flee to this country, Holland, Germany and Switzerland, in the middle of the sixteenth century, and continued to come up to the French Revolution. A rough calculation, based on the records still existing of church registers and acts of naturalization and the records still extant in France, places their numbers between 1550 and 1789 at a conservative estimate of 250,000; a not extravagant estimate when one takes into account the large families they had. The Threadneedle Street French church, whose registers begin in 1600 and end in 1840, contains thirty thousand entries of births and marriages. The Canterbury French church has about the same number. London alone had forty refugee churches. The Bristol French church was one of the smaller churches, and its registers, beginning in 1687 and ending in 1744, contain 600 entries. Then there were churches at Plymouth and Stonehouse; Exeter, whose registers are lost; Dublin, Portarlington, whose registers exist; and very many others of which they are lost; with smaller settlements all over the southern half of England, which serve as a basis for calculation, which the Returns of Fugitives sent in by the Intendants of provinces show to be fairly correct, if one takes five as the average in a family. When one considers that the population of Great Britain at the end of the eighteenth century was under 6,000,000, the infusion of French blood was of such proportions as to have influenced the character of the English race very considerably from the physical point of view alone: especially as the refugees, for two generations at least, married very largely among themselves, and had large families, the mortality amongst the children, so far as can be judged from a comparison between the English and French registers, being much smaller.*

The French Returns of Fugitives from 1680 to 1685 show that the greater number fled in the years 1682–1683. It is to

* Or to put the calculation in another way: assuming that 50,000 marriages took place between 1550 and 1789, and a mean of five to the family, we get the figure of 250,000 of purely French blood.

HUGUENOT PEDIGREES

By CHARLES E. LART

FELLOW OF THE ROYAL HISTORICAL SOCIETY
FELLOW OF THE HUGUENOT SOCIETY of LONDON
MEMBRE CORRESPONDANT DE LA SOCIÉTÉ DES ARCHIVES DE POITOU

Editor of
"Jacobite Extracts from the Parochial Registers of St. Germain-en-Laye." The "Protestant Registers of Caen : Loudun : Le Rochebeaucourt," etc.

VOL. I

"O Seigneur, Tu as été notre Refuge
de l'une génération à l'autre."

CLEARFIELD

Originally published
London, 1924–1925

Reprinted for
Clearfield Company, Inc. by
Genealogical Publishing Co., Inc.
Baltimore, Maryland
1992, 1995, 1997, 2002

Library of Congress Catalogue Card Number 67-28595
International Standard Book Number: 0-8063-0207-0

Made in the United States of America

be remembered that the Revocation of the Edict of Nantes was only the final and culminating blow, and had been preceded by Edict after Edict, each of which curtailed some privilege granted to Protestants by Henry IV and caused an increase in the emigration.

It is a curious fact that the great nobles, such as the families of La Rochefoucauld—of which three separate branches came to England—of Duras, Ruvigny, Bourbon-Malauze and others, left no posterity who continued their great traditions and emulated their history. The great sailors and soldiers, like Gambier, the three Ligoniers, and a host of others of lesser note: the inventors, engineers, divines, writers, actors, lawyers, like Brunel, Jacquard, Casaubon, Thélusson, D'Urfey, Garrick, Romilly, all came from the ranks of the lesser families—the "petite noblesse," the merchants, bankers and artisans.

There is nothing about which there has been so much misconception as the question of "noblesse." There is no analogy between the English nobility of to-day and the French "noblesse" of the sixteenth and seventeenth centuries. The English nobility begins with the baron: the lowest rank of the French noblesse was the "écuyer," or esquire—"armiger." It was the rank of "écuyer" which alone constituted nobility. "Noblesse," in the reign of Louis XIV was more analogous to the peerage, baronetcy, knightage and landed gentry of to-day—with the added resemblance that the easiest way of acquiring it was by money, either by the purchase of a "fief" or some official post, such as "conseiller" or "secrétaire du Roy." The baron, comte, etc., was merely a seigneur—"écuyer"—whose property was a barony, etc., larger than a parish.

The terms of French nobility are not analogous to modern English terms. "Ecuyer" and "esquire" certainly are near relations; but "seigneur," always translated literally "lord," is not always synonymous with "earl" or "baron," but generally simply "lord of the manor." Neither was "gentilhomme" the equivalent of "gentleman," which usually signifies a person of education, manners or social position; the French term being strictly applied to those of ancient race—though not necessarily of means or great landed property—whose origin was lost in the Night of Time. It was the one title which even the King could not create : for, though he could create an " écuyer " by Letters-Patent or by sign manual on the skin of a drum, as Henry of Navarre did on the field of Coutras, he could not make a " gentilhomme," who was the product of race and time : nor could he unmake him, for " once a gentilhomme always a gentilhomme."

" Noble homme " is generally taken to mean " noblesse " ; but, although it did so in earlier days, it had long ceased to do so in the seventeenth century, and was then universally used to designate a bourgeois who had bought a fief. The term " bourgeois " itself never was used in a derogatory sense, but simply to denote a non-noble person. In the thirteenth and fourteenth centuries it was an honour sought by great nobles to be made " bourgeois " of some town, and was then equivalent to " freeman."* Seigneur and sieur originally were the same, but in the seventeenth century " sieur " is invariably used in deeds when speaking of a bourgeois who owned a fief, while " seigneur " is used to denote an esquire or one of higher rank.

Feudalism lasted till the Revolution as an organised system and died a violent death, and did not, as in England, undergo a gradual change ; but it had entirely lost its old original life and vigour. Its functions had been taken over by the bureaucratic system of centralization perfected by Louis XIV, who carried out on a larger scale the idea of curbing the power of the Nobility, which had often before curbed the power of the Throne. By opening the door still wider to the coveted rank of " écuyer " he created a multitude of small seigneurs and " anoblis," while he attracted the higher nobility to his Court at Versailles, where they basked in the splendours of " Le Roi Soleil." The King smiled on his courtiers, but ruled France through his Intendants.

But, though the feudal system was sapped of its former strength and usefulness as an administrative system, it still retained its old forms. " Nulle terre sans seigneur, nul seigneur sans terre " was still in theory the rule. Nobility derived from the possession of a fief, and was not a personal and hereditary rank in essence.

In earlier days the possession of a " terre " implied

* X . . . bourgeois, de Caen, *means* X . . . bourgeois by status, of Caen ; *but* X, bourgeois de Caen, *is* X . . ., freeman of Caen.

obligations. The seigneur was the administrator of his territory, over which he was lord, holding his Court and administering justice, even to life and death. He was subject to his over-lord, whom he followed to the wars, with such vassals as he was called upon to bring in obedience to " ban " and " arrière-ban." He was also responsible for defending his vassals and tenants against attacks on their rights. Exempt from taxation himself, he paid the blood tax, or " impôt du sang," and paid for his privileges by personal service. As province after province became subject to the Crown as over-lord, instead of a number of semi-independent and often rebellious petty principalities and dukedoms, more and more power passed into the hands of the King. The abjuration of Henry of Navarre brought his kingdom into that of France, and the last of the independent provinces, Roussillon, came finally under the French Crown in the reign of Louis XIV—the first King of France who was able to say with truth " L'état, c'est moi."

The Crusades and the religious wars of the sixteenth century had done their part in weakening the feudal nobility, in whose ranks many gaps had arisen ; and it had become necessary from time to time to repair them, since the administration of the country suffered. Louis XIV, though he wished to weaken the power of the feudal system, had no intention of reducing it, but to mould it to his own ends, and at the same time to raise more money for his wars and ambitious schemes. He therefore opened fresh roads to " noblesse," and enlarged those already existing.

Impoverished by the wars of religion and desirous of raising money to live at Court, the greater nobility as well as lesser, were selling or mortgaging their estates to the rich merchants of the towns. Anyone who had money to invest bought a fief or even part of one.* The " noble fief " was

* A parallel is found in Jersey and the Channel Islands. Anyone can buy a seigneurie or manorial fief in the market and call himself " Seigneur de La Trinité," " de La Ferte," etc., because he becomes *de jure* and *de facto* its seigneur. He is not, however, a " lord " in the sense that a baron or peer of the realm is a " lord," but is a lord of the manor. If he sells it he ceases to be its seigneur.

The title of " Vicomte de Jersey " was not a nobiliary title, but an administrative one, equivalent to bailiff : " Vice-comitis," the deputy of the Comte, or Earl.

exempt from taxation, and the new owner hastened to acquire " noblesse," by one or other of the many means now opened up : generally by buying an " office " or " charge " such as " secrétaire " or " conseiller."

The possession of noble fief did not necessarily confer an immediate nobility—in other words, make the owner an esquire. It was necessary to hold it for three generations—*i.e.*, " homage à tierce foy " : he became an " anobli," and is spoken of as " noble homme " in official documents : in other words, it " took three generations to make a gentleman."

We can study the same process in every village churchyard in England to-day. The local maltster or big farmer or merchant—all honour to him !—put his son into the Law, and he, in his turn, sent his son to a public school or college—and died a " gent," as his tombstone records ; the son makes a good marriage, enters the Army or Church, and the process is completed, although the third generation is often inferior to the founder of the family, whose worth and character are not always transmitted to his descendants.

These facilities for increasing the number of petty seigneurs led to unforeseen evils in the succeeding century ; for the roturier, whether peasant or artisan, had to bear the whole burden of taxation, and, the call of ban and arrière-ban having fallen into desuetude, the whole of military service fell on his shoulders, one of the causes, as de Tocqueville shows, of the Revolution. They also led to a flood of unauthorised claimants.

To the early creation of " noblesse " by " chevalerie " and the direct investiture for personal services by the king, and " noblesse par fief à tierce foy," were added nobility by " Lettres Patentes " and " Lettres d'Anoblissement " registered in the Cour des Aides : " noblesse de robe " by legal office : " noblesse par finance," or the holding of a post under the provincial treasury, this being bought and farmed out to subordinates, a favourite method of acquiring the rank of " écuyer."

These last " charges anoblissantes " were divided into three classes : (i) those which conferred an immediate nobility, transmissible to descendants ; (ii) those which conferred nobility transmissible after a certain number of years—which was twenty years in the case of presidents, councillors and other officials of the Grand Conseil ; (iii) those which gave hereditary title to esquire after three generations—*i.e.*, " à tierce foy."

The splitting up of large domains gave rise to a multitude of small seigneuries and fiefs, a process which reached its highest point under Louis XIV. This phase of social life is severely criticised by Molière in his *Ecole de Dames* :—

" Je sais un paysan qu'on appelait Gros-Pierre
Qui, n'ayant pour tout bien qu'un seul quartier de terre,
Y fit tout à l'entour faire une fosse bourbeux
Et de Monsieur de l'Isle en prit le nom pompeux."

One of the necessary conditions incumbent on the " anobli " was to " live nobly " and not to commit any " acte de derogéance," one of which was to pay taxes. The Edict of 1656 directly imposed the payment of taxes every 40 years, partly in order to stop the multiplication of petty seigneurs, and partly to raise money.

Since all the world was flocking to acquire " noblesse," and the title was being assumed by a large number of persons who had no right to it, a " Recherche de Noblesse," or Visitation, was ordered by the King to be made in 1666–68, in each province, under d'Hozier, King of Arms, through the Intendants. All who claimed or used the title of " écuyer " were ordered to attend and show their proofs. Those who could not produce any were fined as " usurpateurs," and forbidden to lay claim to the rank. Few of the old noblesse attended, deeming it derogatory, and were fined ; but no other steps were taken, since their claims were beyond dispute, and they were not, as in the other case, " renvoyés."

The rank of " esquire," however, did not necessarily raise its possessor to an equality with the older families. The honours of Court, for instance, were reserved for those who could trace unbroken descent from the year 1400, without known " anoblissement." In the eighteenth century the same condition was imposed for commissions in the Maison du Roy : a descent from the year 1500 was necessary to become a Page in the Royal stables : four degrees of noblesse for a commission in the Marine regiment : three degrees for the troops of the Colonies : four degrees for entrance into the Royal schools : one hundred and forty years of noblesse for St. Cyr.

Admission to the orders of knighthood was severely restricted : nine degrees of nobility on the father's side were required by the Order of Saint Lazare. The Order of Malta required eight quarterings on the father's and eight on the mother's side.

Some misconception is prevalent as to the right to claim the title of Baron, Comte, etc., by families of Huguenot descent from an émigré who bore the title. Since the title of "Baron," "Comte" or "Marquis" was purely a territorial and administrative one, it followed that if a family in the person of the chief, no longer possessing a barony, comté or marquisat to administer, lost by any means the "terre," they no longer called themselves seigneurs of it, an exception, of course, being in the case of the esquire, where a family had held a fief so long that they were known by the name of the seigneurie and not by their family name, which in the case of some had long fallen out of mind. But it was the "terre" or seigneurie which was erected into a barony or marquisat, and not the person who possessed it.

In all cases where by death or partition the barony or marquisat passed out of the hands of a family who had possessed it, the title of Baron, Comte or Marquis passed to the next holder, if he held the original seigneurie which had been "erected" into a barony, etc.

As a matter of fact, the original owner, even if he sold or alienated the greater part, retained his title as long as he still kept the château and châtellenie. Although he might only be co-seigneur, he reserved the honours—*i.e.*, the "litre," or funeral enclosure—the family tomb—and "bancs et droits d'encensements" in the church, and the "droits d'aubaine," "lods et ventes," "prescriptions," etc.

In the eighteenth century nobles at Court began to assume the title of Baron, Comte, etc., before their family names, and in the nineteenth century, in the case of titles of the Restauration, the custom grew ; but in the reign of Louis XIV this was not so. St. Simon, in his *Mémoires*, protested against this usage as an absurdity.

The highest French authorities on the French noblesse

are unanimous on this point, that the title depended on the "terre," and was not intrinsically a personal one, and could not exist without it.

The refugee himself was known by his title—though not always—as a matter of courtesy, since there was a certain doubt as to whether he might not be allowed to return and be reinstated; but he could not, and did not, transmit it to his descendants.

It is not, however, to nobility of race, but to nobility of character, that the Huguenot pedigree owes its interest. With the steadfastness of the Puritan or Catholic, the Huguenot combined a cheerful gaiety of character and "élan" which certainly the Puritan did not possess, and, in addition, a steadfast loyalty to the King who had persecuted them so cruelly—a loyalty, we may safely say, which was never entertained by Puritan, Covenanter or Catholic.

In the year 1778 M. de Villiers, sub-delegate of the Intendance of Orléans, was ordered to make a report on alleged scandalous assemblies, "opposées aux lois et aux ordonnances du Royaume." The complaint was made by the curé of Chatillon-sur-Loire, who petitions the King to forbid meetings of Protestants "qui scandalisent avec raison les Bons Catholiques."

M. de Villiers summoned the chief Protestants of Chatillon and held an enquiry, after which he sent a report to the King. The report is a long one, but one point reported is interesting and bears on this question. One of the rules of these meetings which so scandalised good Catholics, more especially, and more probably solely, the curé of Chatillon, was the following: "de les édifier, de les instruire en commun, de prier Dieu pour le Roi et toute la famille roialle: pour la tranquillité de son état: pour tous hommes qui sont nos frères."

And this was after more than two hundred years of persecution far worse and more cruel than Puritan or Catholic non-juror ever had to suffer, and after Jean Calas had been publicly broken on the wheel only eighteen years previously.

It was not the King, but his councillors, against whom the French refugees took up arms in the service of England, Holland and Germany; and, in spite of all their enemies could say or do against them, they coined the saying " Foy d'un huguenot "—who always kept his word.

" C'est mon plaisir " is the motto of a noble family: " C'est mon devoir " is a better one; and it has been, in the main, the motto of our Huguenot ancestors, some of whose pedigrees are here recorded.

* * * * * *

The Editor does not claim that a pedigree is complete or without errors—no pedigree can ever be so. The object has been to write as complete and exact a one as is possible from unpublished as well as printed sources, as a basis and material for future history, especially from MS. sources; for printed works are scattered all over the world, and can be preserved, while MSS. are unique and are kept in one place, and their loss is irreparable. With the prospect of aerial warfare of the future, it is certain that many stores of MS. archives will be irremediably lost.

The basis of many of the pedigrees is the MS. and printed works of d'Hozier, Anselme, de Courcelles and other official authorities; but wherever a pedigree has been in whole or in part reprinted, it has been enriched with additions and notes. D'Hozier and other official authorities generally ignored or only partially mentioned Protestant branches, which were counted as dead and extinct, and their memory blotted out.

The Editor takes this opportunity of acknowledging his indebtedness and thanks to the President and Council of the Huguenot Society of London for allowing him to reprint and use some of those pedigrees published in their " Proceedings," and to Mr. Wagner, their author. In no case is any one published in this series without addition and correction. He also begs to acknowledge his indebtedness to all authors, living and dead, whose works have been consulted or laid under contribution, such as MM. Haag, Agnew, Lièvre and others.

No rigid and hard-and-fast rule has been followed in publishing a pedigree. A short one of only four or five generations is often as interesting as one of double that number, provided it bridges the gap between the family in France and in England, Holland and America. Neither has a pedigree always been continued to the present day, if sources readily accessible exist for that purpose. In some cases it has happened that it has been comparatively easy to write a complete pedigree of many generations in France, and one or two in England, whereas the task of bringing it down to the present day or to the end of the eighteenth century would entail many months of search and great expense. It is not the Editor's object to produce complete pedigrees to date in every case, but to preserve the testimony of unpublished and perishable manuscript sources.

In succeeding volumes it is proposed to add an appendix containing such fresh additions to previous pedigrees as may be found.

Although families will be distributed as far as possible in equal alphabetical sequence, no fixed rule will be observed, *i.e.*, more may be found under A, B or C, etc., than under other letters, or *vice-versa*.

In conclusion, the Editor wishes to offer his best thanks to all the authorities of the British Museum and Public Record Office, London; the Bibliothèque Nationale, Archives Nationales, and the Société de la Protestantisme Francaise, Paris; the archives of Amsterdam and Leyden, Holland, for their courtesy, help and advice. To the many Archivistes of Départements, and finally and specially to MM. l'Abbé du Bois, Dangibeaud, de Beaucorps, P. Beauchet Filleau, Bourde de la Rogeris, Guillemard, M. Kuhner, Luard, Mangin, Millot, de Morel, Pannier, Ravenel, le Comte de St. Saud, P. de Vaissière, le Vicomte de Vaux de La Foletière, M. N. Weiss, and to so many other kind friends, a list of whose names would fill many pages.

C. E. L.

Authors' Club,
2, Whitehall Court, S.W.1.

Abbreviations :—a.e.b.=a été baptisé or baptisée; b.=born, né; bapt.=baptised; sr.=sieur; sgr.=seigneur; daur.=daughter, fille; Dlle.=demoiselle; d.=died.

D'ABZAC

Arms : D'argent, à la bande d'azur, et à la bordure d'azur chargées de 9 besants d'or, 3, 3, and 3, d'azur.(A)

Alias, d'argent, à la bande d'azur, chargée d'un besant d'or : à la bordure du second chargée de 10 besants du troisième :

Alias de 8 besants d'or.

Crest : A bust of the Queen of Cyprus.

Known by various deeds and charters (abbeys of Cadoin, Uzerche, Dalon, etc.) from the beginning of the twelfth century. N. . . . d'Abzac gave lands to his wife 1100, and left Hélie and a daur. Hélie is named in a donation, 17 June 1158, to the chapel of Limeuil, and to the Abbey of Uzerche 1174. Jacques d'Abzac, Governor of Bergerac, 1187, etc. Charters of the Abbey of Dalon 1224, 1231, 1246.

First Branch de La Douze

I. Hugues d'Abzac, 1st of the name, damoiseau, sgr. in part de Clarens 1314. Ancestor of all the Branches of the family existing to-day ; mentioned in various deeds 1287–1317. Left among others :

II. Hugues d'Abzac, known by various deeds and charters, and by the part he took on the English side in the wars. Will dated 1360. He was buried in the church of Monzie, in the tomb of his ancestors. He married, 1st, Dlle. Marguerite de Neuville ; 2nd, Dlle. Alais de La Cropte, widow in 1st marriage of Pierre Vigier, a daur. of Fortanier de La Cropte, damoiseau d'Abzac, and of Ponce de Leuville. He left : (*a*) Gui, who succeeds, III.; (*b*) Hélie, damoiseau, of the parish of Monzie [1349]; (*c*) Adhémar, a monk, of Tourtoirac [1340]; (*d*) Marguerite, wife of Bernard de Porchmalet, 23 July 1348.

III. Gui d'Abzac, or Guinot, damoiseau, sgr. de Montastruc and other places, known by various deeds 1334–1364. Married Dlle. Bertrande de La Pradelle, of an ancient family of Couze, near Monleydier-sur-Dordogne. Qualified as Damoiseau de Monzie 17 July 1347. He left, among others : (*a*) Adhémar, IV., who succeeds ; (*b*) Hélie, celebrated in the annals of Guienne and the Crusades.

IV. Adhémar, or Aimar, d'Abzac, damoiseau, sgr. de La Douze, Montastruc, La Cropte, Bellegarde, Beauregard, Siorac, etc., well known in the wars of Guienne. D. after 15 Ap. 1414. He married, in 1373, Dlle. Guillemette, or Guillonne, de Boniface, daur. and heiress of Lambert de Boniface,(B) and left: (*a*) Olivier, who succeeds, V.; (*b*) Bertrand, author of the Branch of Montastruc; (*c*) Tristan, damoiseau, sgr. de Badefols-sur-Dordogne, Clarens and other places. Fought on the English side in the wars of Guienne; (*d*) Gantonnet, author of the Branch de La Prade; (*e*) Margnese, wife of Leonard de Graulier; (*f*) Brunissende, wife of Pierre Mosnier, damoiseau.

V. Olivier d'Abzac, sgr. de La Douze, de La Cropte, Rullac, Sénillac, Mayac and Beauregard, squire to Charles Duc d'Orléans, whom he followed in the wars in Burgundy. Married, by contract passed in the château of Saussignac in Périgord, Dlle. Jeanne de Barrière, daur. of Amalric de Barrière, chev., sgr. de Rullac, and of Dlle. Huguette de Guerre. This contract gives many details of his fiefs, lands and feudalities. He left by her: (*a*) Gui, or Guinot, who succeeds, VI.; (*b*) Hélie, chanoine; (*c*) Jean, damoiseau de Beauregard; (*d*) Jeanne.

VI. Gui d'Abzac, sgr. de La Douze, damoiseau, sgr. de La Douze, Rullac or Reillac, Sénillac, etc. B. 1400 or 1401. Made a contract with his brother Jean, 3 June 1447. Founded Masses for the souls of his father and mother and his aunt, the Marquise d'Abzac. He d. at La Douze, 10 Aug. 1478. In his will, dated 29 July 1478, he declares himself to be 78 years old. He married in 1425 or 1426 Dlle. Agnès de Montlouis, daur. of Pierre de Montlouis, sgr. de Labutat. She died 5 Nov. 1472, in her house at Périgueux, called "Rossal," and was buried in the chapel of the Cordeliers. By this marriage he left: (*a*) Pierre, Archbishop of Narbonne; (*b*) Jean, who succeeds in main line; (*c*) Hugues, a monk, prior of La Faye; (*d*) Jean, archpriest of St. Médard d'Excideuil; (*e*) Bernard, Canon of St. Etienne, Dean of St. Front, Périgueux; (*f*) Guillaume, Marquis de Mayac, author of the Branch de Mayac, VII.; (*g*) Jean, chev. of the order of St. John of Jerusalem, killed in a sea-fight against the infidels; (*h*) Jeanne, wife of Pierre de Goth, éc., sgr. de Pelatignoux;

(*i*) Louise, married, in 1408, Antoine de Carbonnières, éc., sgr. de Pellevezy; (*j*) Agnès, or Anne, wife of Jean de Grossolles, chev., sgr. de Flamarens and Baron de Montastruc; (*k*) Jeanne, wife of Raimond d'Aitz, sgr. de Meymy; (*l*)Catherine, married by contract dated 2 Sept. 1471, Antoine de Grossolles, son of Etienne, sgr. de Caumont en Lomagne.

VII. Guillaume d'Abzac, 6th son of Gui, sgr. de La Douze, and of Agnès de Montlouis, is known by many deeds and charters 1478–1517. His will is dated in his château of La Douze, 8 Feb. 1511, in favour of his children. He was still living 1 July 1517. Buried before the altar of St. Catherine in the church of St. Saturnin de Mayac. He married, 3 Sept. 1476, Dlle. Antoinette de La Cropte, daur. of the late Monot de La Cropte, sgr. de La Faye, and of Philippe Flamenc. Her will is dated 1 July 1517. They left: (*a*) François, who succeeds, VIII.; (*b*) Guillaume d'Abzac de Mayac, legatee of his father 1511; (*c*) Antoine, called the youngest son in his father's will; (*d*) Philippe, a nun of St. Clair, Toulouse, 1511; (*e*) Marie, ditto; (*f*) Antoinette, wife of Raymond de La Vergne; (*g*) Jeanne, wife of Jean de Comarque; (*h*) Hélène, wife of François de Ranconnet; (*i*) Alix, wife of Jean de Albusso; (*k*) Jeanne d'Abzac de Mayac (the younger), wife of Jean de Bayly, sgr. de Razac (in 2nd marriage).

VIII. François d'Abzac de la Douze, éc., sgr. de Mayac et de Limeyrac, universal heir of his father, 8 Feb. 1511. Known by various deeds and charters. He married, 7 Aug. 1511, Dlle. Sobiranne, or Souveraine, de Paleyrac, daur. of Bertrand de Paleyrac,(C) co-seigneur de St. Pompon, living at Belvès, near Sarlat. She made a will dated, in her château of La Roche-Jaubert, near Excideuil, 17 Aug. 1567, in favour of her children (*a*) Pierre, who succeeds, IX.; (*b*) Gui, curé of Gonzelles; (*c*) François, author of the Branch of Sarrazac and Limeyrac; (*d*) Gabriel, sgr. de La Chouzedis, who married Catherine de La Roche-Jaubert; (*e*) Guillaume, or Guillem, a monk; (*f*) Jeanne, who married, 16 May 1553, Jean de Maignac, sgr. de Mazerolles, in Angoumois, and de Boissic. He gave a receipt to Pierre d'Abzac, his brother-in-law, for the sum of 2,000 livres, as the marriage portion of his wife, dated 12 Sept. 1553.

IX. Pierre d'Abzac de Mayac, éc., sgr. de Mayac, etc., signed a contract, with his father, François d'Abzac, between himself and Raimond de Salignac his father-in-law, relating to the portion of Marguerite, his wife. He is known by deeds and charters of 1542, 1545, 1551, 1552, 1554, 1555, 1557, 1575. His will is dated 30 Oct. 1575, in the church of Mayac, where he is buried in the tomb of his ancestors. His wife, Marguerite, whom he married, 7 Sept. 1540, was the daur. of Raymond de Salignac,(D) éc., sgr. de Rochfort, in the Limousin, and of his wife, Dlle Françoise Béchide, Dame de Rochfort. Marguerite d'Abzac made her will at Mayac, 18 May 1572, in favour of her children: (*a*) François, who succeeds in the main line: (*b*) Gui, author of the Branch of Villars and St. Pardoux; (*c*) Bardin, author of the seigneurs de Cazenac and Mondiol,(E) X; (*d*) Souveraine d'Abzac de Mayac, married 18 Feb. 1564, François de Cussac, éc., sgr. de Cussac, near Bergerac, son of Jean de Cussac and Dlle. Jeanne de Martin; (*e*) Marguerite d'Abzac de Mayac, married, 18 Feb. 1571, Léonard Roux, éc., sgr. de Lussan and St. Front-la-Rivière, in Périgord, son of Pierre Roux, éc., sgr. de Lussan.

X. Bardin d'Abzac de Mayac, éc., sgr. de Limeyrac, Cazenac, Mondiol and other places,(F) 3rd son of Pierre, and Marguerite de Salignac de Rochfort, legatee of his father and mother by deeds dated 18 May 1572, and 30 Oct. 1575; married, by contract dated 5 Ap. 1592, Dlle. Françoise, Dame de Cazenac, in the parish of St. Coux-sur-Dordogne, and Mondiol. They made a joint will, Dec. 1617, in favour of their children: (*a*) Louis, who succeeds in his line; (*b*) Charles, author of the Branch of Bigaroque, Falgueyrac, etc.; (*c*) Henri, sgr. de Mondiol.

XI. Henri d'Abzac, éc., sgr. de Mondiol, lieut. in the company of Louis d'Abzac, his eldest brother, in the regiment de La Douze. He married, 1 Oct. 1639, Dlle. Anne de Baisselance, daur. of Jean de Baisselance,(G) Pasteur at Limeuil and Le Bugue, 1626–1637. They left: (*a*) Pierre, éc., sgr. de Mondiol, d. *s.p.* 26 Ap. 1667; (*b*) Marc,(H) XII.; (*c*) Henri, who left France at the Revocation and went to Ireland, where he married Dlle. Marie d'Abzac de La Boissière, sister of Jeanne-Isabeau d'Abzac de La Boissière, wife of his brother

Marc. Her sister Jeanne d'Abzac de la Forêt, b. at Le Bugue, in Périgord, *circ.* 1645, also came to Ireland with her nephew and niece about 1701, where she appears in the Dublin French church registers. (Will, P.C.C., Abbot, 130). D. 1729.

XII. Marc d'Abzac, éc., sgr. de Mondiol, b. 1655, married his cousin, Dlle. Jeanne-Isabeau d'Abzac de La Boissière, daur. of Isaac d'Abzac de La Boissière and of his wife Marguerite de Barraud du Fournil. He left by his wife, who was not living in 1714: (*a*) Jean, born at Limeuil in 1681; (*b*) Henri, b. at Limeuil,(I) XIII; (*c*) Catherine, who married, 9 July 1715, at the French church of Spring Garden, London, by licence, Isaac Blanché de Feyrac.(J)

XIII. Henri d'Abzac, éc., sgr. de Mondiol, born at Limeuil 11 Jan. 1677; d. at Dublin, March 1750; married Dlle. Magdeleine Elizabeth d'Ortoux, daur. of Captain d'Ortoux, at Dublin, in 1711. She d. there 14 Nov. 1763 (will dated 8 Aug. 1761. Pr. 29 Nov. 1763. P.C.I.). Henri d'Abzac was lieut. in General Stewart's Regt., 1704–5: major and captain of a company, 20 Dec. 1722, Otway's Foot: commission renewed in 1727: serving in 1736. His will is dated 6 March 1748. Pr. 6 June 1750. (P.C.C. 194, Greenly.) They had 8 children (see Dublin French church register): (*a*) Marc Henri, b. 30 Jan. 1712: presented by his grandfather, Marc d'Abzac, sgr. de Mondiol: d. young; (*b*) Jeanne Magdeleine, b. 6 June 1713: d. young; (*c*) Louise, b. 28 June, 1714: d. young; (*d*) Catherine, b. 1 Aug. 1715, wife of Major Edward Molesworth; (*e*) Henri Pierre, bapt. 4 Aug. 1717, d. 20 Aug. 1721; (*f*) Anne Victoire, b. 20 Nov. 1726: presented by Isaac de Feyrac and Dames Anne La Columbine and Victoire d'Abzac: d. 5 Ap. 1799; (*g*) Jeanne, born in Minorca: married, 19 Aug. 1761, at Dublin, Sir Morgan Crofton, Bart.: d. at Dublin 27 June 1798; (*h*) Henri-Joseph, who succeeds, XIV.

XIV. The Rev. Henry Joseph d'Abzac, D.D., Fellow of Trinity College, Dublin. Born in Minorca, 1737: d. 12 May, 1790. (Will dated 14 Nov. 1788. Prob. 27 May 1790. P.C.I.) He married Catherine, daur. of Colonel Pigou, 1 March 1774. She d. 12 Dec. 1818, aged 65. (Her will is dated 8 Nov. 1817. Prob. 31 Dec. 1818.) They had 12 children: (*a*) Marc Henry, b. 1784, d. 1803; (*b*) Henry, b. 1781, captain 45th Regt. of Dgns.: d. of wounds received at the battle of Albuera, 7 June 1811, aged 30: buried at Dublin, 9 June 1811: (*c*) Magdalen, d. 13 Aug. 1840: married, 11 Ap. 1803, Reuben Caillaud Mangin; (*d*) Catherine, bapt. at St. Anne's, Dublin, 10 Feb. 1776: d. 1850: married, in 1801, Alexander Mangin, of Southampton; (*e*) Harriett, bapt. at St. Anne's, Dublin, 29 Feb. 1777: buried there 1 March 1778; (*f*) Jane, d. 5 July 1801, aged 22: buried in the Huguenot Cemetery, Dublin; (*g*) Another Harriett, wife of Dr. Wilson, d. *s.p.* 1842; (*h*) Anne, d. 14 Feb. 1861: married 1825 the Rev. William Veysey; (*i*) Susanna (Suzette), d. 12 Jan. 1853, aged 68: buried in the Huguenot Cemetery, Dublin; (*j*) Julia, living unmarried in 1798; (*k*) Charles, d. young; (*l*) Colombine, d. young.

NOTES

The family of d'Abzac, one of the most ancient and illustrious families of Périgord, ramified into many branches, too numerous to cite. Several of its members went to the Crusades, and one was Archbishop of Narbonne (1484). Amongst its alliances were those of d'Hautefort, de Beaumont, de Chasteigner, de Boniface, de Gontaut, de Narbonne-Taleiran, de Bourbon-Malause.

(A) The English branch bear one besant.

(B) Arms: Ecartelé 1 and 4 d'or semé de fleurs de lys, azur (Boniface), 2 and 3, gueules, à la fasce d'or (de Vals).

(C) Arms: D'azur, à la croix d'argent, cantonnée de 4 pals d'or; à la bordure de gueules, chargée de 10 besants d'or. (Paleyrac).

(D) Arms: D'or, à 3 bandes de sinople. (Rochfort de Salignac).

(E) The branch of the seigneurs de Cazenac and Mondiol is omitted by d'Hozier in his Armorial General.

(F) Marguerite d'Abzac de Mayac et de Limeyrac, who married Louis Perry, sgr. de La Chaussée, was probably a daughter of Bardin d'Abzac. (La Chesnaye-des-Bois.)

(G) The Baisselance family sent Protestant members to England.

(H) de Courcelles is clearly wrong in making Henri d'Abzac the founder of the English Branch, instead of Marc.

(I) Naturalised 25 May 1702: " Henry Dabjac, son of Marc Dabjac, by Jane his wife, born at Limeulh in Guienne."

(J) Their son, Colonel Joseph Blanchard (Blancher) de Feyrac, d. 31 Jan. 1782, aged 66; buried 2 Feb. at Stephen's Green, near Merrion Row, Dublin; born 20 Ap. 1716; bapt. at Les Grecs French church, London. His godfathers were Joseph Comte de Vivans and Louis de Feyrac; godmother, Mlle. Jeanne Dabsat La Forest. The family of de Vivans came from the neighbourhood of Le Bugue. Nicolas Simeon d'Abzac, Vicomte de Gérac, d. 4 Dec. 1710. (Hug. Cemetery, Merrion Row, Dublin.)

The whole pedigree of d'Abzac will be found in d'Hozier, Anselme, etc.

BOYBELLAUD

Arms : D'azur, une arbre, d'argent.

I. Charles Boybellaud, or Boisbellaud, Juge d'Ozillac, in Saintonge, seneschal de La Châtellenie d'Ozillac in 1573. His wife is not known : he left two sons : (*a*) Hyppolite, who succeeds, II. ; (*b*) François, author of the Branch of Ozillac.

II. Hyppolite Boybellaud, sieur de La Morillière, left several children by his wife, whose name is not known, among others Pierre, who succeeds, III.

III. Pierre Boybellaud, sieur de La Morillière ; married, 9 June 1658, Dlle. Marie Richeteau, daur. of the Juge-Lieutenant of the Barony of La Fontaine, who brought in dowry 5,000 livres Tournois, and 300 livres of property. They left : (*a*) Jacques, who succeeds, IV. ; (*b*) Marie, wife of Jérémie Boybellaud, sieur des Lizards, Juge Seneschal des Roys et Puypellard en Fontaine, in 1668. Of the two daughters of Jérémie Boybellaud (i) Marie, married Pierre Françoys, avocat at Bordeaux ; (ii) Judith, married her cousin, Gaston Boybellaud.

IV. Jacques Boybellaud, sieur de La Morillière, married (i) Judith Maignac,(A) by whom he had 8 children, amongst whom (*a*) Philippe, Docteur en Médicine, who succeeds, V. ; (*b*) Jean, who left with his brother for Les Isles ; (*c*) Jérémie, a surgeon, who emigrated and practised at Port de Paix, Saint-Domingo : married in 1690 : he lived at Trois-Rivières, parish of N. Dame de Paix, and died there in August 1713 ; (*d*) Jacques, Procurator Fiscal of Jonsac in 1738. (ii) After the death of his first wife, Judith Maignac, Jacques Boybellaud married Jeanne Rivé, and d. 1709.

V. Philippe Boybellaud, Doctor, married his cousin Jeanne Maignac, of Fontguyon, parish of Antignac, and left 3 daurs. : (*a*) Jeanne, wife of Jean Sauvaistre ; (*b*) Suzanne, wife of Pierre Arnaud in 1733 ; (*c*) Catherine, wife of Jacques Boybellaud, sieur de La Chapelle.

BOYBELLAUD

Branch of Ozillac.

I. François Boybellaud, avocat, brother of Charles Boybellaud (*v. ante*), was born *circ.* 1530, and d. aged 63 in 1593. He had married before 1567 Louise Thibaudeau, daur. of Jean Thibaudeau, sieur de Cormier, near Saintes, and of Dlle. Jeanne de Prahec, by whom he left: (*a*) Denys, who succeeds, II.; (*b*) Jean, author of the branch of Montacier; (*c*) Christophe, Sergent Royal de La Châtellenie d'Ozillac, who married Hélise Péraud, and d. before 1612, leaving (i) Christophe, Sergent Royal, who married in 1612 Marie Jailler, daur. of Daniel Jailler and of Marie Amaniou; (ii) Jehan, a witness to the marriage contract of his brother Christophe, and who was a merchant tailor at Ozillac. This sub-branch migrated to Tugérac, in 1655, after the devastation caused by the troops of Condé.

II. Denys Boybellaud, b. *circ.* 1568, inherited the office of Notaire-Royal from his father, and replaced him as Procureur-Fiscal, 14 March 1594. He married Gabrielle Tiers in 1595, and had 4 children: (*a*) Denys, who succeeds, III.; (*b*) Séphora; (*c*) Daniel, sr. de Barbeyrac, d. 1671, leaving all his property to his niece Suzanne Boybellaud; (*d*) Catherine, wife of Etienne Jailler, Notaire-Royal. Denys Boybellaud d. in 1631 or 1632, aged 64, and left directions in his will to be buried in the cemetery of the "R.P.R." near his wife: he left 6 livres for the poor of the Protestant Church.

III. Denys Boybellaud, 2nd of the name, married in 1621 Anne Moreau, by whom he had 6 children: (*a*) Jean, who succeeds, IV.; (*b*) Denys, sr. des Combes, a soldier, d. at Paris 27 Nov. 1660; (*c*) Jean-Jérémie, sieur des Lizards, Notaire-Royal in 1678, Juge-Lieutenant of the Barony of Ozillac, and Juge Sénéchal des Roys et Puypellard, married in 1671 Dlle. Marie Boybellaud, daur. of Pierre Boybellaud, sr. de La Morillière (or Mouillière), and of Marie Richeteau; (*d*) Gabrielle, d. Sept. 1694, at Pignes; (*e*) Marie, wife of Guy Pryou, surgeon at Ozillac; (*f*) Suzanne, wife of Abel Boybellaud, sr. de La Parge. Denys Boybellaud, III, was nominated Procurator Fiscal for the Marquis d'Ozillac, on the death of his father, in 1632, by Léon de Sainte-Maure, Comte de Jonsac, Marquis d'Ozillac.

IV. Jean Boybellaud, sieur de La Poyserie, b. 1622, was Procurator in the Court of Parlement of Guienne. He abjured Protestantism at St. Vincent de Marcillac, 22 Aug. 1647. Married, 29 Aug. 1647, Jeanne Chastillier, by whom he left 6 children: (*a*) Anne, d. young; (*b*) Gaston, who succeeds, V.; (*c*) Hyppolite, who married, 23 Feb. 1680, Daniel Jailler, sieur de La Chaillauderie, son of Jean Jailler, sieur de La Chaillauderie, and of Marie Amaniou; (*d*) Hector, sieur de Puylaudard,(B) a captain in the regiment of St. Pol, and in the regiment de Navarre in 1688: he had abjured, but his conversion was renounced owing to the influence of his family: he soon afterwards fled to England, where he died, 10 Aug. 1703; he had made a division of his property with his brothers and sisters, and received a share of 1,600 livres; (*e*) Marie-Anne-Alexe, wife of Jean Caunière, sr. du Sort: she had 4 children.

V. Gaston Boybellaud, b. 1649, avocat en Parlement, lived at La Réole. He married, 1st, 18 June 1676, Armie de Cazeaux, widow of Jean Babin, sieur Desmaries, daur. of Pierre de Cazeaux, Minister at Saintes, and of Esther Moreau, who remarried Cézar de Pourceul, sgr. des Clies. Armie de Cazeaux d. 29 Aug. 1683, in the Protestant faith, leaving (*a*) Armie Boybellaud, b. 19 Sept. 1680, who married, 9 June 1697, Alain Joulain, sgr. de Seutre; (*b*) Marie-Anne, b. 1681, wife of Joseph Ferry Landreau in 1708; (*c*) Uranie Boybellaud, who married her cousin Isaac Boybellaud, son of Auguste Boybellaud, sieur de La Chapelle. Gaston Boybellaud remarried, 2nd, in 1687, Judith, his cousin-german, daur. of Jean-Jérémie Boybellaud, sr. des Lizards. By this second marriage he left: (*d*) Jean-Gaston, who succeeds, VI.; (*e*) Philippe, b. *circ.* 1695, sgr. des Lizards, who married in 1723 Dlle. Henriette Démédys, nouvelle catholique, of Fontaine, daur. of Daniel Démédys, sieur des Combes, and of Suzanne Beau.

VI. Jean Gaston Boybellaud, b. 6 March 1690, d. 4 Sept. 1803, with whom the Cadet Branch ends.

Branch of Montacier.

II. Jean Boybellaud (*v. ante*), sieur de Montacier, 2nd son of François Boybellaud, avocat, of Ozillac, was b. *circ.*

1567. Notaire-Royal. Married Suzanne Pillet, by whom he had 6 children: (*a*) Marc, sieur de Montacier, or Montassier, who succeeds, III.; (*b*) Jean, sieur de La Chapelle (see later), b. at Ozillac *circ.* 1610; (*c*) Isaac, sieur de la Barrière (R.C. branch); (*d*) Elizabeth, married *circ.* 1630 Jérémie Pillet, apothecary, who at her death remarried, in 1641, Séphora Jailler; (*e*) Dorcas, wife of Isaac Molangin, sieur de La Chérante; (*f*) N . . . , wife of François Francorps, sr. de Chalon, in the parish of Ozillac.

III. Marc Boybellaud, sieur de Montacier, "gentilhomme ordinaire de La Fauconnerie du Prince de Condé." He married Suzanne Fonteneau, and left one son, Marc, IV.

IV. Marc Boybellaud, 2nd of the name, a student of theology in 1672, was admitted into the ministry in 1674 at the Synod of Marennes. Minister at Montausier in succession to Pastor Mauzy: then at Marennes (2 Nov. 1682 to 1684). As Pastor of Montauzier, he assisted at the Provincial Synod of Mauzé, 29 Sept. 1677. In 1678 he assisted, with Auguste Boybellaud, ancien of the church of Ozillac, at the Synod of Jonsac, and at Barbézieux in 1682. He was imprisoned in 1684, and passed several months in prison with his colleague Loquet, minister of Marennes. On his liberation he escaped to Holland, and is mentioned at Amsterdam in 1685. Signed the Confession of the Walloon Churches at Rotterdam. He was elected second Preacher in the town in 1706. By his wife, Marie Védeau, he left 4 children: (*a*) François, sieur de La Terre-Nouvelle, who succeeds, V.; (*b*) Henri, sieur de Lislemarais; (*c*) Henriette, naturalised 18 March 1710 at Amsterdam; (*d*) Anne, who married Samuel Menot, sieur de La Guernerie, at St. Ciers du Taillon, and left a son Samuel and a daur. Anne, who became the wife of Jacques Tabois, merchant, of Ozillac. Marc Boybellaud d. at Tortosa, 24 July 1707.

V. François Boybellaud, sieur de La Terre-Nouvelle, b. 1680; avocat. He is generally known by the soubriquet "Terrenouvelle." At or about the date of the Revocation he followed his father to Holland, and his property was finally confiscated, 20 Aug. 1726, and divided between his nephews, Samuel Menot and Jacques Tabois (série T.T.

Arch. Nat. 106 $\frac{A}{V}$). He is mentioned in the Armorial of 1696 as "François Boisblaut, sieur de Terrenouvelle," where his arms "parlantes" are given. He was present at the marriage of his uncle, Jean Boybellaud, sieur de La Chapelle, 1 Aug. 1672, in Paris, with Andrée Vallet, widow of Jean Vachon. François Boybellaud married Marie Grilhon,(c) and left a daur. Marie, wife of his nephew Peter Louis d'Aulnis, sr. du Caillaud. Marie Drilhon was naturalised at Amsterdam 17 March 1710. His brother, Henri Boybèllaud, sr. de Lislemarais, entered the army of the United Provinces, and became a major-general. His will is dated 30 Oct. 1722. (Pr. Marlbro, 207 P.C.C. Pts. translated out of French). He is described as Sir Henry Boybellaud de Montacier, Kt., major-general, and colonel of a regiment of Foot. The will was made in presence of his niece, Mrs. Mary Boybellaud de Montacier, daur. of his elder brother François, Lord of Terrenouvelle, and of his sister-in-law, his (François') wife, Marie Grilhon, "which niece is wife of Peter Lewis D'Aulnis, Esq.,(D) my nephew, Lord of Du Caillaud, Lt.-Col. in my regiment." He leaves a house at the Hague, near the Turf Market, to his sister Henriette de Boybellaud de Montacier and Lislemarais, and to Mary Grilhon (Drilhon), his sister-in-law. He mentions Angélique D'Aulnis as sister of Peter D'Aulnis (de La Lande) and wife of François D'Aulnis de La Lande. François Boybellaud de Terrenouvelle was an officer in the English army.

Branch of La Chapelle.

III. Jean Boybellaud, sieur de La Chapelle,(E) second son of Jean Boybellaud, sgr. de Montacier, and of Suzanne Pillet, was b. at Ozillac, *circ*. 1610. He married, 1st, 1 Jan. 1640, Judith Morineau, daur. of h. homme Jehan Morineau, sieur du Pible, and of Anne Rangeard. The witnesses to the marriage were Marc Boybellaud de Montacier the elder, his brother, and his brothers-in-law Isaac Malangin, sieur de La Chérante, and François Francorps, sieur de Chalon, Daniel Boybellaud, sieur de Barbeyrac, and other relatives. By this marriage he left: (*a*) Auguste, who succeeds, IV.; (*b*) Josué; (*c*) Isaac; (*d*) Judith, d. young; (*e*) Suzanne; (*f*) Pascal. He married, 2nd, Andrée Le Valet, widow of Jean Vachon, sieur de La Béraudière, he being 62 and she 50. The "promesses de mariage" were published at La Rochelle by "acte notariée," 14 June 1672. The marriage took place in Paris at Charenton 7 Aug. following, in presence of his brother, Marc Boybellaud; his nephew, Marc Boybellaud, student of theology, sieur de St. Marc. By this 2nd marriage he left a son, Armand Boybellaud,(F) b. at Ozillac in 1676. He studied at Bordeaux and, after 1685, emigrated to England and went to his grandfather, Isaac du Bourdieu.(G) He passed two years in Ireland, and then became minister at Wandsworth French church, and, in 1711, of the French church of the Artillerie. In 1725 he was elected pastor at the Hague, where he d. in 1746, aged 70. Author of many theological works. (P.C.C., Edmunds, 251.) His wife was Anne Hebert.

IV. Auguste Boybellaud, eldest son of Jean Boybellaud and Judith Morineau. Bapt. 2 Ap, 1643 in the Temple at Fontaine by Hamilton, the minister, and relative of the family by marriage. He was received as avocat in the Parlement de Bordeaux, where he lived till 1680. He married there his cousin, Isabeau du Bourdieu, granddaughter of a Pastor Bourdieu of Bordeaux, who abjured, 20 May 1682. By this marriage he had (*a*) Isaac; (*b*) Pascal; (*c*) Elizabeth, wife of Pierre Blanchard, notaire, after she had abjured at Fontaine.

NOTES.

A family of Saintonge, neighbourhood of Jonsac, ennobled by hereditary legal office.

(A) The Maignac family lived at Jonsac and its environs, where they had property. Isaac Maignac, or de Maignac, was pastor at Barbézieux, and died there 1676. He had married Dlle. Anne de Chièvres, daur. of Pierre de Chièvres, sgr. de Curton, and of Dlle. Marthe de Mergey. Her sister Rachel was wife of Samuel Drilhon [1668] and afterwards of Pierre Rossibe, or Rouibe, a pastor. Another sister, Renée, married the Pasteur de Royère, minister of Coutras. She appears in the Témoignages of the French church of Threadneedle St., London, in 1687. Her brother, Jean de

Chièvres, sgr. des Citernes, was the only son who remained Protestant, and fled to Holland after 1685; an officer in the Regiment of Orléans. Pierre de Chièvres, the father, had married on 25 Dec. 1627, Eleonore de Montalembert, of a noted Protestant family of Saintonge and Poitou.

(B) Hector Boybellaud, sieur de Puylaudard, d. at Portarlington, and was buried there 10 Aug. 1703. Lieutenant en pension. His heir was Mr. Daulnis de La Lande. (Register Portarlington Fr. Ch.)

(C) Drilhon in French church of Portarlington registers. The translator of the will of Henri Boybellaud (Marlbro, 207, P.C.C.), is probably responsible for the change to Grilhon. The Drilhon family came from Barbézieux, in Saintonge. She was buried at the Hague, 28 March 1718.

(D) The family of d'Aulnis, or Daunis, de La Lande was of Saintonge: seigneurs du Caillaud, Lomadé, etc. Captain François d'Aulnis de La Lande, of La Rochelle, married Angélique Judith de La Lande, his cousin, daur. of Pierre d'Aulnis de La Lande by his second wife, Angélique Boybellaud: he had previously married Henriette Boybellaud de Montacier, daur. of General Henry Boybellaud.

The will of Angélique Judith Boybellaud was proved (P.C.I. 1752) leaving her plate to her four children, Peter, Angélique-Henriette, Jane and Charles.

By his first wife, Henriette Boybellaud, Pierre d'Aulnis du Caillaud left a daur. Marie (will P.C.I. 1764), who married Captain Henri d'Aulnis de La Lande, who left by her Henri De Lalande of London; John De Lalande, who went to Virginia, and Anne Henriette, who married Captain Paul Mangin (b. 1700, d. 1797).

The last male representatives of this family in England were Abraham Lalande, b. 1752, of the H.E.I.C.S., d. 1844; and General Carey Lalande, b. 1754, also of the H.E.I.C.S., who lived and died in India. Of their three sisters, Jane and Catherine Lalande died unmarried; the third was Mrs. Waller.

Peter d'Aulnis du Caillaud, by his 2nd wife, Angélique Boybellaud, left a branch in Holland, now represented by Baron d'Aulnis.

(E) A Pierre Boybellaud appears in the Témoignages of

the French church of Threadneedle St., London, 24 June 1750. Témoin, Mr. Barbault. He may be the officer, " de La Chapelle," mentioned by Haag, in the Dutch army in 1750.

(F) His will was made 29 Aug. 1739, before Samuel Favon, notary, at the Hague, and proved Sept. 1746. (P.C.C., Edmunds, 251.) Armand Boibellaud, sieur de La Chapelle, minister of the Walloon church at the Hague. He mentions that his late father left him part of his estate in France, of which his two brothers, Isaac and Pascal, are now (in 1739) in possession, by virtue of the Edict of Louis XIV. He leaves this property to them. He leaves all he possesses outside France to his wife, Anne Hebert, through whom the bulk of it came to him. He makes her sole heiress and executrix, and mentions property in England, Holland and elsewhere; MSS., household goods, etc., and excludes all brothers and nephews who might claim. The other executor was Charles Chais, his esteemed friend and colleague. (Trans. out of French.)

(G) Isaac Du Bourdieu was pastor at Bergerac, where he married Marie de Costebadie. At her death, he married, in 1660, Jeanne de Poytevin. He studied at Montauban in 1629. Pastor at Monpellier 1650 to 1682. At this latter date he was banished by the Parlement de Toulouse, on account of the procès caused by the false accusation brought against Isabeau Paulet of having abjured. Isaac Du Bourdieu emigrated to London with his son, Jean, and grandson, and became minister of the French church of the Savoy, where he d. at the end of the year 1699. According to Quick, he still preached when he was 95 years old. (*Dictionnaire des Pasteurs de l'Eglise Reformée de France*, MS. 592, Bib. de la Soc. de la Protestantisme Fr.)

Jean Armand Du Bourdieu was also a minister at the Savoy French church in 1701. D. 1726.

Jean Du Bourdieu, son of Isaac Du Bourdieu and of Marie Costebadie, or de Costebadie, of Bergerac, was minister of this church in 1685, and d. in 1720. His will (P.C.C., Shaller, 173) describes him as " Minister, living in the Parish of St. Martins-in-the-Fields, London." He left directions to be buried with his father in the French Chapel of the

Savoy; after leaving legacies to the French poor, and to six old-established French ministers assisted by the Royal Bounty, he leaves an annuity to his son Peter, Rector of Kirby-over-Karr, Yorks; to his son Armand, an annuity. He mentions his grandson John, son of Armand. Property to his two daughters Anne and Elizabeth, still at Monpellier, on condition of coming to England and becoming Protestant.

According to Frain, a Pierre Du Bourdieu, son of a governor of Bergerac, left a son Samuel, who married, 25 Dec. 1681, Rachel Lemoyne, who d. before he emigrated to South Carolina. His second wife was Judith Dugué, by whom he had a son Samuel, born in Carolina. He married, 3rdly, Louise Thoury, and left a son Louis-Philippe Du Bourdieu, born in Carolina.

It is clear, however, that Frain's statement is incorrect, for Samuel Du Bourdieu, who married, 20 Jan. 1682, Rachel Lemoyne at Vitré (Reg. Prot.), was son of Olivier Du Bourdieu, écuyer, seigneur du Rocher, who married, 3 May 1648 at Vitré, Marie de Gennes, and left 9 children, of whom Samuel was the second, bapt. at Vitré, 25 March 1650. Pierre Du Bourdieu, son of Samuel, and Rachel Lemoyne, was bapt. at Terchant, in Brittany, 10 Sept. 1682. Samuel Du Bourdieu emigrated to Carolina in 1685. (Prot. Registers Vitré.) Rachel Lemoyne was bapt. 11 March 1654, and d. 1 Jan. 1683 at Vitré; she was daur. of Pierre Lemoyne, seigneur des Grands Prés, and of Marguerite Lemoyne.

* * * *

NOTE.—The Boybellaud family went to Holland at an early period. " Steve (Etienne) Boiblo, jeune homme de France," is found at the Hague, fiancé of Maria Wynants Struys, 12 Aug. 1640.

A Boybelleau de Roche was received into the church of Amsterdam, 26 May 1646, by Témoignage from Breda.

Samuel Boybelleau was received at Amsterdam by Témoignage from Vianen, 19 Aug. 1646. He married Catherine Van Offeringh, and several of their children were baptised at Amsterdam, where he was buried, 16 June 1649.

BUOR DE LA LANDE

Arms : d'Arg. à 3 coquilles de gueules, 2 and 3.

I. Guillaume Buor, valet, sgr. de La Lande, accompanied Saint Louis on his crusade to Africa in 1270. He signs the marriage contract of his son Maurice in 1311 " le mercredi avant Saint-Jean l'Evangeliste." (Contract passed at La Roche-sur-Yon.)

II. Maurice Buor, éc., sgr. de La Lande, married in 1311 Letice Des Florens, and had : (*a*) Guillaume, III.; (*b*) Maurice, valet, author of the Branch of Pasquinay; (*c*) Amaury, who married Dlle. Jeanne Ancelon, daur. of Henri Ancelon and Jeanne Freslon. These three brothers made an " acte d'accord " in 1345, regarding their rights and succession ; (*d*) Marguerite, who married Hugues de Bazoges in 1336.

III. Guillaume Buor, éc., sgr. de La Mothe-Freslon, received various homages in 1384, 1385, 1398. He married, after 1356, Marie Ancelon, who brought him by dowry the seigneurie of La Mothe-Freslon (Paroisse de Champs St. Père). He d. in 1392, leaving : (*a*) Guillaume, who married Dlle. Marguerite Catus, *s.p.*; (*b*) Jean, who succeeds, IV.; (*c*) Maurice.

IV. Jean Buor, éc., sgr. de La Lande, Gerbaudière, and La Mothe-Freslon. He made a deed of agreement, 1 Dec. 1392, with Jean Ancelon, sgr. de l'Isle Bernard, and Jeanne Ancelon, his sister. Jean Buor was chamberlain to Jean, Duc de Berri, captain of the château of Civray, captain of Luçon in 1404. He was present in Paris at a levy in the quality of Knight Banneret, with a knight and eight esquires under his banner, 9 May 1414, and in 1419 he commanded a company of 30 esquires and 15 archers. He married, *circ.* 1401, Dlle. Marguerite de Bellosac, by whom he had: (*a*) Maurice, who succeeds, V.; and Marie, married, by contract dated 14 Feb. 1416, Georges Foucher.

V. Maurice Buor, chev., sgr. de La Mothe-Freslon, La Lande Buor, and La Gerbaudière: échanson to Jean, Duc de Berri, Comte de Poitou, and captain of La Grange-du-Jard, 1 Oct. 1410. He married, by contract dated 14 Feb. 1416, Marguerite Foucher, daur. of Jean Foucher, éc., sgr. de La Sausaye, and of Marie Samin. Maurice Buor did homage for his fief of La Mothe-Freslon, 27 March 1438, to the Seigneur d'Amboise, Vicomte de Thouars. He left: (*a*) Jean, who succeeds, VI.; (*b*) Marguerite, who married, 1440, Olivier Poitevin, chevalier. They sign an agreement with their brother Jean, 13 June 1448.

VI. Jean Buor, éc., sgr. de La Lande Buor, La Gerbaudière, and La Mothe-Freslon: is known by several acts and commissions 1445, 1453, 1467. He married, by contract dated 9 Dec. 1443, Jeanne Fresneau, daur. of Jean Fresneau, éc., sgr. de La Fresnaye, and of Rose de Maillé, and had by her: (*a*) Louis, who succeeds, VII.; (*b*) Pierre, éc., sgr. de La Mothe; (*c*) Joachim; (*d*) François, a priest; (*e*) Jehanne, wife of Pierre Marchand, éc., sgr. du Plessis-Marchand; (*f*) Françoise, wife of Jehan Escoubleau de Sourdis; (*g*) Rose: all of whom figure in an act of 7 March 1480.

VII. Louis Buor, éc., sgr. de La Gerbaudière, received an act of homage from Etienne Serneron, éc., sgr. de Boislambert, 20 June 1480. He married Dlle. Marie de Granges, daur. of Jean de Granges, éc., sgr. de Puychenin, and of Dlle. Mauricette Aumosnier. They left one son, François, who succeeds, VIII.

VIII. François Buor, éc., sgr. de La Gerbaudière, married Gillette Jousseaume, *circ.* 1503, and left: (*a*) François; (*b*) Gillette, wife of Jacob de Bessay; (*c*) Pierre, author of the Branch of La Lande, IX.; (*d*) Jehan, Canon of Luçon.

IX. Pierre Buor, éc., sgr. de La Lande-Buor, married 6 July 1545, Dlle. Anne Lingier, daur. of Jean Lingier, chev., sgr. du Plessis-Tesselin, by whom he left: (*a*) Jean-Baptiste, who succeeds, X.; (*b*) Elie; (*c*) Josias; (*d*) Bienvenue, who had a legacy from her aunt Gillette, Dame de Bessay, in 1555: she married Nicolas de Rivecour, éc.; (*e*) Diane, wife of Jean de Goulaine, éc., sgr. de Barbin; (*f*) Louise, wife of Jean Massé, éc., sgr. de la Maumenière; (*g*) Rebecca; (*h*) Foy.

X. Jean-Baptiste Buor,(A) éc., sgr. de La Lande, who married, 20 July 1582, by contract (notaires Pilon and Trouplier) and in 1585, according to Protestant rites in the Temple of La Rochelle, Dlle. Olympe de Lespinay, daur. of Pierre de Lespinay. Jean-Baptiste Buor was one of those who broke down the doors of the parish church of Bouffière, 24 May 1613, to bury one of their co-religionists. He left by his wife Olympe: (*a*) Charles, who succeeds, XI.; (*b*) Elie, sgr. de La Hermière et La Negrie: married in 1637 Dlle. Olympe de Goulaine. He maintained his noblesse, 23 Sept. 1667, before the Intendant Barentin. Left several children, one of whom, Pierre Buor, passed to England in 1689; another, Isaac, sgr. de La Morinière, also went to England with his son in 1689; (*c*) Jaquette.

XI. Charles Buor, éc., sgr. de La Lande-Buor, was sentenced to death in 1622 for robbery and violence to his mother, but the sentence was commuted to confiscation and fines by an arrêt dated 26 July 1634. His property was divided between his brother and sister, Elie and Jaquette Buor. He married, in 1631, Dlle. Anne Garripaud, and left: (*a*) Gilles, éc., sgr. de La Lande, d. 1663, as appears by a contract of marriage of his widow Madelaine de Goulaine, daur. of Gabriel de Goulaine, chev., sgr. des Mortiers-Garnier, and of Louise Le Maistre de Garrelaye, with Philippe Janvre, chev., sgr. de La Mosnière; (*b*) Gabriel, who succeeds, XII.; (*c*) Renée, married 21 Nov. 1667, to François Bellanger, éc., sgr. de Launay, and secondly, 24 Nov. 1678, Henri de La Varenne, sgr. de La Chalonnière, a widow in 1687, when she was arrested with others on a boat on the Loire, as they were trying to escape to England.(B)

XII. Gabriel Buor,(C) éc., sgr. de La Lande, answered the Ban de Poitou, in 1689, 1690, 1691, at which dates he must have been a "Nouveau Converti." He married in 1661 Anne Prévost, a Protestant like himself, though both "Nouveaux Convertis" at the Revocation. They left a son, Gabriel, who continued the succession, but both Gabriel Buor, the father, with his wife, a daughter, Charlotte,(D) and a granddaughter escaped to England, where they appear on the Assistance Roll for London, 1701-1710. Their goods were confiscated and given to their son Gabriel, who remained in France as a R. Catholic. (*Protest. de Poitou*, Lièvre, III, 214.)

NOTES.

This family must not be confounded with that of d'Aulnis de La Lande, also of Poitou. The name La Lande is a common name of fiefs throughout France. Various members of both families emigrated to England.

Charles Buor, of Poitou, 22 years of age, appears on the List of Abjurations of the London French church of the Savoy, 23 June 1700. Brought up since the age of 8 in the Church of Rome, where he took the habit of the Cordeliers. He was probably the Charles Buor, son of Isaac and Magdalen his wife, born at Monteyn, in Poitou, naturalised in 1713. His administration (P.C.C. Dec. 1716) was granted to Alexander Geoffrey de La Touche, cousin and next of kin. Captain Alexander Geoffrey de La Touche married Angélique Buor : his son, Charles Benjamin, was baptised, 20 July 1714, in the French church of the Artillery, London : also Gabriel 16 July 1715. Charlotte Pujolas, née Buor, was godmother to both.

(A) Jean Baptiste Buor was godfather, 17 Feb. 1586, at La Rochelle, to Charles Bodin, son of René Bodin, sieur de La Blandrière, and of Antoinette de Besse "escuyer, seigneur de La Lande Buor." (Reg. Prot. La Rochelle.)

(B) Lièvre, *Hist. des Protestants de Poitou*, III., 29.

(C) Gabriel Buor de La Lande was godfather, 28 May 1692, to Charles Olivier Gabriel, son of Hector Parmenion Gourdeau, esc., sgr. de Montigny des Besson, and of his wife, Dame Louise [de] Genays. The second godfather was Mr. Olivier, Marquis de La Musse. The godmothers were Dame Marie Beringhuam (de Béringhen) and Dame Marie Anne Dugast, wife of Gaston Pompée de Goron, sgr. de St. Germain de Thenie (Fr. ch. Le Carré, London).

The family of Chauvin, seigneurs de La Muce (or La Musse) were seigneurs de Ponthus (or Pont Hue). The château was one of the "maisons seigneuriales" where Protestants were allowed to hold services, and where marriages and baptisms were celebrated.

BUOR DE LA LANDE

Bonaventure de La Musse was governor of the town and château of Vitré, in place of his nephew, M. de Montmartin, in August 1590, and died there, 3 March 1592. His son David married at Vitré, 1st, 8 March 1592, Dlle. Philippe Gouyon; 2nd, 28 Nov. 1593, Dlle. Sara du Boys, Dame de Baulac, and d. at Crauzon, near Brest, while on service in the army, and was buried as a Protestant at Vitré, 10 Nov. 1594, leaving a son, David de La Musse, b. at Vitré, 1 Dec. 1594, bapt. 6 Ap. 1595, who was President of the Assembly at La Rochelle in 1621. (Baird.)

Olivier de La Musse, godfather to Hector Gourdeau in London in 1692, was son of Haut et Puissant César de La Musse, chevalier Marquis, baron banneret, seigneur de Ponthus, who d. in his château, where he was buried, 8 Sept. 1676, aged 65, and of his wife Dame Claude-Ursuline de Champagné, "Marquis et Marquise de La Musse" (Prot. Reg. Sucé). He was arrested on the Isle de Rhé as he was escaping, and was imprisoned for two years at La Rochelle. He was then expatriated and sent to England, where he lived for twelve years, when he went to Virginia and founded the town of Manakin, or King William's Parish.

According to Baird, "*Huguenots in America*," Cézar de La Musse was son of Bonadventure de La Musse. This, however, is incorrect, as the latter d. in 1592. It is probable that he was son of David de La Musse. (Arms: De gueules, à 9 besants d'argent, 3, 3, 3.)

Charlotte de La Lande Buor, spinster, "30 years of age," married 20 Dec. 1703, at St. Martin's-in-the-Fields, London, Denis Pujolas, bachelor, aged 40, of St. Anne's, Westminster. She was bapt. 27 March 1681 at Vieillevigne.

Isaac Buor [sr. du Blizon] with Aymée [de Goulaine] his wife, and Francis, their son, were made Denizens, 9. Ap. 1687. They had another son, Gabriel, bapt. 12 Feb. 1680. (Reg. Prot. Vieillevigne.)

Gabriel Buor [sr. du Perraut] with Marguerite [Mandin] his wife; Gabrielle and Israelite, their daughters, were made Denizens, 9 Ap. 1687. Israelite was bapt. 25 Feb. 1679. (Reg. Prot. Vieillevigne.) They had another son, Isaie Fleurant, bapt. 8 March 1676: his godfather was Isaac Buor, éc., sgr. de La Morinière; and Gabriel, bapt. 26 May 1677 (Reg. Prot. Vieillevigne).

Israelite was godmother, 11 Oct. 1691, to Israelite, daur. of Monsieur Antoine Cougot and Dlle. Antoinette de Gineste, of Puylaurens, in Languedoc (Fr. ch. of Southampton), and also 12 Jan. 1694-5 to Charlotte Israelite, daur. of Monsieur Jean Thomas, of Cauvisson, Languedoc (Fr. ch. Southampton). A Jean Buor was godfather in this church, 6 Dec. 1699, to Rebecca, daur. of Gerard de Vaux, of Castres.

Esaie Buor de La Morinière emigrated with his son Peter in the spring of 1689 (Lièvre, *Protestants de Poitou*, III, 214), who was naturalised 25 May 1702: "Son of Esaya Buor de La Morinière, by Ann his wife, born at St. Hilaire, in Poitou." This is probably Isaac, son of Elie (see X.). Lièvre says that a Buor du Perreau married an Englishwoman, Marie Roy, and came back to France with her and died in May 1702. She had a child and asked leave to go to Nantes, probably with a view to escaping. This Buor possibly was Gabriel Buor, sr. du Perreau, above.

The family of De Goulaine, allied with those of Buor and La Musse, seigneurs de La Tour-Gosselin, du Breil, and other places in La Vendée, was one of the most ancient and illustrious in Brittany, and was related by marriage in early days to the Royal Houses of France and Brittany. The fief of Goulaine was made a marquisat by Louis XIII. in Oct. 1621, in favour of Gabriel de Goulaine, seigneur de Loroux. Charles de Goulaine, captain in the army, is on the Oath Roll Naturalisations, 11 Nov. 1698. Charles de Goulaine, son of Samuel, by Charlotte his wife, b. at Laudonnière, in Brittany, was naturalised 10 June 1713. Another Charles de Goulaine, son of Charles de Goulaine, by Anne his wife, b. at the Hague, was naturalised 10 June 1713. The family settled in Ireland, where they appear in the registers of the French church of St. Mary, Dublin.

"Armes de concession" France et d'Angleterre, mi-parti. Devise, "A celluy-ci, à celluy-là, j'accorde la couronne."

* * * *

The earlier part of this Pedigree is given by M. P. Beauchet-Filleau.

CHAMIER

Arms: D'azur à la fasce d'or, chargée d'un cœur de gueules: acc. de 3 roses, 1 and 2 d'argent.

I. Adrien Chamier, avocat at Avignon, became a Protestant, and was Pastor of St. Romans, in Dauphiné, then of Pouzin, and afterwards of Privas, in the Vivarais. He was appointed to Montélimar, in Dauphiné, and was drowned by his horse falling into a pit of water, whilst on his way to attend a colloque.(A) He married a Dlle. Fournier, of Annonay, and left a son Daniel, who follows, II.

II. Daniel Chamier, b. in 1565, minister of the Protestant church at Montélimar, and afterwards at Montauban, in Guienne. Professor of Theology in the Academy there, and secretary to the Assembly at Loudun in 1596. Transferred to Vendôme, Saumur, and lastly to Châtellerault. In 1598 he was chosen to assist in drawing up the Edict of Nantes, and was President of the National Synod at Gap in 1603, Deputy to the Court of Henry of Navarre from the National Synod of La Rochelle, 1607, Vice-President of the National Assembly at Saumur in 1611, and chosen as Deputy from the Reformed Churches of France to the Assembly of the United Provinces of the Netherlands in 1618, but was not allowed to attend it, by the King's orders. He was killed by a cannon ball at the siege of Montauban in the general assault on the town by Louis XIII., 17 Oct. 1621. He had married Mlle. Portal, who survived him, leaving a son, Adrien, III, and three daughters.

III. Adrien Chamier, b. 1590, d. 1671, aged 81; married Madeleine Alard, and left: (*a*) Jacques, docteur and avocat, who remained at Montélimar and married Marie Bourselle, by whom he had (i) Adrien, pastor at Château d'Alais, Dauphiné, who fled to Holland, where he appears on a list of those assisted in 1686 (Commission Walloune, I. 2, 13): he came to England and d. in Essex; (ii) Antoine, broken on the wheel at Montélimar, aged 28; (*b*) Daniel, who succeeds, IV, and 5 daughters.

IV. Daniel Chamier, second and youngest son of Adrien and Madeleine Chamier, b. 1628, was pastor at Beaumont, and succeeded his father at Montélimar. He came to England and d. of fever, 29 Jan. 1676, aged 47. He married, 10 Dec. 1659, Madeleine Tranchin, of a Dauphiné family, b. at Geneva 1 Sept. 1628. She came to England with her son Daniel, and was buried at St. James's, Westminster, 17 Jan. 1709. By his wife, Madeleine Tranchin, he had: (*a*) Daniel, who succeeds, V; (*b*) Isaac,(B) b. 10 May 1667, who came to England, and 4 daurs., of whom three are known; (*c*) Madeleine, b. at Beaumont, 16 Nov. 1662: d. in England in 1745: she is godmother to Anne Louise Guybert, daur. of René Guybert, of Noirmoutier, Poitou, 2 Ap. 1698 (Fr. Ch. Reg. Le Carré and Berwick Street, London); (*d*) Jeanne, b. at Beaumont 26 Aug. 1669, d. at Edinburgh 7 March 1729; (*e*) Marie, said by Haag to have been born at Beaumont in 1664.

V. Daniel Chamier, b. 11 Jan. 1661, at Beaumont, in Périgord, studied at Die and Geneva, where he matriculated in 1682, and went to Neufchatel in 1685, where he was appointed a minister, 1 June 1686. He stayed there till 1691, when he went to England, arriving 26 May 1691, with his mother and sisters, wife and son. He was appointed one of the French church ministers in London, and was minister of the Glasshouse Street church, and elected to the Walloon French church in April 1692. He d. 15 July 1698, aged 37 years and six months. Buried at St. James's, Westminster. He married Anne Françoise Huet, daur. of a minister at Neufchatel, 9 Dec. 1689, who came with him to England. He left by her 5 sons and 2 daurs.: (*a*) Daniel, b. at Neufchatel 1690, d. 1694 or 1695; (*b*) Adrien, b. 1692, d. 1694; (*c*) Daniel, who succeeds, VI.; (*d*) Jeanne Magdeleine, b. 25 Oct. 1694 (Glasshouse Street Fr. ch.); (*e*) Pierre; (*f*) Jean, b. 16 Nov. 1697, who was secretary to Dr. William Wake, Archbishop of Canterbury, d. 11 May 1765; (*g*) Marie, or Marie-Anne; (*h*) Robert, a posthumous child, b. 1698, d. 1748, wounded at Dettingen.

VI. Daniel Chamier, of St. Stephen's, Coleman Street, London, b. 21 Nov., bapt. 1 Dec. 1696, at the Fr. Ch. of the Tabernacle. He made his Témoignage, 25 March 1739, with his brother Jean and sister Judith. Their father,

Daniel Chamier, is the witness (Threadneedle Street Fr. Ch.). Died 17 Nov. 1741, and buried at the chapel of St. Faith, St. Paul's Cathedral. He married, 2 Sept. 1719, Dlle. Suzanne de La Méjanelle, daur. of Mr. de La Méjanelle and Judith his wife, and sister of Marie-Anne de La Méjanelle, wife of Philip de Vismes, of St. Mary Aldermary, merchant: she died at Southampton, 16 Dec. 1787, aged 85. By his wife Suzanne he left 4 sons and 5 daurs.: (*a*) Daniel, bapt. 13 June 1722 (Fr. Ch. of the Savoy): he went to Maryland; (*b*) Jean, bapt. 25 Sept. 1723 (*idem*), d. at Arrah, 1770; (*c*) Gérard, bapt. 2 Sept, 1724 (*idem*); (*d*) Antoine, b. 6 Oct. 1725, bapt. 19th at Threadneedle Street Fr. Ch. He was Under-Secretary of State in 1767: deputy Under-Secretary for War 1772: M.P. for Tamworth: d. *s.p.* 12 Oct. 1780, aged 55 (Musgrave Obit.): he married Miss Dorothy Wilson, 3 Oct. 1753 (Vic. Gen. Lic.); (*e*) Judith, bapt. 2 Feb. 1721 (Fr. Ch. of the Savoy), who married, 4 Ap. 1753 by licence, the Rev. Jean Deschamps, at the Mile End Chapel, Middlesex (Lic. 19 March), and d. at Winchester, 27 Dec. 1801, aged 80. Their son John Ezechiel Deschamps assumed the name of Chamier pursuant to the will of his uncle, Antony Chamier, by Royal Licence, 20 Oct. 1780 (see Deschamps); (*f*) Suzanne, bapt. 5 Oct. 1726, godmother in 1754 to her nephew, Jean Ezechiel Deschamps, 4 June (Fr. Ch. of the Savoy); (*g*) Magdeleine, bapt. 7 March 1727; (*h*) Marie Anne, bapt. 8 Dec. 1729; (*i*) Anne, bapt. 27 June 1736.

NOTES.

(A) Said by Haag to have been minister at St. Romans before 1660, and lived at Nismes till 1674, after leaving Privas, and to have lived to over 100 years old.

(B) Isaac is said by Haag to have abjured and remained in France.

COLUMBINE

I. François Columbine,(A) or La Columbine, a physician, of Clelles,in Dauphiné,settled at Norwich, *circ*. 1685, where he married Anne La Caux, daur. of Pierre La Caux, a refugee minister from Castres ; appointed Pastor of the French church at Norwich in 1689. She d. in 1741, and was buried at St. Michael at Plea. François Columbine d. in 1699, and was buried, 29 May, at St. Clements. They had three sons and four daughters: (*a*) Pierre, II.; (*b*) François, bapt. at St. Clement's, 13 Feb. 1692, and buried there 22 Ap. 1720, not married; (*c*) Paul, bapt. at St. Clement's, 16 Feb. 1698, d. 30 Aug. 1784, aged 85 (Fr. Ch. Reg). Buried at the French church, Norwich. He married Esther Waller, daur. of Simeon Waller, alderman, of Norwich, and mayor in 1745. She d. 3 Feb. 1779, aged 74, and was buried at the French church; (*d*) Olympe, bapt. at St. Clement's, Norwich, 12 March 1693; (*e*) Anne, bapt. at the French church, 28 July 1695; (*f*) Susanne, third daur., bapt. at St. Clement's 8 Oct. 1696, and buried there 27 Oct. 1708 ; (*g*) Michelle, bapt. . . .

II. Peter Columbine, born 13 Nov. 1697; d. 11 Dec. 1770, aged 73; buried at the French church, Norwich (St. Mary the Less). He was sheriff in 1751, mayor 1755.(B) He married, 8 Sept. 1719, Mary Anne, daur. of Gaston Martineau, of St. Peters, Hungate, Norwich, a surgeon, formerly of Dieppe, d. 1780, 6 May, aged 86. He left by her 6 sons and 3 daurs.: (*a*) Pierre, or Peter, bapt. 3 Dec. 1721 at the French church, Norwich.(C) Married Amelia Hardyngham, who d. 13 Jan. 1821, aged 78: they had a daughter Amelia, or Melia, who d. 30 Jan. 1829, aged 48; (*b*) François, bapt. 6 Ap. 1723 at the French church, Norwich: alderman of Norwich, sheriff 1769, mayor 1776, d. 21 Feb. 1808, aged 85. He married Susanna Maria Mason, daur. of Thomas Mason, of Swaffham, by whom he left a son Francis Columbine junior, merchant, who married Elizabeth, widow of Henry Headley. She d. 19 — 1790, aged 28, and was buried at North Walsham: they left a son Peter Columbine, and a daur. Susanna; (*c*) Paul, b. 29

Nov. 1730, d. at Necton, 1821, aged 91, Rector of Little Plumstead: married, 1st, Elizabeth Brewer, daur. of John Brewer, who d. 1760, aged 25, buried at Langley. He left by her one daur., Elizabeth, who married 8 Nov. 1787, William Mason, of Necton, high sheriff of Norfolk: she d. 12 June 1849, leaving posterity. Paul Columbine married, 2nd, Catherine Skottoe, 24 Oct. 1772, at St. Luke's Chapel, Norwich Cathedral; (*d*) David Columbine, III.; (*e*) Arthur; (*f*) Marie, b. 22 May 1726, wife of Hewet Rand; (*g*) Anne, b. 4th, bapt. 12th July 1720; (*h*) Harriet; (*i*) Sarah.

III. David Columbine, b. 1733, d. 2 Nov. 1819, aged 86. Sheriff of Norfolk in 1772. Married Theodora Martha, daur. and heiress of . . . . Dyball. She d. 21 Sept. 1816, aged 73 (Reg. Fr. Ch. Norwich). Both she and her husband were buried at the French church, Norwich. They had: (*a*) David, IV.; (*b*) Theodora Martha, b. 30 Dec. 1756, d. 28 July 1801; married Thomas Blake,(D) of Skottoe, *a quo* Robert Blake-Humfrey, of Wroxham House; (*c*) Peter, d. 9 Oct. 1810, aged 73 (Reg. Fr. Ch.). His wife, Elizabeth Brunton, d. 3 Nov. 1799, aged 28. She was the 2nd daur. of . . . . Brunton, and sister of Mrs. Merry, the actress, and of the Countess of Craven; (*d*) Sarah, d. 15 Dec. 1817, aged 50; (*e*) Harriett, d. in 1861 at Edinburgh, wife of Thomas Corlett, merchant, of London: left a son, Thomas Corlett.

IV. David Columbine, merchant, of Norwich, married 16 Dec. 1800, Ann, daur. of Peter Elwin, of Booton. He d. 22 July 1845, aged 78, at Notting Hill, Middlesex, leaving a son David Columbine, solicitor, who married twice and d. *s.p.*

NOTES.

(A) Anna Columbine, sister of François Columbine, or La Columbine, married, 15 June 1699, Noah Violas, or Violard, at St. Luke's chapel, Norwich Cathedral.

(B) His portrait, by Stoppelaer, is in St. Andrew's Hall, Norwich.

(C) Peter, son of Peter and Mary Columbine, bapt. at

the Octagon Chapel, Norwich, 8 Sept. 1737. He may have been another son Peter.

(D) For pedigree of Blake, see Carthew, East and West Bradenham.

* * * *

Monuments and tombstones, Norwich:

Mary Columbine, an infant, buried 1765.
Peter Columbine, aged 6, 1766.

COSTEBADIE

Arms (on seal): 2 chevrons, in chief 3 stars, in base a lion rampant.

I. Jean Costebadie, bourgeois, and consul of the town of Tonneins, in the Agenais, married Marie Bonis and left by her 6 children: (*a*) Jean Costebadie, a Protestant minister, who left a son Cirus; (*b*) another Jean Costebadie, sr. de La Trille, b. at Tonneins, pastor at La Linde, 1626: secretary to the Duc de Candalle, 1660–65. He married Jeanne Vallois, who appears as godmother to Abraham Costebadie de Bazats, son of François and Anne de Bazats, bapt. 18 Jan. 1647 by Maître Costebadie. She d. Mar. 1682, aged 55 (Prot. Reg., Bordeaux); (*c*) Jean-Jacques, II, or Jacob as he is called in the marriage settlement of his son Jean; (*d*) François Costebadie, d. 1661, leaving one son by his wife, Marie Baucon; (*e*) Jeanne; (*f*) Marie, wife of Pierre de Vaüze, whose daur. Marie was the wife of a Protestant minister, Abraham Galliné: d. *s.p.*

II. Jean-Jacques Costebadie, b. *circ.* 1590 at Tonneins, a Protestant minister and author of several works. He was educated at Montauban, and afterwards at Geneva,(A) where his entry is recorded—" J. Costebadius Thoneinensis, Nov. 4 1614." His first post was at La Brède, from whence he removed to La Salinde. Jean-Jacques, or Jacob, Costebadie was the pastor of Clairac in 1661, when he retired, from age and infirmities, and d. in 1674. He had married, in 1637, Marie Braunes, daur. of Daniel Braunes and of his wife, Anne Roi, and left 5 children: (*a*) Jean, who emigrated to England, ancestor of the English Branch, III.; (*b*) another Jean, mentioned in the marriage contract of his elder brother as " Jean puisnay." He d. in 1715, *s.p.*, leaving a will in favour of his sister Anne, with reversion to his brother Jean, if he should return to France (Test. par Lebon, Not. Royal); (*c*) Jeanne, whose marriage contract, dated 2 Nov. 1676 (Reg. Prot. Tonneins) to Jean Costes, merchant, of Bordeaux, describes her as " Jehanne de Costebadie,(B) damoiselle, fille de feu sieur Jacob Costebadie, bourgeois, et de Braune, damoiselle "; (*d*) Marie Costebadie, who married Jean Coutry, apothecary, of Bordeaux. She is mentioned in the Armorial of 1696 as "Marie Costebadie, veuve de N . . . . Courtoide (*sic*) bourgeois de la ville Bordeaux." The coat attributed to her is a complicated piece of heraldry, with a dove, 3 cypress trees, a heart and darts, a crescent, 2 carp in a river, but bears no resemblance to the arms engraved on the seal still preserved in the family, with the exception of 3 stars, or, on a chief azure; (*e*) Anne Costebadie, married Antoine du Vignau, surgeon, of Bordeaux, 20 Oct. 1708, at the church of St. Simeon, Bordeaux.

III. Jean Costebadie, b. at Tonneins, *circ.* 1640; educated at Geneva, where he graduated 15 Oct. 1668. He was ordained minister 11 Nov. 1668, by the laying on of hands by M. Garisolles, pastor of Castelmoron, at the Synod of Basse-Guyenne, held at Monpazier. He became minister of Argentat and remained there till 1683, when he removed to Beaumont, in Périgord. He married, 12 Feb. 1673, at Argentat, Jeanne Echaunie,(c) daur. of Pierre Echaunie and Anne Gril, or Greil, widow of le sieur Bétut, sgr. de Nonars, whom she had married before she was 18.

His marriage contract describes him as "Ministre de l'église prétendue reformée de la présente ville, fils naturel et légitime du sieur Jacob de Costebadie, et de demoiselle Marie Braunes, habitans de Tonneins-Desoubs, en Agennois." The marriage took place in the house of "demoiselle Anne de Greil, veuve du Sieur Pierre Chaunies, en la ville d'Argentat, Bas-Limousin, Viscomté de Turenne." His father being old and infirm, his place was taken by Jean Costebadie, his younger brother, who acted as "procureur" for his father in the marriage settlement. Considerable sums of money were settled by both parties: his wife brought him a dowry of 5,000 livres from her father's side, and 3,000 from her mother. Among the articles included in the settlement were "un lit de serge de Seigneur vert, avec la couverture trainante; le tout garni de frange de soie, et de linge à sa discreption." Jean Costebadie left 7 children by his wife, Jeanne Echaunie, of whom only 5 are recorded: (*a*) Pierre, who travelled in Italy, Germany and Turkey, and was killed in action in the army of William of Orange, in the

Low Countries; (*b*) Jean Jacques, who was taken to England as a child, and continues the succession, IV.; (*c*) Jean Gril or Greil Costebadie, who married, 6 July 1710, Marie Guillot,(D) in the French church of Spring Gardens, London (Jean Gril Coste Badie); (*d*) Jeanne, b. 1681, wife of N . . . de Martret, sgr. de Bétut; (*e*) Lucie, d. in 1769 at an advanced age. For many years she had carried on a law-suit against her cousin Anne Echaunie. According to Tamizey de Larroque, Jean Costebadie left France in 1684,(E) taking two of his children with him, and leaving his wife and 5 others in France. He settled at York in 1686, and in 1704 they are mentioned on a roll of French refugees assisted by the English Government (Jean Costebadie, sa femme et quatre enfants). The tradition is that both he and his wife made several journeys to France between 1684 and 1688. It is certain, however, that Jeanne and Lucie remained in France, and that their mother did not leave till 1687 (série T.T. 117). Jeanne was left at Argentat, aged 5, and Lucie at Tonneins, aged 4. In the request made by their guardians that the property of their father and mother should be handed over to them, it is stated that they were "abandonnées dès leur plus tendre enfance par ceux qui leur avoient donné la naissance." Jean Costebadie had left his property in the hands of MM. Rose et Pasquier, merchants of Tonneins. The property was taken over by the Receveur des Domaines in 1688. Lucie was placed with some Nouveaux Catholiques of Tonneins at a pension of 140 livres. Jeanne was left at Argentat with a guardian called de Pradeaux. At his death, in 1699, she was admitted into the convent of the Ursulines of Beaulieu, where she abjured. Marie Costebadie, who married Isaac du Bourdieu of Bergerac before 1660, may have been another daughter of Jean Jacques Costebadie, II.

IV. Jean Jacques, or Jacob, Costebadie, b. at Argentat in 1684, the year of his father's exile, and was brought to England in 1686. Naturalised 5 Anne. (John Costebadie, son of John Costebadie, by Jeane his wife, born at Argentat, in Auvergne, in France.) He held the Stamp Office at York for some years, and was a Proctor in the Ecclesiastical Court. He d. in 1758, and was buried 31 Oct. at St. Michael le

Belfrey, in an altar tomb in the churchyard to the east of the church. There is a monument in the church recording several charities left by him. He married Rebecca, daur. of Humphrey Robinson, of Thicket Priory, son of Richard Robinson and Jane Akroyd, of Foggathorpe, who d. in 1670. He left by her 3 children: (*a*) Jacob, who continues the line, V.; (*b*) Henry, Commander R.N., d. *s.p.* at Acomb, near York, aged 81; (*c*) Rebecca, wife of John Clough, of York, and Newbold Hall, Proctor and banker.

V. Jacob Costebadie, b. in 1724, bapt. at St. Michael-le-Belfrey, York, 3 March 1724–5; appointed to the Akroyd exhibition, being of founder's kin, and was educated at Jesus College, Cambridge. He was Rector of Wensley for 53 years, 1750–1802, where he died aged 78. He married a Miss Rutter, of Houghton-le-Spring, and left two children: (*a*) Jacob, VI.; (*b*) Anne, wife of the Rev. Thomas Lund, Rector of Barton. Jacob Costebadie, or Costobadie, b. 1758, was appointed to the Akroyd scholarship in 1775. He succeeded his father as Rector of Wensley in 1802, and held the living for twenty-six years, and died there, 8 Nov. 1828. Previously to becoming Rector of Wensley he held the college living of Graveley, Cambs, and was Fellow and tutor of his college. He had married, July 1796, Anne, daur. of the Rev. Dr. Milnes, of Newark, by whom he left 11 children: (*a*) Henry Palliser Costobadie, of West Barton in Bishopsdale, curate of Wensley, and Rector of Husbands Bosworth, Leicestershire. He married Louisa, daur. of Samuel Judd, of Stamford Baron, by whom he left 3 sons: (i) Clermont Hugh Costobadie, capt. 3rd D. Gds., d. in India; (ii) Henry, d. young; (iii) Henry Holmes Costobadie, Lt.-Col. R.H.A., of the Hermitage, Stamford Baron, who married Gertrude Elise Lucas, youngest daur. of George Vere Braithwaite, of Edith Weston Hall, Rutland; and 3 daurs.: (iv) Caroline Laetitia, wife of Captain Nelson Thomas; (v) Henrietta Louisa, d. abroad; (vi) Charlotte Kate, wife of James Sullivan Bowdoin, Boston, Mass.; (*b*) Hugh Palliser Costobadie, Vicar of Kings Norton, Leicestershire. Appointed to the Akroyd scholarship 2 Aug. 1822.; d. 28 March 1887 and was buried at Kings Norton. He married Fanny Burnett, daur. of the Rev. Frederick Lateward, Rector of

Perivale, Msex., and left: (i) Akroyd Palliser Costobadie, b. 6 Aug. 1853. Married in 1887 Mary Ann Stevens, of New Zealand; (ii) Frederick Palliser Costobadie, b. 9 Aug. 1856; married 20 Sept. 1881 Mary Laetitia, daur. of the Rev. James Beauchamp, Rector of Crowell, Oxon; (iii) John Palliser Costobadie, b. 17 Aug. 1864; (*c*) Akroyd Costobadie, of Thornton Rust, Wensleydale, b. in 1805; married a Miss Chapman; (*d*) George Costobadie; (*e*) Charles Costobadie, b. 1811, d. 5 June 1867, aged 56: 51st Regt: buried at Wensley: married a daur. of General Currie; (*f*) James Costobadie, major in the army 1852. Married Laura, youngest daur. of John Kingston, Commissioner of H.M. Stamp Office, by whom he left: (i) William, b. in 1855, a civil engineer, who married his cousin Mary, daur. of Stafford Hotchkin, of Woodhall, Lincs.; (ii) Harry, b. 1857; (iii) Gerald, b. 1864, major Loyal N. Lancs Regt.; (iv) Isabel, b. 1859; wife of Major Cuffe-Wheeler, R.N.; (*g*) William Costobadie, b. 1814, d. 1832; Lieut., R.N.; (*h*) Elizabeth Anne Costobadie, married Thomas Grubbe of Eastwell Hall, Devizes, 21 June 1821, b. at Gravely 14 Ap. 1801; (*i*) Mary, b. at sea, wife of Richard Lucas, of Edith Weston, Rutland; (*j*) Charlotte, wife of John Humphrey, of Kibworth Hall, Leicestershire; (*k*) Fanny, d. in 1878.

NOTES

(A) Haag, *La France Protestante*, IV. 73.

(B) This genealogy affords an example of the assumption of the particle " de " before the family name. The Costebadie family were not ennobled either by charge or office.

(C) Pierre Echaunié, bourgeois, of Argentat, had 5 children: (*a*) Pierre, avocat; (*b*) Jeanne, wife of Jean Costebadie; (*c*) Jean; (*d*) Pierre, the younger; (*e*) Lucie. Details of the family are given in the Procès instituted in 1718 by claimants for the property of Jean Costebadie and his wife (Série T. T. 117, Bordeaux). This suit ended in 1727. It is stated therein that Jeanne Echaunie did not go to England till 1687, and took four male children with her. This accounts for six of the children. A Mary Costebadie appears in London in 1711, when she received an Oath Roll naturalization; no details are given, but she may well have been the seventh child, and one of the two brought to England by the father in 1684. Jean Costebadie is stated to have left his wife and 5 children at Tonneins (T. T. 170).

(D) Jean Gril Costebadie married Marie Guillot "dans l'église de Springarden 6 juillet 1710." By Mr. Jean Dubourdieu, Min. de la Savoye. Licence Arch-Bishop of Canterbury. His daughter Jeanne Marguerite was bapt. 26 May 1711 at the Savoy French church. The father was of Covent Garden. His son Jacob was bapt. 2 Aug. 1716, *id.* The godfather was Jacob Costebadie. Jean Costebadie was 2nd Lt. in Sibourg's French Foot at Alicante in 1709. Commission dated 2 Ap. 1706. Lt. 23 Aug. 1712. On half-pay 1740.

(E) Jean Costebadie was naturalised 19 March 1705–6. "Son of John Costabadie by Marie his wife, b. at Argentat (*sic*) in Limosin in France." His son Jacob was naturalised 8 Ap. 1707. "Son of John Costebadie by Jeane his wife, b. at Argentat in Auvergne in France."

The family possess among other heirlooms an iron seal with the arms—two chevrons with 3 stars in chief, and a lion rampant in base. Crest, a church on a hill, in allusion to the name (Coste, a hill; abadie, a church). Motto: "*In hoc saxo templum meum aedificabo.*" A gold and sapphire ring, and a Genoese coin weighing 8 grains, 2 inches in diameter, bearing the inscription DUX · ET · GUBERNATORES · REIP · GEN (obverse) ET · REGE · EOS · 1641 · I · SES. which were bequeathed by Jean Costebadie with the proviso that they were never to be parted with except in case of dire necessity.

Jean Costebadie, sgr. de La Trille, left a daughter Eleonore, who married, 9 Feb. 1684, at Bordeaux, Théophile Garnier, sieur de Lisle, son of Théophile Garnier, sieur de Laborde, and Catherine Audebert, of Caumont. Jean Costebadie or Costabadie is described as "Secrétaire de feu le duc d'Epernon."

DESCHAMPS

I. Jean Deschamps,(A) minister, b. at Bergerac in Périgord, 1667. Left France in 1685, and went to Geneva, where he remained three years, and afterwards to Butzow, in the Duchy of Mecklenburg. Removed to Berlin in 1730 and died there in the same year, aged 63. His wife was Dlle. Lucrèce de Maffée,(B) of Dauphiné, whom he married in 1701 or 1702. She d. in Dec. 1739, aged 68, leaving 8 children, three of whom died young: (*a*) Gabriel, b. 1703, page to the Grand Duke of Mecklenburg-Strelitz: abjured and returned to Rouen; (*b*) Jacques, b. at Butzow, 1708: studied theology at Geneva and Marbourg and returned to Germany; (*c*) Jean, who follows, II.; (*d*) Antoine; (*e*) Sophie.

II. Jean Deschamps, b. at Butzow, 27 May 1709, and 30 years pastor in that place. He was chaplain to the Queen of Prussia and was appointed, in 1737, Court preacher in the household of Frederick William, Prince Royal of Prussia, and, in 1740, tutor to his sons. He fell into disgrace owing to his attacks on Voltaire, then at the zenith of his fame, and went to England, arriving in London, 25 March 1747. He had already been proposed as pastor of the French church of the Savoy when he was offered a chair as Professor of Philosophy at Cassel by Prince William of Hesse, and in consequence refused it. Was ordained by the Bishop of London in Duke Street Chapel, Westminster, and entered on his functions in June 1749. In 1756 he assisted Israel Antoine Aufrère, minister of St. James's, and on his death, 5 Ap. 1758, aged 92, he asked permission to succeed him, which was not granted. He remained pastor of the Savoy Church till his sudden death, 23 Aug. 1767. He was on the Commission of the Royal Bounty for the relief of poor French Protestants. Married, 4 Ap. 1753, Judith Chamier, and left six children, three of whom died young: (*a*) Jean Ezechiel, III., the eldest son, took the name of Chamier (see Chamier Ped.); (*b*) Dorothée-Sophie, b. 21 Sept. 1755, bapt. 12 Oct., Savoy; married John Mackie and d. at Vevey in 1819; (*c*) Suzanne-Judith, b. 7 Oct. 1759, bapt. 9 Oct.

Savoy; married the Rev. Thomas Cave Winscom, Vicar of Wirkworth, and d. in 1820.

III. Jean Ezechiel Deschamps, or Chamier, b. 30 May, bapt. 4 June 1754 (Savoy), entered the East India Civil Service in 1772, and became chief secretary to the Government and a Member of Council in the Madras Presidency. He assumed the name of Chamier by Royal Licence, 20 Oct. 1780, pursuant to the will of his uncle, Antony Chamier, d. 23 Feb. 1831, buried in the cemetery of St. George's, Hanover Square. He married Georgina Grace, daur. of Admiral Sir William Burnaby, Bart., at Madras, 1 Oct. 1785. She died, 14 May 1826, and was buried at Stoke, near Guildford. They left six sons and five daughters. (See Burke's *Landed Gentry*.)

NOTES

(A) An ancient family of the Périgord, according to tradition, of which, however, there is no proof. One of the sisters of Theodore de Béze married the fifth ancestor of Jean Deschamps, I.

(B) Daughter of Nathaniel Maffée and Isabeau Archer, both of whom left France and died in a foreign country. Nathaniel, or Nathan, de Maffée left two sons, Pierre and Nathan de Maffée, also fugitives. Gabriel Deschamps, after his return to France, claimed the property of his mother Lucrèce de Maffée, in 1738. The property of Pierre de Maffée was claimed by Étienne Blanc in 1740; Pierre having left France in 1692, a claim to this property was also made by Nathan de Maffée, officier des Dragons, in 1736–1738, grandson of Nathaniel de Maffée, and nephew of Pierre de Maffée (Biens des Religionnaires). The family came from Grenoble.

FONNEREAU

Arms (English): Gules, 3 chevronets argt. on a chief azur, a sun in splendour.

I. Zacharie Fonnereau of La Rochelle, married Marguerite Chateigner before 1677, and had

II. Claude Fonnereau,(A) b. at La Rochelle 22 March 1677; sent to England at the age of 12, at the Revocation; d. 8 Ap. 1740. Married secondly, 15 June 1738, at St. Antholins, London, Anne Bochon, mentioned in his will. By his 1st wife, Elizabeth, daur. of Philippe and Anne Bureau,(B) of La Rochelle, whom he married 16 Oct. 1698, at St. Mary Magdalen, Old Fish Street, London, he left: (*a*) Zachary Philip, who succeeds, 4th son, III.; b. 31 Jan 1705/6; bapt. at the French Church of St. Martin Orgars; d. 15 Aug. 1778; bur. at St. Peter's, Cornhill; (*b*) Thomas, of Christchurch, Ipswich, M.P., b. 27 Oct. 1699; bapt. at St. Swithin's, Cannon Street, London; d. in 1779; (*c*) The Rev. Claude Fonnereau, D.D., Rector of Clapton, Northants, b. 14 Ap. 1701; bapt. by the Rector of St. Swithin's, Cannon Street; alive in 1759: he married, 24 Ap. 1728, Ann, daur. of the Rev. William Banbury, Rector of Great Catworth, Hunts; they left two sons: (i) Peter, d. a bachelor, 16 Sept. 1759; (ii) Claudius, b. 17 Ap. 1729; bapt. at Clapton, Northants; (iii) Frances Eliz, b. 30 May 1730; (iv) Anne, b. 8 July 1731; (*d*) Elizabeth Frances, b. 2 May 1702. She married, 13 May 1729, Jacques Benezet,(C) merchant, at St. Stephen's, Walbrook; (*e*) Abel, b. 10 Ap. 1703, d. 1753: he married, 21 Feb. 1731/2, at Oxford, Elizabeth, daur. of Francis Heywood; (*f*) Anne, b. 12 Oct. 1704: she married, 5 Feb. 1734/5, Philip Champion de Crespigny; (*g*) Peter, b. 5 March 1709/10, d. a bachelor 1743; (*h*) Mary Anne, b. 9 July 1711; married Professor Martyn of Cambridge, at Chelsea; (*i*) Elizabeth, b. 2 Nov. 1712; she married Mr. de Hauteville, who was buried at Broxbourne; she was buried at St. Antholin, Budge Row.

III. Zachary Philip Fonnereau, married Marguerite, daur. and co-heir of George Martyn, of Odington, co. Gloucester, and of his wife Cary Cave Malcher, at Whitehall Chapel,

13 Ap. 1738. She d. 8 June 1778, aged 61, and was buried at St. Peter's, Cornhill. They left: (*a*) Philip, b. 17 June 1739, d. 17 Feb. 1797, IV.; buried at Greenwich; (*b*) Martyn, b. 19 March 1740/1, d. a bachelor, 18 May 1817, buried at Wargrave, Bucks; (*c*) Charlotte, b. 28 Jan. 1741/2, d. 15 Nov. 1806, buried in the cemetery of St. George's, Hanover Square; (*d*) Fanny, b. 7 Jan. 1743/4, married George Stainforth, junior, 22 March 1777, at St. Peter, Cornhill, d. 10 Jan. 1827: he d. 20 Sept. 1815, *s.p.*; (*e*) Thomas, b. 21 Jan. 1745/6, d. 26 Dec. 1788, buried at Topsham, Devon: he married, 19 Oct. 1786, Harriet, daur. of John Hanson, of Reading, and Ann his wife, Harriet Fonnereau, d. 2 Feb. 1832, aged 65, buried at Reading. Thomas Fonnereau left by her: (i) John Zachary, b. 29 Dec. 1787, d. at Douai 22 Sept. 1822: he married, 11 May 1822, at the British Embassy, Paris, Caroline, daur. of Robert Sewell, of Jamaica and Gerrards Cross: she re-married at his death the Rev. S. Whitelock, of Kirby Underdale, 29 Nov. 1831; (ii) Thomas, a posthumous child, d. at Bushey, Herts, 1850, aged 61: buried at Aldenham.

IV. Philip Fonnereau, married, 15 Dec. 1763, Mary, daur. of Armstead Parker and Eliz: Rogers. She was b. in 1740, d. 5 Jan. 1775, and buried at St. Mary-le-Bone. By her he left: (*a*) Elizabeth Margaret, b. 3 Jan. 1765, d. 23 Jan. 1841, buried at Aldenham; (*b*) Isabella, b. 15 March 1766, d. unmarried in 1848; (*c*) Mary Ann, b. 17 Feb. 1768, d. 1 June, 1844, buried at Aldenham: she married, 30 Ap. 1790, in Bishopsgate Church, George Woodfield Thelusson, 2nd son of Philip and Ann Thelusson; (*d*) Philip, b. 5 Aug. 1778, and baptised at Scarborough 10 Sept., d. *s.p.*

NOTES

(A) Claude Fonnereau was naturalised 25 March 1698. "Born at La Rochelle, in France, son of Zacharia Fonnereau and Margarette his wife. The family of Chateigner was numerous in Saintonge, and a branch became seigneurs of Cramahé. It was distinct from that of Chastaigner, of Poitou.

A George Fonnereau was admitted to the Pest House Hospital in 1710. (Haag, Vol. 5, 6, 2 edit.)

(B) The Bureau family of Saintonge and Poitou came to England. The preacher, Bureau, imprisoned in 1720, is mentioned by Lièvre (*Histoire des Protestants de Poitou*). An interesting letter written by Thomas Bureau, of Niort, to his brother, a bookseller in London, dated 30 Aug. 1685, giving details of the Dragonnades in Poitou and the cruelties suffered by their mother, is in the Bodleian Library, Oxford. (Rawll MSS. 984.)

(C) The Benezet family came from Calvisson, in Languedoc, but migrated to St. Quentin about the year 1681. John Stephen Benezet settled in London. His son Antoine was b. at St. Quentin, married Joyce Marriott; he went to America and took up the slave question; d. aged 71, and was buried in the Friends' burying ground, Philadelphia. Jacques, or James, Benezet, husband of Elizabeth Françoise Fonnereau, was brother of John Steven, or Jean Etienne, Benezet. (See Agnew, *French Prot. Exiles.*)

For Thelusson, see Burke's *Landed Gentry*, etc. See also Cussan's *Hertfordshire* and Agnew, *French Prot. Exiles*.

DE GENNES

Arms : d'Hermines, à la fasce de gueules.

Alias, d'azur, à 3 renards rampant d'or : 2 en chef, 1 en pointe.

Alias, many other coats, differing. (d'Hozier Armorial.)

I. Jean de Gennes, married Dlle. Marie Rouxigneul and left Guy, who succeeds, II. (Vitré Par. Reg.)

II. Guy de Gennes, sr. de La Mothe, married Dlle. Mathurine Ravenel, and d. 14 Feb. 1606, leaving : (*a*) Guy, who succeeds, III.; (*b*) Jacquine, b. at Vitré, 11 Feb. 1561, wife of Jean Lemogne : she d. 29 Nov. 1597 ; (*c*) Jean, b. 8 May 1565.

III. Guy de Gennes, sr. de Chalonges, married, 3 June 1584, Dlle. Marie Godard, daur. of Gilles Godard, and of Dlle. Gillette Ravenel. She was b. at Vitré, 25 March 1565, and d. 24 June 1616 : her husband, Guy de Gennes, d. 10 July 1616, leaving 12 children : (*a*) Guy, who succeeds, IV.; (*b*) Catherine, b. 1 Nov. 1590 ; (*c*) Jean, b. 26 Nov. 1591 ; (*d*) Marie, b. 30 Nov. 1593 ; (*e*) Anne, b. 31 Jan. 1595 ; (*f*) Anne, b. 17 June 1596, married 26 Feb. 1623, Jean Beauvoir ; (*g*) Pierre, b. 22 Aug. 1597 ; (*h*) Catherine, b. 18 May 1600 ; (*i*) Daniel, b. 29 Aug. 1601 ; (*k*) Jacquine, b. 26 Jan. 1603 ; (*l*) Jeanne, b. 7 Ap. 1605 ; (*m*) Esther, b. 2 Oct. 1606.

IV. Guy de Gennes, sr. de Chalonges, b. 14 Nov. 1589, married, 13 Sept. 1620, Dlle. Louise de Hemestre. He was one of the elders of the Protestant Church at Vitré ; d. at Izé, 24 Nov. 1657, and was buried at Vitré. He left : (*a*) Jeanne, b. 12 Ap. 1625, married 29 Aug. 1649 Thomas Boisramé, and d. 25 June 1661 ; (*b*) Pierre, b. 22 June 1627 ; (*c*) Jean ; (*d*) Pierre, b. 6 Dec. 1629 ; (*e*) Guy, b. 3 July 1631.

V. Pierre de Gennes, married 14 July 1652 Dlle. Suzanne Nouail, or Noël, daur. of Pierre Nouail, sgr. de La Daudrairie, avocat, and of Jeanne Grislel, and left : (*a*) René, b. 27 Oct.

1654 ; (*b*) Pierre, b. 4 Nov. 1658, who abjured at St. Malo, 22 Nov. 1685 ; (*c*) Daniel, sgr. de La Picottière, who abjured at St. Malo, 22 Nov. 1685, aged 27 years. He lived at St. Malo and Morlaix after 1685. Author of the English Branch, VI.

VI. Daniel de Gennes, (A) sr. de La Picottière, married Dlle. Judith Ravenel, by whom he left 11 children. Their marriage is not found in the Protestant Register at Vitré, nor in the Catholic Register : it probably took place after 1685 at St. Malo, where the birth of one son, François, is recorded : (*a*) Judith-Suzanne, b. 13 Ap. 1688, d. 16 Ap. 1688 (Vitré Parish Reg.) ; (*b*) François, b. at St. Malo, 30 May 1689 ; (*c*) René David, b. at Vitré 7 June 1690 ; (*d*) Joseph-Michel, b. 5 Jan. 1692 at Vitré ; (*e*) Anne-Marie, b. 22 March 1695 at Vitré ; (*f*) Marthe-Suzanne ; (*g*) Daniel ; (*h*) Judith ; (*i*) Philip ; (*j*) Jean-Daniel, VII ; (*k*), Françoise, godmother, 7 March 1732/3, to Guillaume des Vories, at Portarlington ; (*l*) Daniel Antoine.

VII. Jean-Daniel de Gennes, Colonel in the British Army, married Dlle. Françoise d'Orval, daur. of Antoine Hullin, sgr. d'Orval,(B) and of Dlle. Suzanne Gouyguet de St. Eloy,(C) 1 Sept. 1720 at Sunbury-on-Thames (see Dalton, Army List). He d. at Portarlington, 8 Dec. 1766 ; his wife Françoise d'Orval d. aged about 63, 13 Oct. 1776, also at Portarlington. They had 8 children : (*a*) Joseph-Jacques,(D) b. at Portarlington 19 Aug. 1728, d. there 28 Aug. 1759 ; (*b*) Judith, b. before 1731, eldest daur. and co-heiress who married, 19 Feb. 1752, at Portarlington, George Frazer, of Parke, and Cuba House, Banagher ; (*c*) Moyse, b. 5 Oct., bapt. 7 Nov. 1731, at Portarlington : his godfather was Antoine d'Orval, maternal grandfather : proxy for Moyse de St. Eloy, maternal great uncle, d. 23 Feb. 1734-5 ; (*d*) Marie-Anne, b. 3 Dec. 1733, bapt. 1 Jan. 1733-4 : her godfather was Guillaume Portal, capitaine de cavalerie, proxy for Edouard Ravenel : her godmother was Suzanne d'Orval, maternal grandmother, proxy for Marie Anne de Gâtine ; (*e*) Caroline, b. 7 Feb., bapt. 12 March 1738, at Portarlington ; (*f*) Louise Françoise, b. 18 Aug. 1744 ; (*g*) probably a son Paul, who was godfather, 2 July 1755, to

Françoise Frazer, daur. of George Frazer and Judith Suzanne de Gennes ; (*h*) a son Nathaniel is mentioned by Dalton (Army List).

NOTES.

(A) Daniel de Gennes and his wife Judith Ravenel remained in France as " Nouveaux Convertis," as late as 1736, when they applied for leave to sell property at Vitré. The memoir states that they had been R.P.R. for 46 years : " l'un et l'autre seuls héritiers de leurs Pères et Mères morts. Ont des petits héritages à Vitré . . . deux maisons et autres pièces de terre dans la paroisse de Dizé, St. Martin, etc." Another memoir connected with this application states that " Daniel de Gennes, sieur de La Picottière et Judith Ravenel, son épouse, nectés de La Religion Prétandue Reformée, ayant demeuré à St. Malo plus de 15 ans, et à Morlaix 28 ans, faisant un petit commerce, ce voijeant en des aages avancés et ce voulant Retirer à Paris Requiescent très humblement du Roy . . . de vandre . . . deux petites maisons en la ville de Vitré, Paroisse de Notre Dame." (Série T.T.124.) He had abjured 22 Nov. 1685 at St. Malo. They appear to have left France immediately afterwards, for Daniel de Gennes died in London in 1739, where he made his will (P.C.C. Henchman 127) dated 26 March 1737 (1738 N.S.) and proved by Judith de Gennes his widow, to whom administration was granted. He describes himself as son of Pierre de Gennes, sieur de La Picotière, and of Susannah Nouail: born at Vitré 4 Nov. 1658, according to a certificate given by the late sieur de la Follière and John Godard, " anciens " of that church, dated 20 Oct. 1671. He states that he has five children living, three sons and two daughters, to whom he had given successively 69,000 livres French money, for which he has receipts, except for the portion given to his youngest daughter, Mrs. Maxwell. He had a sum of £5,100 invested in the Public Funds in the names of his son, " the Major," and his sister to enjoy the interest thereof during their lives. He mentions property in France, which was not to be sold without the consent of Joseph Michel, his son, living in Paris. He also mentions his grand-daughter and god-daughter Judith de Gennes, in Ireland : a mortgage in Dublin on a house in the name of her father. He desired to be buried at Marylebone, near his sister. The will is translated out of French by Peter St. Eloy, and was proved 13 June 1739. Etienne du Pont, of St. Anne's, Westminster, and Jeanne Margaret Bistord, wife of Peter Tirel, of St. Anne's, appearing. His wife Judith Ravenel was sole residuary legatee for life. His daughter Marthe Suzanne de Gennes married 22 Nov. 1719, " écuyer Charles Théodore de Maxüel, capitaine dans le régiment de Gauvain au service de sa Majesté Britannique": she is described as daughter of Daniel Degennes, sieur de La Picottière et de Dame Judith Ravenel, dem. à Morlaix en Bretagne." The marriage took place in the house of Lord Stair, ambassador at Paris, in presence of Mr. Savile Bradley, chaplain to the Duke of Richmond and Rector of Earnly, in Sussex; the Earl of Stair, Judith Ravenel, René David de Gennes, Ph. de Gennes, Anna Maria de Gennes, Marthe de la Favelle; Alfred Devole Kershoven, De Martine, Louis Henri Daumenil, Laurent François Prévost de Boisbily. (Fr. Church of the Savoy Registers.)

The family of Maxüel or Maxwell was originally of Scottish origin, but had been settled in France since the fifteenth century. Several of its members left France at the time of the Revocation. Etienne de Maxüel, sgr. de La Fortière, left in 1681 by permission of the King. His brother Jacques, sgr. des Champs, entered the service of the Prince of Orange and the Duke of Zell. Etienne de Maxüel was living near Pont-au-de-mer. He went to Berlin, where he is mentioned in a List of Deputies in 1688. Pastor at Hanover. (MS. Court, 617, 1.)

(B) The d'Orval family came from Normandy, where they possessed several seigneuries near Alençon and in the Beauce. Gidéon de Calmesnil, chev., sgr. d'Orval, de Canon, et de Chenneville, etc., claimed property left by the English branch, in 1720: " tant en son propre nom, qu'en qualité de père et tuteur légitime et naturel de l'enfant dont Dame Marie-Anne Hellouin son espouze de luy authorisée," etc. She was living in the parish of St. Pierre, Caen. (Série T.T. 125.) The Hellouin family was ennobled in 1604 by office of " secrétaire du Roy " in the person of Jean Hellouin, who resigned it in favour of his son Jean, in 1627. Arms, d'azur au chevron d'or, acc. en chef de 3 étoiles de même, et en pointe d'une pointe de lance renversée, d'argent.

(C) Probably daughter of Isaac Gouyguet de St. Eloy, sieur du Tertre, and bapt. at Cleusné 1 Jan. 1664. Her mother was Jeanne Doudart. (Prot. Reg. Cleusné). He was b. at Plumy, in Brittany, son of Isaac, by Jane (Jeanne) his wife. Naturalised 24 March 1699; captain in Sir Neville Granville's regiment; "had served his Majesty for ten years past and had a large family, and no home to go to." (Nat. List.) The family of Gouyguet were seigneurs de St. Eloy, du Plessis, du Tertre, and other places, and bore for arms: d'azur, à une croix engrêlée d'argent, cantonnée de 4 roses de même.

Another Isaac Gouyguet de St. Eloy married Dame Marguerite Leblanc, and had a daur., bapt. at Cleusné, near Rennes, 24 June 1685: presented by Henri Gouyguet, her uncle. Several members of the family emigrated in 1685 and in 1715.

(D) A Joseph de Gennes is on the Irish Half Pay Lists in 1756, 2nd Lieut. in Sir John Bruce's regiment, which was broken in 1748.

JANVRE DE LA BOUCHETIÈRE

Arms: D'azur, à 3 têtes du Lion d'or lampassées et couronnées de gueules. (Poitou and Ireland.)

I. Geoffroi Janvre, sgr. de La Bouchetière, and his wife Dlle. Aldama de Lambertye, or Lambert (de Lamberto), founded the parish church of Clavé in 1005 (Cartulaire de l'Abbaye de St. Maixent). Several seigneurs, amongst whom was a Janvre, signed a charter by which Guillaume IV., Comte de Poitou, gave property to the abbey of Bourgueil in 1019. Geoffroi Janvre left 2 sons by his wife Aldama: (*a*) Aimery, who succeeds, II.; (*b*) Archambaud, Archbishop of Bordeaux, seigneur de St. Maixent by virtue of being abbot.

II. Aimery Janvre, sgr. de La Bouchetière, married, before the Thursday before the Feast of St. John the Baptist, 1032, Dlle. Agnès de Parthenay, sister of Guillaume II. de Parthenay. She made an agreement to build a church, before that date, in the parish of Saint Lin (1032) (Cart. de l'Abbaye de St. Maixent), known by deeds of 1040 and 9 Dec. 1058. They left a son, Archambaud, III.

III. Archambaud Janvre, sgr. de La Bouchetière, consented with Agnès de Parthenay, his mother, to the gift of a farm (La Froine et du bois de Nanteuil), in 1058, for the repair of the tomb of St. Maixent. He is known also by a deed of the abbey of Bourgeuil-en-Vallée, 1060. He married Dlle. Hélène de Savary, and left: (*a*) Archambaud 2nd, who succeeds, IV.; (*b*) Aimery, who gave much property to the abbey of Chatelliers, near the seigneurie of La Bouchetière, and was first abbot.

IV. Archambaud Janvre, sgr. de La Bouchetière, married before 1089 Dlle. Pétronille de Varèze, daur. of Bertrand de Varèze, who gave the church of Varèze to the monastery of St. Jean d'Angély in 1077. Known by deeds and charters dated 18 Dec. 1089, and 1095, the Thursday after the Feast of St. Peter, when he founded a Mass for the repose of his wife's soul. At this date he had 3 young children, whom he commends to the care of Garnier, Abbot of St. Maixent.

In 1103 he made a second gift to the chapel of St. Jean in the church of St. Saturnin at St. Maixent. Took part in the First Crusade and was taken prisoner (Cart. de l'Abbaye de St. Maixent). By his marriage with Dlle. Petronille de Varèze he left 3 children: (*a*) Hélie, V.; (*b*) Pierre, Abbot of St. Maixent; (*c*) another Hélie, who left for the Second Crusade in 1147, with his nephew Archambaud.

V. Hélie Janvre, sgr. de La Bouchetière, 1st of the name, married before 8 Nov. 1119 Dlle. Agnès de Ste. Maure, as is known by a deed of gift by him, his wife Agnes de Ste. Maure, and his sons Pierre and Archambaud, of a house and vineyard at La Trinité, to the church of La Trinité at Poitiers. She was probably the daur. of Guillaume de Ste. Maure, Vicomte de Tours, and Dlle. de Cassenote, Dame de La Haye. They left: (*a*) Archambaud, 3rd of the name, VI.; (*b*) Pierre.

VI. Archambaud Janvre, sgr. de La Bouchetière, known by a deed of gift in 1119, and one of 28 Feb. 1146. Went to the Second Crusade in 1147, and left his wife Alianore Chenin and his children under the guardianship of his uncle Pierre Janvre, Abbot of St. Maixent, and in case of his death, as guardian of his children (Titres et chartres de l'Abbaye de St. Maixent). He died in the Crusade and left with others, Hélie, who succeeds, VII.

VII. Hélie Janvre, seigneur de La Bouchetière, married 30 Jan. 1164 Dlle. Préjente de Tonnay-Charente, daur. of Armand, sgr. de Tonnay-Charente. He was not living 17 July 1176, when his widow Préjente, guardian of his children, executed a deed of partition with Bertrand Chenin, regarding the succession of Dlle. Auzie Chenin, sister of Bertrand Chenin and Alianore Chenin. They left 2 children: (*a*) Guillaume, who succeeds, VIII.; (*b*) Bertrand, alive 17 July 1176.

VIII. Guillaume Janvre, sgr. de La Bouchetière and Veuzé, married 20 Sept. 1194, Dlle. Jeanne de Volvire, daur. of Renault de Volvire, sgr. de Ruffec. In 1208, 19 Dec., he and his wife Jeanne bought the fief of La Chaignée for Pierre, her brother. Guillaume Janvre accompanied Louis, son of Philippe II., in his attack on the English, as an esquire, and was killed at Avignon in 1226, aged 64, leaving a son Jean, who succeeds, IX.

IX. Jean Janvre, 1st of the name, sgr. de La Bouchetière, married Dlle. Lectice de Surgères, daur. of Guillaume Maengot, sgr. de Surgères and Dampierre, and of his wife, Dame Berthoumée d'Allemoigne, and left a son Archambaud, who succeeds, X.

X. Archambaud Janvre, 4th of the name, sgr. de La Bouchetière and Veuzé, married (lundi après la St. Barnabé, apôtre, 1242) Dlle. Pétronille de Chaunay, daur. of Guillaume de Chaunay, sgr. de Champdenier and Javarzay. By consent of his wife he settled his seigneurie of La Bouchetière on the monks of the Abbey of St. Maixent in 1247, before leaving for the Crusade to the Holy Land with St. Louis. In the event of his death, he charged Dame Lectice de Surgères, his mother, and his wife Pétronille to release as much of this land as possible. He was killed near Massourah, defending the king, 1250. In 1256 his wife, mother, and children released the fief of La Bouchetière. He left : (*a*) Jean, who succeeds, XI.; (*b*) Geoffroi, who married in 1268 Dlle. Marie Chasteigner, daur. of Guillaume Chasteigner, sgr. de Paillès ; (*c*) Honore, mentioned in a deed of 1256.

XI. Jean Janvre, chev., sgr. de La Bouchetière and Veuzé, married in 1266 (le mardi après St. Pierre) Dlle. Jeanne de Montmorenci, who d. 11 Dec. 1274, daur. of Bouchard de Montmorenci, sgr. de Montmorenci, and of Isabeau de Laval. He is mentioned in deeds and charters of 1268, 1270, 1271, 1273, 1275 ; d. in 1287, and was buried in the church of the Cordeliers of St. Maixent, 19 April, leaving Archambaud, XII.

XII. Archambaud Janvre, 5th of the name, chev., sgr. de La Bouchetière and Veuzé, married, 18 Feb. 1288, Dlle. Agathe Voyer, daur. of Renault Voyer de La Haye, chev., sgr. de Paulmix, in Touraine, and left : (*a*) Jean, who succeeds, XIII; (*b*) Thomas, known by a deed of 1320.

XIII. Jean Janvre (dit Bagoulin), chev., sgr. de La Bouchetière, Veuzé, des Loges, and La Chauvellière, married, 23 Oct. 1323, Dlle. Marguerite de La Rochefoucauld, daur. of Aimery de La Rochefoucauld, sgr. de Maraton, Balsac and Bayers, and of Dauphine de La Tour, daur. of Bernard, sgr. de La Tour, in Auvergne. Jean Janvre served in Flanders under Philip of Valois, and left: (*a*) Jean, who succeeds, XIV.; (*b*) Guillemette, wife of P. de La Garde.

XIV. Jean Janvre, " noble écuyer," sgr. de La Bouchetière and Veuzé, married 26 Jan. 1355, Dlle. Marie de Rogre, daur. of Guillaume de Rogre, chev., sgr. de Rouvre, near Cherveux, and of Jeanne Poupart. He is known in various deeds and charters of 14 Aug. 1381, 1386, 26 Oct. 1389, 1390. He left: (*a*) Jean, who succeeds, XV.; (*b*) Perrot, d. *s.p.*, 13 Oct. 1436.

XV. Jean Janvre, sgr. de La Bouchetière, married, 26 Oct. 1389, Dlle. Marguerite Chenin, daur. of Gauvin (d. at that date), chev., sgr. de l'Isle Bapaume. Jean Janvre was living 9 Ap. 1409 and left: (*a*) Jean, who succeeds, XVI.; (*b*) Philippe, wife of Jean Sergente; (*c*) Marguerite, married before 1436, Louis Corignon; (*d*) Jeanne, married before 1436, Alain Leschatté; (*e*) Catherine: all mentioned in a deed of partition, 13 Oct. 1436.

XVI. Jean Janvre, 6th of the name, sgr. de La Bouchetière and Chauvellière; married, 21 Jan. 1410, Dlle. Thomasse Corignolle (Corignon), daur. of Haubert Corignon, chev., sgr. du Vivier-Estraing, in Angoumois, sister of Louis Corignon, above. Jean Janvre qualifies as " haut et puissant " in deeds of 26 July 1432, 8 Aug. 1435, 16 Dec. 1439, 28 May 1450, 27 May 1456. He left: (*a*) Mathurin, who succeeds, XVII.; (*b*) André, d. before 15 June 1440; (*c*) Isabeau, married, before 15 June 1440, Mathurin Rourtheau, éc.; (*d*) N.... Janvre, wife of Anthoine Chevallier, éc.

XVII. Mathurin Janvre, éc., noble et puissant sgr. de La Bouchetière, Veuzé, Fougères, Sermont, and La Chauvelière, married, 9 Feb. 1436, Dlle. Jeanne de Pérusse d'Escars, daur. of Ardouin, and of Hélène de Roquefeuille. He accompanied Marie d'Anjou in a pilgrimage to St. James of Compostella as " premier écuyer " and " chevalier d'honneur." By his wife Jeanne d'Escars he left 7 children : (*a*) Alain, who succeeds, XVIII. ; (*b*) Jean, elder brother of another Jean ; (*c*) Jean, the younger ; (*d*) Madeleine, married, 16 June 1483, Christophe Eschallas, son of Pierre, sgr. de Maillé, and of Catherine de Vers ; (*e*) Marguerite ; (*f*) Souveraine ; (*g*) Jeanne, called sister of Madeleine in her marriage contract, 16 June 1483.

XVIII. Alain Janvre, sgr. de La Bouchetière, Fougères, Sault, Sermont, Chauvelière, etc. ; married, 29 Ap. 1474, Dlle. Anne de La Porte de Vézins, eldest daur. of René de La Porte, chev., sgr. de Sermont, and of Dame Jeanne des Ridelières. Known by various deeds. Will dated 17 Aug. 1486. He left six children : (*a*) Léon, sgr. de La Bouchetière, Veuzé and Sermont, married Dlle. Anne Janvre before 8 June 1503 ; d. before 16 Aug. 1516 *s.p.*; (*b*) Georges, married, *circ.* 1500, Dlle. Marie de Preuilly, and left one daur., who d. young ; (*c*) Jean, who succeeds, XIX. ; (*d*) Gabriel, known by a deed of partition with his brothers, 8 June 1504 ; (*e*) Renée, married before 8 June 1528, Jean de Granges de Surgères, chev., sgr. de La Gard, etc.; (*f*) Jeanne, known by a deed of partition, 18 June 1517, with her brother Georges Janvre, relating to the property of Alain Janvre and Anne de La Porte, her father and mother.

XIX. Jean Janvre, sgr. de La Bouchetière and des Loges, married, 12 Jan. 1501, Dlle. Françoise Chabot, daur. of Louis Chabot, sgr. du Luc, near Champdenier, younger brother of Messire Artur Chabot, sgr. de Laleu, and left : (*a*) Georges, who succeeds, XX. ; (*b*) Gabriel, sgr. de Blévinières, La Charprée, and Fougères, chev. de St. Louis, and gentilhomme ordinaire de la chambre to François I. He married, 16 Nov. 1529, Dame Jeanne de Pérusse-d'Escars, daur. of Geoffroi de Pérusse-d'Escars, sgr. d'Escars-Juillac, Ségur, etc., and of Françoise d'Arpajon, daur. of Gui, Baron d'Arpajon, Vicomte de Lautrec, and of Marie d'Aubusson, Dame de Monteil ; (*c*) Marguerite.

XX. Georges Janvre, sgr. de La Bouchetière, Veuzé et La Chauvelière, married by contract, 31 May 1528, Dlle.

Marguerite de St. Georges, daur. of Noble et Puissant Guichard de St. Georges, sgr. de Vérac, Couhé, Boissée and Chavagnac, etc., and of Anne de Mortemer. D. 20 June 1536. His widow Marguerite remarried, 11 Dec. 1537, Noble et Puissant Louis des Granges, chev., sgr. de Montfermier. By his marriage with Marguerite de St. Georges he left: (*a*) Philippe, who succeeds, XXI.; (*b*) Renée, who married, 13 June 1551, René de La Longueraire.

XXI. Philippe Janvre, 1st of the name, chev., sgr. de La Bouchetière, Veuzé, Boisbretier, des Loges, La Chauvelière, etc., chev. de St. Louis, gentilhomme ordinaire de la chambre, was a minor under the guardianship of his mother, 20 June 1536, and had as tutor and guardian, 3 June 1538, Louis des Granges de Surgères, chev., sgr. de Montfermier. He married, 5 July 1558, Dlle. Madeleine de Thory, sister of Antoine de Thory, chev., sgr. de Boumois and La Roullière, and daur. of Noble et Puissant René de Thory and of Dame Anne Asse, his wife. He was ordered to leave France on account of his religion by an order of the king dated 16 Oct. 1585. His departure was delayed by ill-health by permission of Henry III. On the accession of Henry IV. he was made a gentleman of the chamber, chevalier de St. Michel and conseiller d'état. D. between 1597 and 1599. Will dated 14 Aug. 1596. He left: (*a*) Daniel, who succeeds, XXII.; (*b*) Susanne, who married, before 7 May 1596, René Bonnard, sgr. de Marais; (*c*) Marie, who married before 7 May 1596, Philippe Gellier, sgr. de La Tourlégat and Preuilly; qualified as "Haut et Puissant chevalier."

XXII. Daniel Janvre, 1st of the name, chev., sgr. de La Bouchetière, Veuzé, Boisbretier, Tourlégat, La Moussière, Lussay, La Ruichardière, et Moulin-Neuf, married, 21 Oct. 1600, Dlle. Renée de Malmouche, daur. and heiress of Louis de Malmouche, sgr. de La Moussière, and of Dame Elizabeth de Parthenay, daur. of Haut et Puissant Antoine de Parthenay, sgr. de Guéray. Daniel Janvre was dead in 1640 and his wife before 1633. He left by her 6 children: (*a*) Philippe, who succeeds, XXIII.; (*b*) Daniel, chev., sgr. de La Tour-Bouchetière, who married 1st, 20 Oct. 1648, Dlle.

Aymer, daur. of Louis Aymer, sgr. de Corignon, Germon and Breilbon. Maintained his noblesse, 23 Aug. 1667. 2nd, Dlle. .... Béjarry de La Grignonière; (*c*) Artus Janvre, author of the Branch de Quinchamps; (*d*) Anne Janvre, who married, 25 Aug. 1633, Daniel de Gréaulmes, Haut et Puissant chevalier, sgr. de Merduval; (*e*) Renée, Dame de Lussay, who married, 14 July 1637, Louis Duchesne, chev., sgr. de Vauvert. She d. 9 Jan. 1640; (*f*) Judith, living on the 9 Jan. 1640; (*g*) Elizabeth, who married before 8 Feb. 1640, Antoine Vasselot, sgr. de Reynier.

XXIII. Philippe Janvre, 2nd of the name, chev., sgr. de La Bouchetière, La Moussière, Chasnais, St. Lin, Boisbretier, Barrejau, and du Vignault; married Dlle. Marguerite d'Auzy, daur. of Gédéon d'Auzy, sgr. de l'Estortière and Chausseray, and of Dame Judith de Neuport. Maintained his noblesse, 1667. He is known by several deeds, dated 9 Jan. 1640, 7 Ap. 1653, 8 Aug. 1657, 8 May 1663, 26 Jan. 1670, 8 July 1679, and qualifies as "haut et puissant seigneur." He and his wife made their joint will, 6 Dec. 1652, in favour of their children: (*a*) Daniel, who succeeds, XXIV.; (*b*) Philippe, author of the Second Branch de La Moussière; (*c*) Charles, author of the Branch of the Seigneurs de l'Estortière.

XXIV. Daniel Janvre,(A) chev., sgr. de La Bouchetière, Boisbretier, St. Lin, La Barrejau, qualified as "H. & P. seigneur" in deeds dated 8 Aug. 1657, 5 July 1658, 8 May 1663, 8 July 1679. He married, as a Protestant, 8 Aug. 1657, Dlle. Olympe de Châtaigner,(B) whose will is dated 5 July 1658, daur. of H. et P. Messire Charles de Châteigner, chev., sgr. de La Grollière, and of Dame Anne de Machecoul. He maintained his noblesse in 1667, and seems to have conformed, since he appears in the Recherche de la Noblesse of 1697. He left France with his son, but returned. He left a son Charles, who succeeds, XXV.

XXV. Charles Janvre, sgr. de La Bouchetière, Remouillé, de l'Ardière, married, 2 May 1684, Dlle. Marie-Anne Falaiseau, of Paris, daur. of Samuel Falaiseau, éc., and of Dlle. Madeleine Dufour. She d. 20 Ap. 1734 at Dublin.

(Reg. Fr. Ch. St. Patrick.) Soon after their marriage Charles Janvre de La Bouchetière, with his mother Olympe, his father Daniel Janvre, his wife Marie-Anne Falaiseau, left France and went to England, where he was naturalised 7 Nov. 1698. He received a brevet as Colonel of Horse, 22 Feb. 1694, and later became Lt.-Col. of a regiment of Dragoons commanded by Lord Galway in Portugal, 20 Feb. 1709. On his way to Portugal he was taken prisoner by the French, but released. (State Papers, Dom. Anne.) On 24 June 1710 he succeeded Lord Galway in command, on his resignation owing to failing eyesight. Colonel Janvre de La Bouchetière was sent, in 1719, by the English Government to Poitou, owing to his influence among the Protestants, at the request of the Regent of France, who had information that Cardinal Alberoni, Minister of State to King Philip V. of Spain, was making attempts to stir up a rebellion among the Protestants of Poitou. De La Bouchetière reported that the " Nouveaux Catholiques " were opposed to any disloyal movement. He d. in 1720. A pension of £50 was granted to his widow. By his marriage with Marie-Anne Falaiseau he left 4 sons and 8 daughters : (*a*) Charles, naturalised 10 June 1713, " son of Charles La Bouchetière, by Mary his wife, born at Ghent in Flanders, XXVI.; (*b*) Louis, ensign in Lieut.-General Meredyth's Regiment of Foot (1st Bn. Lancs Fusiliers), 5 Ap. 1723 ; Lieut. 10 Jan. 1736, wounded at Fontenoy ; on half-pay 1761 ; (*c*) Henriette, b. 1693 ; married, at Dublin, 21 Aug. 1720, Cirus Guinebald de La Millière.(C) She is described as the eldest daur. of " Charles Janvre, chevalier, sgr. de La Bouchetière, de Haut Poitou, colonel de dragons, et Dame Marie de Falaiseau, de Paris. Henriette d. at Dublin 2 Oct. 1775, aged 82 ; (*d*) Marguerite, b. at Ghent, 23 Oct. 1696, d. at Dublin 11 Jan. 1788,(D) aged 92. She is described as second daur. of Charles Janvre, chev., sgr. de La Bouchetière, de Poitou ; (*e*) Françoise-Jeanne, b. Feb. 1699, and d. aged 3 months 20 May 1699, buried in the French cemetery at Dublin ; (*f*) Daniel, b. in 1700, d. aged one year 14 Nov. 1701, at Dublin (St. Patrick's) ; (*g*) another son, not named, who d. in Dec. 1703, aged one and a half years ; (*h*) Susanne Olympe, bapt. in the French Church of St. Mary, Dublin, 9 Dec. 1705 : she married Monsieur Jacques Pelletreau, Pastor of the

United French Churches of St. Patrick and St. Mary, Dublin: d. 22 May 1788: described as the third daur. of Charles Janvre de la Bouchetière and Marie Anne Falaiseau. Suzanne Pelletreau, their daur., married 16 Aug. 1776 Monsieur François Bessonet, of Nyon, in Switzerland, Pastor of the French Church of St. John, Dublin. She d. 20 March 1818, aged 70; (*i*) Charlotte, bapt. 17 Jan. 1707. Sponsors, Charles Janvre and Marguerite Marianne (Janvre), brother and sister.

XXVI. Charles Janvre, sgr. de La Bouchetière, was a cornet in La Fabrèque's Dragoons, his father's regiment, commission dated 24 Feb. 1709. He appears to have exchanged to the Infantry on the disbanding of La Fabrèque's Dragoons in 1712. This regiment was almost destroyed at the Almanza. In the year 1742 fifty out of a hundred and ninety-nine names of officers' widows were French. Charles Janvre de La Bouchetière was 1st Lieutenant in Bisset's Foot, 5 Dec. 1721; Capt.-Lieut. 1 March 1738, and was serving in 1740. His brother Louis was on half-pay, in 1760, of La Forey's Marines, 2nd Lieut. (W.O. Commission.)

NOTES.

(A) Daniel Janvre de La Bouchetière was imprisoned in 1692, as a Protestant, in the Abbey of St. Jouin, and in 1699 he was imprisoned again as " mal converti." He was alive in 1702.

(B) The family of Châtaigner was one of the earliest to embrace the reformed doctrines. One of its members, Philippe Châtaigner, Abbess of St. Jean-de-Bonneval, near Thouars, corresponded with Calvin, in 1549, with a view to leaving her convent and going to Geneva. This she did in the year 1557, with eight of the nuns, leaving only one remaining in the convent.

Daniel Châtaigner, grandfather of Olympe Châtaigner, was deputy for Brittany at the National Synod of France in 1631.

The family of Châtaigner, sgrs. de Cramahé, was from La Rochelle, and not related to that of Poitou. This family emigrated to Carolina.

(c) Cirus Guinebald de La Millière, son of Florent and Mary Anna, his wife, b. at Nantes in France, was naturalised 23 March 1708-9. Florent Guinebald de La Millière d. at Dublin 14 July 1728. Other members of this family were naturalised in England. Armand Guinebault de La Millière, b. in Poitou, son of Florent de La Millière, by Mary his wife, nat. 11 Ap. 1700. Charles Guinebauld de La Millière, b. at Poise (?) in France, son of Charles, by Jane his wife, nat. 4 May 1699, attested by Barth. Arabin and Reuben Caillaud. Commission as Lieutenant 10 Aug. 1689. Florent Guinebauld de La Millière was nat. 13 Nov. 1698 in Dublin (Oath Rolls, K. Bench, 1691-1711.) Henry Guinebault de La Millière, son of Florent, by Mary his wife, b. in Poitou, France, 9 July 1714. (Disbanded Officers Nat.) Alexander de La Millière was on half-pay in 1709, Brig.-Gen. Wade's Regt. He is probably the same officer who was a cornet, with Charles Janvre de La Bouchetière, in La Fabrèque's Dragoons, raised in 1706 for service in Portugal from the disbanded regiments of William the Third's army, and cornet in Miremont's Dragoons, raised in 1695 in England. The family was existing in Dublin at the end of the eighteenth century. Cirus Guinebald de La Millière, of Dublin, d. 3 Nov. 1729, captain in the Regiment of " Barie." His will (P.C.C., Auber, 35) was made at Dublin. He leaves directions to be buried in the French churchyard of St. Patrick and St. Mary Abbey. He left half his estate to his wife, Henriette Janvre de La Bouchetière (" Henriette Janvre de La Millière "), and half to Alexander and Charles, his two sons. His executors were his brother, Captain Henry Guinebald de La Millière, Colonel John Trapaud, and Alderman John Porter. A family of La Vendée. Arms: De gueules, à 3 roses d'argent.

(D) Marguerite de La Bouchetière, Dublin. 26 Dec. 1787. (Musgrave's Obituary.)

LEGGE

Arms : Mi-parti d'azur et d'argent, au cheval de l'un dans l'autre ; acc. de 3 lions mantelés du même.

I. Guillaume Legge,(A) " Grand Justicier de Paix," said to have been the father of

II. Richard Legge, an English merchant, having a business house at St. Malo. He married at Vitré, or St. Malo, as a Protestant, Rachel Lemoyne, 19 Oct. 1608, and left a son Richard, III.

III. Richard Legge, éc., sgr. de l'Espine, married 10 Jan. 1636, Dlle. Renée Leconte, daur. of Pierre Leconte, sgr. de Gerard, and of Jacquine de Gennes. She was b. 30 Dec. 1614 at Vitré and d. 27 Aug. 1679, at La Barattière. Richard Legge d. 21 Sept. 1676 at his house of La Barattière, aged 64, leaving 9 children : (*a*) Renée, b. 22 Sept. 1636, at Vitré ; (*b*) Anne, b. 23 Nov. 1639 (*idem*) ; (*c*) Richard, b. 28 Ap. 1642 (*idem*), author of the English Branch, IVa ; (*d*) Pierre, b. 8 Aug. 1643 ; (*e*) Pierre, b. 24 Sept. 1644 (*idem*), mentioned in the will of Anne de Gennes, Dame des Granges ; (*f*) Marie, b. 21 Jan. 1646 (*idem*) ; (*g*) Jean, b. 6 March 1648 (*idem*), sgr. de La Barattière, author of the English Branch, IVb ; (*h*) Jacques, b. 8 Nov. 1649, author of the English Branch IVc ; (*i*) Charles, b. 20 Ap. 1651, maître d'hotel du Duc de Trémouille. He abjured and married Anne Duverger in 1683, and d. at Cornillé in 1711.

IVa. Richard Legge, éc., sgr. de La Motte, married 16 May 1677 Dlle. Susanne de Gennes, daur. of Jean de Gennes, éc., sgr. des Hayers, Proc. Fiscal de Vitré, and Renée Pedron. Richard Legge left by his wife Susanne de Gennes 3 sons and 3 daurs. : (*a*) Renée, b. March 1678 at Vitré ; (*b*) Emilie, b. 4 Feb. 1679 (*idem*) ; (*c*) Jeanne, b. 17 July 1680 ; (*d*) Richard Charles, b. 28 Nov. 1681 (*idem*), who went to England(B) ; (*e*) Pierre, b. 15 Jan. 1684 (*idem*), who went to England(B) ; (*f*) Julien, b. 11 Oct. 1685 (Reg. Prot. Vitré).

IVb. Jean Legge, éc., sgr. de La Barattière, married Dlle. Marie-Anne des Pommars, or de Pommeraye,(C) and left :

(*a*) Jacques Charles, b. at Vitré 13 Feb. 1685, naturalised in London, 25 May 1702: "Charles, son of John Legg by Mary his wife, born at Vittrey in Brittany"; (*b*) Richard, b. at Vitré, 12 Feb. 1687 (Par. Register), naturalised 19 March 1706, "son of John Legg and Mary his wife, b. at Vitré in France."(C)

IVc. Jacques Legge, éc., sgr. de Vauguy, married Dlle. Marie Ravenel, who was b. 27 Sept. 1655, at Vitré, daur. of Daniel Ravenel, sgr. de Cohigné, and of Marie Guerineau, by whom he left 6 sons and 5 daurs.: (*a*) Richard, b. 12 Ap. 1674, naturalised 4 May 1699: "Richard Legge, born at Vitrey in Brittany in France, son of James Legge and Mary, his wife. Richard Legge took the Sacrament 5 March 1698-9 at St. Martin's, Westminster." His commission as ensign is dated 1696 (Commission Book, 3 April); (*b*) René, b. 15 July 1675; (*c*) Jacques, b. 29 July 1677; (*d*) Jean, b. 4 June 1679(D); (*e*) Charles, b. 23 June 1680; (*f*) Renée, b. 11 July 1681; (*g*) Daniel, b. 9 Nov. 1682 (bapt. au château); (*h*) Marie Suzanne,(E) b. 16 Feb. 1684; (*i*) Jeanne, bapt. 17 Dec. 1686 (Par. Reg. Vitré); (*j*) Emée-Suzanne,(E) bapt. 8 Feb. 1692 (Par. Reg. Vitré); (*k*) Renée, bapt. 28 May 1693 (Par. Reg. Vitré).

NOTES.

(A) It has not been possible to identify Guillaume Legge. The family is said, without proof, to be a Branch of the Earls of Dartmouth. "Grand Justicier de Paix" probably means a magistrate or "Haut Justicier" and not a Judge of the High Court. The term "Haut Justicier" means a Seigneur who had the High, Middle, and Low Justice.

(B) Two sons of Richard Legge and Susanne de Gennes are said by Frain to have gone to England—probably Richard Charles and Pierre. They do not appear to have been naturalised.

(C) Jean Legge and Marie Anne (or Anne Marie) had four sons and four daurs., baptised in the parish church of Vitré after 1685. Several of the des Pommares family came to England and were naturalised.

(D) John Legge, who took the Sacrament 21 Jan. 1699-1700 at St. Anne's, Westminster, was probably the son of Jacques

Legge and Marie Anne Ravenel, and whose naturalisation, 11 Ap. 1700, describes him as " born at Vitrey in Brittany in France, son of James Legg and Anne his wife."

(E) The family of Jacques Legge fell into great misfortune in France, and in 1727 were reduced to two daurs. : Marie Suzanne and Suzanne Aimée, who applied to the Comte de Florentin, Secretary of State, to sell property in Vitré, left to them by their father, who died burdened with debts. They are described (Série T.T. 171, xviii) as " issues d'un père de condition et d'une mère de famille." The house at Vitré and property was valued at 5,000 to 6,000 livres. The first application was made in 1711 and the matter dragged on to 1727.

LUARD

Arms : Parti per pale, sable and argent, a lion rampant countercharged holding between the paws a mullet pierced, or, and in chief 2 fleurs de lys countercharged of the field. Crest on a wreath of the colours a demi-lion charged with a fleur de lys and holding between the paws an estoile, both or. Motto : " Prospice."

I. Roger Luard, of the parish of St. Jean, Caen, married Noelle . . . (?), of the parish of Bras, near Caen, and left : (*a*) a son Moyse, II ; (*b*) Marie, bapt. 31 May 1568 : her godfather was Jean Luard, of Vaucelles.

II. Moyse Luard, bapt. 24 Oct. 1563, at Caen : his godfather was Laurence Hallot. Married Ester Harel, of Vaucelles, Caen, and left 7 children : (*a*) Anne, bapt. 1 Nov. 1592, and married, 6 June 1619, Timothée Buisson, of Vaucelles ; (*b*) Jacques, III ; (*c*) Pierre, bapt. 30 March 1594 ; (*d*) Marie, bapt. 12 Ap. 1596 ; (*e*) Michel, bapt. 23 Nov. 1597 ; (*f*) Elisée, bapt. 13 March 1600 ; (*g*) Marie, bapt. 18 July 1604.

III. Jacques Luard, bapt. 18 Feb. 1607 at Caen, married Eve Georget, widow of Guillaume Le Sueur, of Vaucelles, 8 June 1631, and left 5 children : (*a*) Abraham, IV ; (*b*) Pierre, bapt. 15 Jan. 1637 ; (*c*) Jacques, bapt. 8 July 1638, d. 1 July 1654 ; (*d*) Jeanne, bapt. 10 Ap. 1633 ; (*e*) Catherine, bapt. at Caen, and married, 11 Ap. 1660, Elie Le Marchand, son of Pierre, and Marie Le Noble, of Vaucelles.

IV. Abraham Luard, of Vaucelles, " Bourgeois de Caen," b. 29 Ap. 1635, d. at Caen 25 March 1685. Pierre Bonnefoy, his brother-in-law, was present at his burial. He married, 1st, 10 Feb. 1663, Marie Le Mercier, daur. of the late Jean Le Mercier and Suzanne Massiene. Marie Le Mercier d. in 1665. By this marriage Abraham Luard left a daur., Madeleine, bapt. at Caen 22 March 1665 : her godfather was Pierre Le Mercier, her godmother Madeleine Le Hulle, widow of Auguste Badenkop : she died, aged 5, 22 Ap. 1670. Abraham Luard married, 2nd, Jeanne Bonnefoy, by whom he left 3 sons : (*a*) Pierre, V ; (*b*) Jacques, b. 5th, bapt. 7th

Dec. 1670: his godfather was Jacques Bouillin; godmother, Jeanne Cardonville, his grandmother: he d. 12 Dec. 1670, aged 5 days; (*c*) Zacharie, b. 11th, bapt. 12th Nov. 1673: his godfather was Zacharie Bonnefoy, his uncle, brother of Jeanne Bonnefoy; godmother Marie Bouillin, wife of Zacharie Bonnefoy: d. and buried in St. Anne's, Soho London, 6 Ap. 1738 (Will P.C.C. Broadrepp, 6) May 1738: he was on the Oath Roll List in 1709 and married, 16 May 1734, Henrietta Remy, at St. Anne's, Soho.

V. Pierre Luard, b. 28th, bapt. 30th Sept. 1668, at Caen. His godfather was Pierre Bonnefoy, his grandfather. He came to England in 1685 with his mother and brother, Zacharie Luard, and was buried, 14 Nov. 1729, at St. Anne's, Soho, under the same stone as his mother, Jeanne Bonnefoy, according to the directions in his will (P.C.C. 311 Abbott, 29 Ap. 1729). He married, 21 Dec. 1701, at Le Quarré French Church, London, Heleine Samson de Cahanel, daur. of Pierre Samson de Cahanel, of St. Lo, Normandy, who d. in 1728 and was buried, 20 April, in the same grave as her husband. He became a Denizen 24 June 1703. By this marriage he left a son, Pierre Abraham, VI, and a daur., Judith Helaine, b. 1706, bapt. 2 Sept. at the French church, Ryders' Court, London. Her godfather was Elie Le Marchand; godmother, Judith Samson de Desert-Dieu, her aunt. D. and buried at St. Anne's, Soho, 29 Ap. 1728.

VI. Pierre Abraham Luard, b. 15 March 1703, d. at Hackney 22 Feb. 1765; married, 1st, Anne Myré, of a Rouen family, at Putney, 8 Feb. 1725. She d. in 1728, aged 34, and was buried in St. Anne's, Soho. By this 1st marriage Pierre Abraham Luard left a son, Pierre, or Peter, Robert Luard, VII. 2nd, Gabrielle Henriette Gilbert, of Hackney, daur. of the Rev. A. Gilbert,(A) chaplain to the King, b. 1703, by whom he left: (*a*) William, b. 4 May 1741, d. at Genoa, 29 Jan. 1802, who married, 27 Sept. 1764, Anne, the only daur. of John Wright, of the Priory, Hatfield Peverel, Essex (*a quo* the Luards of Witham) (B); (*b*) Henrietta, the 2nd wife of Thomas Davies, of Hackney, whom she married 15 Sept. 1770; (*c*) Olympia, the 2nd wife of Peter Cazalet, of Austin Friars and Woodford, Essex. She died in 1826 and he in 1788, and were both buried in Bath Abbey; (*d*) Zacharie Robert, b. 29 Ap. 1737 at St. Andrews, Undershaft; buried 31 July 1737.

VII. Peter Robert Luard, b. 25 Dec. 1727, d. July 1800, and was buried at St. Mary Abbots, Kensington. Married at St. George's Chapel, Mayfair, 19 Feb. 1754, Jane Bourryau, daur. of Zacharie Bourryau and Sophia Spooner (*a quo* the Luards of Blyborough). By her he left: (*a*) Peter John Luard, VIII.; (*b*) Henrietta, b. 1756, d. 1833, buried at Blyborough: married, Dec. 1791, Hungerford Spooner, her second cousin; (*c*) Francis, b. 1758, married, Nov. 1792, Mary Caroline Shaw; and others.

VIII. Peter John Luard, b. 22 Nov. 1754, d. 23 May 1830 at Blyborough, and buried there. Captain in 4th Light Dragoons and succeeded to the Blyborough property at the death of Mrs. Broadley, his mother's sister. He married, 28 Feb. 1784, Louise d'Albiac, daur. of Charles d'Albiac,(C) and of Susanne de Visme. She was b. 1760 and d. 19 Jan. 1831 at Blyborough, and was buried there. He left by her 9 children and was grandfather of Sidney Luard.

NOTES

Another collateral branch of the Luard family is found at Caen, descended from Jean Luard of St. Jean, Caen, probably a brother of Roger Luard, I.

(A) The Gilbert family descend from Abraham Gilbert, minister at Charenton, Paris, and his 1st wife Gabrielle Colin. Their son, the Rev. James Abraham Gilbert, was the first minister of the French Chapel Royal in 1689. (Arms: Arg. on a chevron sable, 3 roses of the field barbed and seeded ppr.) It was connected, by the 2nd marriage of Abraham Gilbert with Marie, daur. of Samuel Thomasset, widow of Jean Pierre Boulier de Beauregard, with that family portraits of whom are in the possession of the Luard family; also of their daur. Catherine, wife of James Abraham Gilbert, minister, and her husband: Robert and Catherine Myré: and of Peter Abraham and Gabrielle Henriette Luard. The Luard family also have miniatures of Robert Myré, Peter Abraham and Peter Robert Luard by Zincke and Petitot.

LUARD

(B) William Luard and Anne Wright left : (*a*) John Luard, b. 1 June 1766, married 17 Aug. 1795, Charlotte Lucy Kynaston, daur. of Roger Kynaston ; (*b*) Peter, who took the name of Wright, b. 21 Ap. 1767, d. 1 Ap. 1851, married Mary Anne Bennett, daur. of Rev. Samuel Bennett ; (*c*) Henrietta, b. 1765, d. 1851, married Charles Brown ; (*d*) Mary Anne, b. 1778, d. 1817 ; married, 23 Oct. 1796, George Hyde Woolaston ; (*e*) William Wright Luard, b. 1756, d. 1857 ; married, 10 Oct. 1815, Charlotte Farnham, b. 1789, d. 1875, and had many children, amongst whom, Admiral Sir Wm. Luard.

(C) The d'Albiac family came from Nismes.

MONTOLIEU DE SAINT-HIPPOLITE

Arms : Fascé d'or et d'azur de 6 p.p.

Alias: Azure, a fleur de lis or, between 3 crescents in chief, and as many mullets in base, argent: supporters 2 eagles regardant, wings extended and invected ppr. Motto : "Deo et principi," and "Per ardua surge."

I. Guillaume Montolieu, éc., sgr. de Saint-Hippolite et de Caton ; married, 1 Jan. 1541, Dlle. Antoine de Vergèze, and had 4 sons and a daur., Isabeau : (*a*) Jacques, killed at St. Denis in 1567 ; (*b*) François, killed at Moncontour in 1569, with his brother (*c*) Hippolite ; (*d*) Antoine, who succeeds, II. Guillaume Montolieu was killed at Dreux in 1562.

II. Antoine Montolieu, sgr. de St. Hippolite et de Caton, was at the siege of Rouen in 1592 and d. in 1615. He married, 21 Jan. 1582, Dlle. Susanne Dupuy, daur. of Bernardin Dupuy, sgr. de Montmoirac, and of Isabeau de Valabrez, and left 5 sons : (*a*) Jean, killed at Montpellier in 1622 ; (*b*) Antoine, killed in Spain ; (*c*) Claude, who succeeds, III.; (*d*) David,(A) ; (*e*) Pierre ; (*f*) Jacques.

III. Claude Montolieu, sgr. de St. Hippolite, captain in the Regiment of Calvisson in 1636, married in 1622 Dlle. Catherine de Saurin, daur. of Pierre de Saurin, sgr. de Pomaret, and of Marthe de La Mare, and had : (*a*) Pierre, who succeeds, IV.; (*b*) Louis, sgr. de La Coste, in the Regiment d'Auvergne, killed at Nevers ; (*c*) Jacques, sgr. de Montredon, killed in a duel; (*d*) Aymar, sgr. de Montessargues, lieut-colonel of the Regiment de Limousin, who abjured. Maintained his noblesse, 24 Jan. 1669.

IV. Pierre Montolieu, sgr. de Saint-Hippolite, married 11 Feb. 1661, Dlle. Jeanne de Froment, daur. of Nicolas de Froment, sgr. de St. Jean de Ceissargues, and of Marie du Roure, and left : (*a*) Claude, who emigrated to Holland at the Revocation ; (*b*) Théophile, who succeeds in the main line ; (*c*) Jacques, killed at Luxembourg ; (*d*) Louis, a major-general in the Prussian army ; (*e*) David, author of the English Branch, V.(A); (*f*) Aymar, "Conseiller du Cour" in Prussia; (*g*) Marguerite, d. young.

V. David Montolieu,(B) sgr. de St. Hippolite, cr. a Baron of the Holy Roman Empire by the Emperor Joseph in 1706 for his services in Piedmont against France. Came to England in 1688 with the Prince of Orange and was a captain in the French regiment of La Melonière. He became a brig.-general in 1727, major-general in 1735, lieut.-general 1739, general in 1761. One of the original 39 directors of the French Hospital in 1718. He married, 26 Ap. 1714, Marie Molinier, who was bapt. at Nismes, 30 Sept. 1684, daur. of Antoine Molinier, a merchant of Cournonterral and of Allix Baudoin, of a Protestant family of Nismes. The marriage took place at St. Martin Orgars French church, London. Marie Molinier d. in 1777. David Montolieu left by her: (*a*) Elizabeth, bapt. at St. Martin Orgars, 24 Feb. 1714/15; (*b*) Susanne Marie, bapt. at St. Martin Orgars, 11 Dec. 1717: her godmother was Suzanne de Saint-Hippolite, probably a sister of David Montolieu; (*c*) Louis Charles, who succeeds, VI. David Montolieu d., aged 93, at his house in Surrey and was buried at Wandsworth, June 1761.

VI. Louis Charles Montolieu, sgr. de St. Hippolite, 2nd Baron, bapt. at St. Martin Orgars, 18 May 1719, was lieut.-colonel in the 2nd Troop of H. Guards, and a director of the French Hospital in 1759. He married, 26 July 1750, Elizabeth Leheup, of the parish of St. James's, Westminster, daur. of Peter Leheup,(C) of Morden, and of Clara, daur. of William Lowndes, of Winslow and Chesham, Bucks. The marriage took place at the French church of Spring Garden. (Lic. Archbishop of Canterbury.) He left by her 5 sons and 4 daurs.: (*a*) Peter James, b. 6 Ap. 1753, d. young; (*b*) Charles, b. 1 Jan. 1758, d. young; (*c*) David, b. 20 Jan. 1759; (*d*) Louis, b. 15 Dec. 1761, who succeeds, VII.; (*e*) Thomas, b. 25 Nov. 1767, d. 30 July 1805: he married Anne ....(?) (will P.C.C. 655, Nelson); (*f*) Mary Clara, b. 3 July 1751, d. 19 Jan. 1802: married 20 Ap. 1776, Alexander, 7th Baron Elibank, her cousin-german; (*g*) Charlotte Gabrielle, b. 19 July 1754; married, 27 May 1783, Wriothesley

Digby, of Meriden Hall, Warwick ; (*h*) Anne, b. 27 March 1756, married at St. George's, Hanover Square, 16 Dec. 1780, Sir James Bland Burges (afterwards Lamb) ; (*i*) Elizabeth, b. 15 Oct. 1759, married at Darnhill, 19 Aug. 1792, James, 8th Baron Cranstoun : d. *s.p.*

VII. Louis Montolieu de St. Hippolite, F.S.A., entered at Oxford 1779. A partner in Hammersley's Bank, Pall Mall. Married at St. George's, Hanover Square, 3 March 1786, Maria Henrietta, daur. of James Modyford Heywood, of Maristow, Devon, d. 20 May 1817. He had a son, Charles, who died a student at Oxford in 1809, and two daurs., Maria Georgina, who married in 1822 Hugh Hammersley of Pall Mall, and Julia Fanny, who married, 1st, William Wilbraham, capt. R.N., and, 2nd, Sir Henry Bouverie, G.C.B., Governor of Malta.

NOTES.

(A) La Roque and Haag, who follows him, are clearly wrong in assigning David, son of Antoine Montolieu, as the author of the English Branch. The naturalisation act of David Montholieu de St. Hippolite describes him as son of Peter by Jone (Jeane) his wife, b. at St. Hipolitte in Languedoc, May 25 1702.

(B) A portrait exists of General David Montolieu, Baron de St. Hippolite (1669–1761), and one of his wife, Marie Molinier, Baronne Montolieu (1684–1777). She was godmother, 10 May 1772, to Marie Marguerite de Claris de Florian at the French church of Le Carré and Berwick Street, " Mme. Marie Molinse (*sic*) fem. de Mr. Saintipolythe."

James Molinier, her brother, was naturalised 4 May 1699. He was in the 2nd Troop of Guards and had served 8 months. His father, Anthony M., stated to have died in the King's service and been all through the war in the troop. Charles, another brother, b. at Groningen, in Friesland.

(C) The Le Heup family, of St. Lo, was widely spread. A branch settled in Jersey and a refugee of the name went to Limerick, whence it removed to London, where the name is found in the Registers of La Patente French Church.

Thomas Le Heup was made a Denizen, 22 June 1694.

He is probably the same Thomas Le Heup, naturalised in 1722, " son of John Le Heup, by Suzanna his wife, b. at St. Lo in France."

Isaac Le Heup was on a Naturalisation Roll in 1704 and is probably the same Isaac Le Heup, naturalised 19 March 1706, " son of Peter Le Heup, by Susan his wife, b. in Normandy."

A memoir of the Molinier and Montolieu families is found in the Proceedings of the Huguenot Society of London, Vol. X, Pt. 1, p. 156.

RAVENEL

Arms : De gueules, à 6 croissants d'or, 2, 2, 2, surmontés chacun d'une étoile de même : et une étoile aussi d'or, à la pointe de l'écu.

Alias, d'azur, à la fasce d'argent, chargée de 3 mouchetures d'hermine, acc. de 3 renards d'or.

Alias, d'azur, à un chevron d'argent, chargé de 2 raves au naturel, acc. de 3 papillons d'or, 2 en chef affrontés et une en pointe (Armorial de 1696).

I. Robert Ravenel, sr. de Ruillé, one of the founders of the Confraternity of " Marchands d'outre Mer " in 1473. The name of his wife is not known. He left a son, Jean, who succeeds, II.

II. Jean Ravenel, who married Jamette (or Jacquette) Miaulais, and left a son, Jean, who succeeds, III.

III. Jean Ravenel,(A) sr. du Perray, married Marguerite Guesdon, and d. 14 April 1566, aged 30. He left a son, Lucas, or Luc, who succeeds, IV.

IV. Lucas Ravenel, sr. de La Brouardière, married 19 Sept. 1530, Dlle. Andrée de Gennes, and left : (*a*) Pierre, b. 17 June 1553 (Par. Reg. Vitré) ; (*b*) Marguerite, b. 2 Oct. 1555 (*idem*) ; (*c*) Catherine, b. 31 March 1557, godfather Jean Ravenel Perray, godmother Catherine de Gennes (*idem*) ; (*d*) Lucas, sr. de Boisguy ; (*e*) Jean, who married Jeanne Guillaudeau ; (*f*) René, sr. de La Mesriais, who follows, V.; (*g*) Marguerite, married 30 June 1591 Guillaume Lemoyne and d. 30 Aug. 1594.

V. René Ravenel, sr. de La Mesriais, married, 1st, Michelle Le Gouverneur ; 2nd, 11 Aug. 1591, Jeanne Guesdon, and d. 11 Oct. 1622, leaving by his 1st marriage (*a*) Esther, b. 21 March 1591, bapt. at the house of the sgr. de La Musse,(B) married, 1st, 17 Feb. 1613, Jacques Ravenel, and, 2nd, 18 March 1631, at Terchant, Jacques Gauvaing, d. 17 Dec. 1662; (*b*) Suzanne, b. 10 Aug. 1593, married 12 May 1611, Pierre Nogues, d. at La Croixille 7 Sept. 1645 ; (*c*) Jeane, d. 2 Jan.

1625; (*d*) Marie, b. 15 Jan. 1597, d. 1599; (*e*) René, b. 28 Jan. 1599, who succeeds, VI; (*f*) Catherine, b. 13 May 1601, married Pierre Lemoyne 8 Dec. 1619; (*g*) Gillette, b. 22 Oct. 1603.

VI. René Ravenel, sgr. de La Paignerie, married 25 April 1624, Anne Nouail (or Noël) and d. 13 Jan. 1661, leaving by her: (*a*) Suzanne, b. 7 Aug. 1624, married 24 Dec. 1645 Henry de Gennes, and d. 27 Feb. 1681; (*b*) Olivier, b. 30 June 1625; (*c*) Daniel, b. 29 April 1629, who succeeds, VII.

VII. Daniel Ravenel, sgr. de Cohigné, married, 1st, Marie Guerineau 20 Oct. 1652; 2nd, Aimée Lefebvre, 18 Oct. 1663, daur. of Daniel Lefebvre, sgr. du Fougeray, and Marie Bérault, and d. 28 Feb. 1669. By his 1st marriage he had: (*a*) Marie, b. 27 Sept. 1655, wife of Jacques de Legge; (*b*) René, b. 25 Sept. 1656, author of the Branch in America, VIII; (*c*) Emilie, b. 30 Sept. 1657; (*d*) Suzanne, b. 26 Dec. 1658, d. 28 Jan. 1665; (*e*) Daniel, b. 28 Jan. 1660. By his 2nd marriage with Aimée Lefebvre he left: (*f*) Jeanne, b. 17 Jan. 1663; (*g*) Daniel,(C) b. 8 June 1667, author of the English Branch; (*h*) Aimée, b. 14 Dec. 1668.

VIII. René Ravenel, sgr. de La Massais, left France about 1685, and went to Holland, from whence he went to England and America, settling at Charleston, S.C. He married, 24 Oct. 1687, Dlle. Charlotte de St. Julien, daur. of Pierre de St. Julien,(D) sgr. de Malacare, and of Jeanne Le Febvre, at Charleston, S.C., and d. before 1697. He left by this marriage: (*a*) Jeanne Charlotte, b. in 1690, who married 20 Feb. 1709-10, in the "Nouvelle Eglise de Ste. Marie," at Dublin, Jean Corneille, son of Rodolphe Corneille, captain of engineers in the British army. She is described as "Demoiselle Jeanne Charlotte de Ravenell, fille de Monsieur René Ravenell, habitant en Caroline." Among those who assisted at the marriage were "Monsieur le Capitaine D'Arabin, and Madame Jeanne René D'Arabin, oncle et tante de la nouvelle mariée." They had several children (Fr. Ch. Dublin); (*b*) Daniel, b. 1692, who follows; (*c*) René Louis, b. 1694, of Pooshee: he married Susan de Chataigné, or Chataigner, widow of Alexandre Thésée de Chataigner, and daur. of Henry Le Noble and of Catherine

Le Serrurier ; (*d*) Paul François, b. 1696 ; (*e*) Mary Amey, b. 1698, who married her cousin, Paul de St. Julien, son of Pierre de St. Julien de Malacare and of Elizabeth Damaris Le Serrurier.

[Note.—The remainder of the pedigree is printed in " Ravenel Records," printed for private circulation by Henry Edmond Ravenel, of Spartanburg, S.C., to whom I am indebted for the printed work.]

NOTES.

The Ravenel family was one of the most numerous in Brittany, and ramified into many branches ; hence the diversity of its armorial bearings.

(A) Jean Ravenel, III, is not mentioned in the printed Pedigree. His existence, however, is proved by his marriage to Marguerite Guesdon in the Catholic parish registers, which have been ignored by compilers of the Pedigree.

(B) The seigneur de La Musse was Bonaventure de La Musse, sgr. de Ponthus, a noted Protestant, whose château of Ponthus was one of those " maisons seigneuriales " in which Protestants were allowed to meet and hold services. He was Lieut.-Governor of Vitré in 1590, but had died on the third day of March, 1591. Arms : De gueules, à 9 besants d'argt. 3. 3. 3. (See note (C), Pedigree Buor de La Lande.)

(C) Daniel Ravenel, son of Daniel Ravenel, sgr. de Cohigné, and Emée Le Febvre, born at Vitré. Naturalised 24 March 1698-9, Cornet and Adjutant of Macclesfield's Horse in 1694, Cornet to the Colonel (Commission at the Hague 28 Ap. 1697). Commission renewed 1702 and out of the service in 1705. (Dalton, Army List.)

(D) The family of St. Julien de Malacare only appear at Vitré in 1667, when their daughter Aimée was born 7 March, followed by 8 others, all born and baptised there (Reg. Prot. Vitré). Pierre and his wife, Jeanne Le Febvre, with their nine children, fled to England at the Revocation, and thence to Ireland and America. Paul de Saint Julien was Denizen 9 Ap. 1687 and naturalised 23 March 1709, and was godfather to Paul Layard, 27 Ap. 1719, at the French church of the Savoy, London. He was in Ireland in 1713, when he was godfather to his niece, Jeanne Corneille, at Dublin. Pierre de St. Julien was also in Dublin in 1719, when he was godfather to Jeanne Renée Trapaud, 27 Oct. The godmother was Madame Jeanne Renée D'Arabien (Arabin). Madame de St. Julien was godmother to Paul Trapaud, 28 Ap. 1703, at Dublin. Marie de St. Julien married Monsieur Jean Adlercron, a minister, and d. at Dublin 8 Feb. 1706-7, aged 71. She was probably a sister of Pierre de St. Julien de Malacare. Emilie de St. Julien d. at Dublin, 17 Feb. 1707, aged 32. She had married Pierre Du Foussat, officer on pension. Pierre de St. Julien, the father, d. at Dublin, 20 Oct. 1705, aged 70.

His will, translated out of French (P.C.C., Gee, 239) was made in London, 4 Sept. 1704, with a codicil dated 13 Oct. 1705, made at Dublin. When he made his will he was living in the parish of St. Anne, Westminster. He directs that "several jewels, moveables and lumber," belonging to his sister, Madame Adlercron, of which she has a "noate," shall go back to her. His children to share equally in his estate in England, France and other places. His daughter Jane Renata (Jeanne Renée) is mentioned, also his daughter Emilia, and granddaughter, Jeanne Caroline, daughter of Mr. Ravenell, to whom he left "Bedd in back parlour, a Toilette looking glass : two pair of sheets, and 2 douzen of napkins." To his son Louis, plate and diamonds : if he died, to his son Pierre. His copy of Moreri's Dictionary to his daughter Marguerite. His Bible in three volumes to his daughter Emilie. His sword inlaid with gold, to his son Paul, with pistols, silver cupp, and a striking watch. He leaves his shirts, cravats and cloathes to his son-in-law, Mr. Ravenel, in Carolina. Judith Caroline Ravenel also was left a lottery ticket in the Million Lottery. By the codicil, made in the parish of St. Andrew, Dublin, he confirms the previous will, with some alterations, leaving the furniture (the translator writes "moveables" for "meubles") in the house in Dublin to Emilie du Foussat, his daughter, "the Bedd and other articles in the chamber wherein my granddaughter Jeanne Caroline de Ravenel doth lie."

His daughter Marguerite being dead, Moreri's Dictionary is to go to Emilie du Foussat ; the striking watch to go to Madame Adlercron, with the diamonds ; six spoons and six silver forks to Judith Caroline de Ravenel, and his scarlet cloak to his son Pierre.

DE LA ROCHEFOUCAULD

Branche de Fontpastour et de Pardachat

Arms : Burelé d'argent et d'azur, à 3 chevrons de gueules, le premier brochant sur le tout. Devise : " C'est mon plaisir."

Descends from Foucauld, sgr. de La Roche en Angoumois. Known by charter of the Abbey of Uzerche, 1019, with his children.

XVIII. François de La Rochefoucauld, sgr. de Bayers, 18th in descent from Foucauld, married Dlle. Isabeau de Lanes, and had Pierre, who succeeds, XIX., author of the Branch of La Renaudie and Fontpastour.

XIX. Pierre de La Rochefoucauld, éc., sgr. du Parc d'Archiac ; married, 1st, Dlle. Catherine Vigier, Dame de La Renaudie ; 2nd, Dlle. Bonne Gillier, daur. of Bonaventure Gillier, éc., sgr. de Puygarreau, Baron de Marmande, and of Marie Babon de La Bourdasière, by whom he left : (*a*) François, who continues his line, XX. (du Parc d'Archiac) ; (*b*) Pierre, d. young. By his 3rd marriage, with Dlle. Madeleine du Barry, daur. of Godefroy du Barry, Baron de La Renaudie, and of Dlle. Guillemette Louvain, he left : (*a*) Charles, sgr. de La Renaudie, who continues his line, XX. (La Renaudie and Fontpastour) ; (*b*) Gédéon, sgr. du Breuil, who married Dlle. Marie Bouhier, Dame de La Chaussetière, by whom he left a daur., Isabelle, d. young ; (*c*) Jeanne, wife of (1st) Charles Bourzon, sgr. de Cravois et de La Mothe de Gaen, and (2nd) of Jean Casimir d'Augury, sgr. de Couveille et St. Trojan (17 May 1616).

XX. François de La Rochefoucauld, ec., sgr. du Parc d'Archiac et de Rigaudière, made a division of his property with his brothers and sisters, 10 March 1599. He married Dlle. Isabeau Goumard, daur. of Robert Goumard and Dlle. Louise Poussard, Dame de Pougné et La Saussaye, by whom he left : (*a*) François, d. young ; (*b*) Gédéon, who succeeds, XXI.; (*c*) Louis, sgr. de Fontroux, who married his cousin, Elizabeth de La Rochefoucauld, by whom he had a son,

François, who was present at the marriage of Henriette Audoyer, his cousin german, with the sieur de L'Estang; (*d*) Marie, wife of François, sgr. de La Roche-Brusillet; (*e*) Jeanne, wife of François de Prévost,(A) sgr. de La Touche-Imbert et La Piagerie; (*f*) Marguerite.

XXI. Gédéon de La Rochefoucauld, sgr. du Parc d'Archiac et La Rigaudière, married Dlle. . . . de L'Abbé. He was imprisoned in the prison of Château Trompette at Bordeaux, 1690–1701.

By his 3rd marriage, with Dlle. Madeleine du Barry, Pierre de La Rochefoucauld (*v. ante*) left a son Charles, sgr. de La Renaudie, who follows.

XX. Charles de La Rochefoucauld, sgr. de La Renaudie, made a division of property with his brothers in 1641. He had married in June 1608 Dlle. Sara de Verrières, Dame de Fontpastour, and left by her: (*a*) François, who succeeds, XXI.; (*b*) Samuel, d. in 1642; (*c*) Casimir, who made a division of property with his brothers and sisters, while still minors under the guardianship of Pierre de Beaucorps, chev., sgr. de La Grange; (*d*) Elizabeth, already married (in 1642) to her cousin, Louis de La Rochefoucauld; (*e*) Marie, also married at that date to Claude de Villedon, éc., sgr. de Magézis; (*f*) Françoise, who afterwards married André Audoyer, sgr. de St. Hilaire et de Limaudie, in Bas-Poitou, 1648, 9 Nov. The contract was drawn up by Limousin, notaire. André Audoyer is described as "veuf de Marie Roy, chevalier, seigneur de St. Hilaire et La Bretonnière, et de Loirière en Poitou, demeurant en sa maison de La Bretonnière, Paroisse de Gros-Breuil, Principauté de Talmont."

Françoise de La Rochefoucauld is described as "daughter of the late Charles de La Rochefoucauld and of Sarra de Verrière, seigneur et dame de La Renaudie et Fontpastour, demeurant à la maison noble de Magezie."

XXI. François de La Rochefoucauld, chev., sgr. de Fontpastour et St. Coux, etc., married, 26 Aug. 1641, Dlle. Marie de Beaucorps, daur. of Antoine de Beaucorps,(B) and of Dlle. Dorothée de La Faille, his 2nd wife. He was still a minor under the guardianship of Pierre de Beaucorps, sgr. de La Grange, in 1642. D. before 1667. His wife, Marie, was b. in 1623 and d. 17 Dec. 1683, aged 60. (Reg. Pr. Dompierre et Bourgneuf.) They had: (*a*) Charles Casimir, who succeeds, XXII.; (*b*) François, author of the Branch of Pardachat, who will follow XXII.; (*c*) Marie, wife of Pierre du Gûa,(C) (21 July 1669), chev., sgr. du Bois: she d. before 1682, leaving children; (*d*) Bénigne, d. before 1682, unmarried; (*e*) Marguerite, wife of Jacques Gourde, chev., sgr. des Ardilliers, who left a daur., Marie Gourde, wife (1st) of François Gabriel Grimouard, (2nd) of Charles Prévost de La Touche-Imbert, éc., sgr. de Brassac.

XXII. Charles Casimir de La Rochefoucauld, éc., sgr. de Fontpastour, b. 1651, d. 11 Jan. 1679, aged 28 (Reg. Pr. Dompierre et Bourgneuf). Married Dlle. Marie-Françoise de Mazières, daur. of Daniel de Mazières,(D) éc., sgr. du Passage et de Voutron, and of Dlle. Elizabeth de Ste. Hermine, by whom he left: (*a*) Marie-Françoise, bapt. in the Prot. Temple of Dompierre et Bourgneuf en Aulnis, 19 June 1672. Her godfather was Charles de Villedon, éc., sgr. de Magezis, in Saintonge: her godmother was Dame Elizabeth de Ste. Hermine, wife of Daniel de Mazières, sgr. des Fontaines; (*b*) Angélique, bapt. 23 July 1673 (*idem*)(E): godfather, Messire Elie de Ste. Hermine, chev., sgr. de Laigne: godmother, Dame Marie de Beaucorps, veuve de François de La Rochefoucauld, chev., sgr. de Fontpastour, de St. Coux, and other places; (*c*) Elizabeth, bapt. 4 Nov. 1674 (*idem*): godfather, Daniel de Mazières, éc., sgr. des Fontaines de Rouhon: godmother, Dlle. Marguerite de La Rochefoucauld; (*d*) Charles Casimir,(F) bapt. 22 Dec. 1675 (*idem*): godfather, Jacques Gourde, chev., sgr. des Ardilliers: godmother, Dlle. Bénigne de La Rochefoucauld; (*e*) Suzanne-Ester-Aimée, bapt. 25 Sept. 1678 (*idem*): godfather, Messire Joachim de Beaucorps, éc. sgr. de Guillonille: godmother, Dame Olympe du Caillaud, widow of André de Mazières, éc., sgr. de Voutron.

XXII. François de La Rochefoucauld, chev., sgr. de Pardachat, 2nd son of François, and of Marie de Beaucorps, living at Sauzay, near Soubize; married, 1st, Marguerite Bernardeau, daur. of le sieur Bernardeau, sieur de Ronsay. This 1st marriage is not mentioned in official pedigrees, but is substantiated by a baptism at Dompierre, 28 Aug. 1665, of " Samuel Bernardeau, fils de Samuel Bernardeau, sieur de Ronsay et de Jeanne Pagez.(G) Parain, Jacques Pagez, marchand; Maraine, Marguerite Bernardeau, femme de Messire François de La Rochefoucauld, sgr. de Pardachat." She was living in 1687, as appears by a sentence in the Presidial Court of La Rochelle (B. 750). He married 2nd, after 1687, Dlle. Charlotte de Beaumont. By his 1st marriage he left: (*a*) Reuben; (*b*) François, who succeeds, XXIII.; (*c*) Marguerite,(H) who married 7 Oct. 1691, in London, at the French church of Les Grecs, Charles de Ponthieu, son of Daniel de Ponthieu, and of Julienne Thomas his wife, b. at Taillebourg, in Saintonge (Naturalisation Rolls).

XXIII. François de La Rochefoucauld was bapt. 11 June 1684 at La Rochelle. His godfather was Reuben de La Rochefoucauld, his brother. It is not known if he remained in France, as is probable, or left posterity.

NOTES.

(A) The family of Prévost de Touchimbert was a noted Protestant family of Poitou. The following extracts from the Registers of Admissions to St. Cyr, 1689-1793, record the baptisms of three daughters of Casimir Prévost de Touchimbert and his wife Marie Robillard: Diane, bapt. " comme huguenote à Sauzé en Poitou, née en Juin 1673." " Julie Prévost de Londigny, née en Juillet, 1674, baptisée comme huguenote à Sauzé." " Esther-Silvie Prévost de Touchimbert-Liléau, baptisée a Sauzé comme huguenote, née le 6 Jan. 1676."

A Prévost de Touchimbert was imprisoned in the Bastille in 1686 (Lièvre, *Hist. des Protestants de Poitou*).

(B) Marie de Beaucorps died a Protestant, and was buried 17 Dec. 1683, aged about 60, " veuve de Messire François de La Rochefoucauld, sgr. de Fontpastour " (Reg. Pr. Dompierre et Bourgneuf).

(C) Pierre du Gûa, or Dugast, son of François du Gûa, chev., sgr. du Bois et de La Roche-Breuillet, and of Marie de La Rochefoucauld. François was dead at the date of his son's marriage, which took place at Dompierre, 21 July 1669. He went to England with his sons, François and Louis, and made his Reconnaissance in 1687. "Pierre [du] Gua De La Roche-Breuillet, ecquier, seigneur du Bois-des-Marais et de St. Cou en Xtonge, 50 ans. François 19 ans: Louis 14 ans. 27 Fev. 1687 (Reconnaissances, Eglise Française de La Savoye, Londres.)

(D) Daniel de Mazières had another daur., Marie Anne, bapt. 21 March 1667 at La Rochelle. Their son, Benjamin de Mazières, éc., sgr. du Passage et des Voutron, dead in 1673, 10 July, when his widow, Dlle. Hélène le Franc, was maraine to Hélène Henriette de Culant, daur. of Jacques de Culant, sgr. de Landray, and of his wife Marie Grousseau (Reg. Pr. Dompierre). She came to London and was naturalised 16 Dec. 1687. "Hélène le Franc de Mazières." She made her témoignage in the French church of Threadneedle Street, London, 29 Dec. 1696. Françoise Suzanne de Mazières, daur. of Benjamin and Hélène le Franc, married Moyse Viridet, or Véridet, widower, a French pastor at Dublin, 28 March 1683 (Eglise Nouvelle de St. Patrick). Moyse Viridet is described as "fils de feu Jacques Véridet, officier de S. Altesse Royalle Monseigneur le Duc d'Orléans, et de Marie Veroul."

(E) Angélique de La Rochefoucauld. She apparently was the only one of the children who became a Nouvelle Catholique. Françoise de Mazières, her mother, with three daughters, were imprisoned in 1701 in the Convent of N. Dame de Bordeaux, and sent in 1704 to the Convent of the Nouvelles Catholiques at Luçon. Angélique became heiress to her father, Casimir de La Rochefoucauld, and is so described in a suit of 1690 between Pierre Julliot, sgr. des Hommeaux, *versus* Angélique de La Rochefoucauld and Louis de Rancourt, chev., sgr. d'Escour, Monroy, etc. (Présidial de La Rochelle, Sentences, B. VI°, 1630.)

(F) A Louis-Casimir de La Rochefoucauld appears at Canterbury in 1683 as godfather to Louis-Casimir Dutuiller, 4 March. He may be (Louis) Charles Casimir, or another unrecorded Protestant member of the family.

(G) Several members of the Pagez family went to Bristol.

DE LA ROCHEFOUCAULD

A Colonel Gibert de Pagez appears in Dublin in 1715, with his wife, Anne Esther de Goulaine. Their children were baptised in the Nouvelle Eglise de Ste. Marie.

(H) Vicar-General, Marriage Licences, Oct. 1691. Charles de Ponthieu, of St. Anne's, Westminster, gent. Bach. about 29, and Margarett de La Rochefoucauld, 22, of the same, with consent of her father and mother in France, at St. Anne's, Westminster. Her brother Reuben emigrated with her, and made his témoignage at the French church in Threadneedle Street, London, 24 Sept. 1690, and was naturalised 11 May 1699. He was godfather to his brother François in La Rochelle in 1684, and is described as "chevalier, sgr. de Sauzay"; and also to his nephew Reuben Charles de Ponthieu, 14 Jan. 1699, at Portarlington, Ireland; son of Charles, and Marguerite de La Rochefoucauld, when he is described as "frère de la mère." This is the only mention of him which identifies him as son of François de La Rochefoucauld de Pardachat.

A Dame Marie de La Rochefoucauld de Champagné was buried at Portarlington 14 Feb. 1730. She was the wife of Josias de Robillard, chev., sgr. de Champagné, in Saintonge, son of Daniel de Robillard, seigneur de Champagné et de Theron, in the parish of Thénac, and of his wife Judith Poitevin.

Josias de Robillard left France at, or before, the Revocation, leaving property valued at 19,000 livres (T.T. 232). He and his wife, Marie de La Rochefoucauld, appear in a List of Fugitives, 1685, from Saintonge. They left a daughter, aged 4, who was placed in a convent. She was probably Marie Thérèse de Robillard, whose guardian, Philippe Benjamin de Mazières, sgr. du Passage, claimed the property of Josias de Robillard and his wife, "fugitifs de Xaintonge" (Arch. Presidial de Saintes. B). Their son Josias was naturalised in England 24 March 1689, and was called "Joseph Campagne" in the Naturalisation Roll. He died at Portarlington, where he was buried, 4 May 1737, having married Lady Jane Forbes (Granard). The de Robillard family were connected by marriage with that of Prévost de Touche-Imbert (see note (A)). It was still represented at Portarlington in 1793.

DE RUVIGNY

Arms : D'argent, à une fasce de gueules surmontée de 3 merlettes rangées en chef : un franc quartier d'or, chargé d'une huchet de sable, envauchée de même.

Alias, d'argent, à trois massues de sable, 2 and 1.

I. Nicolas Massüe,(A) or Massi, éc., sgr. de St. Aubin en Rivière ; married Dlle. Marie de Licques ; alive in 1519 ; left a son, Thierry, who succeeds, II.

II. Thierry Massüe, éc., sgr. de St. Aubin en Rivière, capitaine de Dommart ; married Dlle. Péronne de Bellangreville, daur. of Guillaume, sgr. de Fresnoye, and of Dlle. . . . . Maudesson, daur. of the seigneur de Crognoison, and left : (*a*) Nicolas, who succeeds, III. ; (*b*) Marc.

III. Nicolas Massüe, éc., married Dlle. Hélène d'Ailly, daur. of Antoine d'Ailly,(B) chev., sgr. de La Mairie, Pierrepoint et Belleval, and of Dlle. Charlotte Famechon, Dame de Belleval, only daur. and heiress of Claude Famechon, at Audainville, 25 Feb. 1565. By this marriage he left : (*a*) Daniel, who succeeds, IV ; (*b*) Françoise, Abbesse d'Espagne (1612-1624), near Abbeville ; (*c*) Rachel, wife of Antoine de Lespine, sgr. de l'Espagne ; (*d*) Suzanne, wife of Jean Matifas, sgr. de La Salle.

IV. Daniel Massüe, éc., sgr. de Ruvigny, Governor of the Bastille ; married Dlle. Madeleine Pinot,(C) widow of Jean Pinot, sgr. de Fontaine, Dame de La Caillemotte, and left by her : (*a*) Maximilien, sgr. de Ruvigny, a lieutenant in the Gardes Royalles, d. *s.p.* ; (*b*) Henri, who succeeds, V. ; (*c*) Rachel,(D), b. 1603, bapt. at Charenton, Paris, wife of Thomas Wriothesley, Lord Southampton ; (*d*) Cirné, b. 28 June 1608 (Reg. Charenton), whose godmother was Anne de Rohan, Duchesse de Sully, and godfather Cirné de Béthune, her son. Daniel Massüe d. in 1611 and his wife, Madeleine Pinot, in 1636.

V. Henri Massüe, or de Massüe, éc., sgr. Baron de Renneval, then Marquis de Ruvigny, lieut.-general in the

French army, President of the Assembly of the Reformed Churches of France, Ambassador to Portugal and Envoy to the English Court; d. at Greenwich 5 Aug. 1689, aged 89. He had married Marie Tallemand, daur. of Pierre Tallemand,(E) merchant, of La Rochelle, and of his 2nd wife, Marie de Rambouillet. The Marquise de Ruvigny d. in London, where she had settled with her son, in 1698, aged 80. By his marriage with her, Henri de Massüe, 1st Marquis de Ruvigny, left: (*a*) Henri, who succeeds, VI; (*b*) Pierre, sgr. de Caillemotte, near Calais: he entered the army of the Prince of Orange and raised, in 1689, a regiment of foot, called "Caillemont's Foot," of which he was first colonel. He was not married and was killed at the Boyne in 1690; (*c*) François, bapt. 6 Feb. 1656, d. before 1685 *s.p.*

VI. Henri de Massüe,(F) sgr. Baron de Renneval, Marquis de Ruvigny, b. 9 Ap. 1648, Deputy of the Reformed Churches of France 1670. He came to England finally with his mother and lived at Greenwich when not on service, and afterwards near Southampton. Louis XIV. retained a close intimacy with his father and himself, and they were allowed to retain their estates and revenues in France. He retired from the French army in 1678 as a brigadier-general on a pension of 4,000 livres and a salary of 1,000 pistoles. William III. created him Viscount Galway and Baron of Portarlington in 1692. Naturalised 24 Dec. 1691, "Henry de Massue de Ruvigny, born at Paris in France, son of Henry de Massue de Ruvigny and Marie Tallemand his wife."(G) He d. at Rookly, near Southampton, in Aug. 1720, unmarried. All male issue of his family having failed, his titles, both French and English, became extinct. The succession to his French estates, however, gave rise to a series of suits by various claimants, of which there is an interesting dossier preserved in the Archives Nationales, Paris.(H)

NOTES.

(A) d'Hozier.

(B) Antoine d'Ailly had an elder daur., Marguerite, wife of Claude du Chesne (1570), from whom descended Claude le Comte, bapt. 6 May 1635, daur. of Charles le Comte, whose mother was Antoinette du Chesne, daur. of Marguerite d'Ailly. The le Comte family was one of the claimants to the succession. Claude le Comte was first cousin four times removed from the 2nd Marquis de Ruvigny.

(C) Haag, and Agnew, who copies him, state that Daniel Massüe married twice: 1st, Madeleine Pinot, by whom he had a daur. Rachel, bapt. 1603 at Charenton, and Cirné, bapt. in 1608; 2nd, Madeleine de Fontaine, Dame de La Caillemotte, by whom he had Henri and Pierre. Madeleine Pinot was Dame de Fontaine when she married Daniel Massüe (d'Hozier), which Haag, who is often incorrect, probably did not know.

From the fact of the Duchesse de Sully and her son being godparents to one of his children, it may be surmised that Maximilien Massue had as his godfather Maximilien de Béthune, Duc de Sully.

(D) Rachel Massüe married, 1st, Elysée de Beaujeu, sgr. de La Maisonfort, and was his widow in 1634, when she married, 18 Aug., Thomas Wriothesley, at Titchfield, Hants. Her portrait exists and is engraved (Evans' Catalogue of Engraved Prints). She d. in 1637, leaving two daurs., Elizabeth, first wife of Edward Noel, Earl of Gainsborough, and Rachel, wife of (1st) Francis, Lord Vaughan, and (2nd) of the Hon. William Russell, afterwards Earl of Bedford.

(E) The Tallemand family came originally from Tournay. François Tallemand established himself in La Rochelle, and was Maire in 1612. His eldest son, Gédéon, was a banker in the town, and in 1634 bought a " charge " of " Conseiller Secrétaire du Roy " and became an " anobli." He married Anne de Rambouillet. His brother Pierre married in Paris, 1st, Elizabeth Bidault, and had 3 children: (*a*) Pierre; (*b*) Paul, who abjured in 1685, but afterwards fled to Switzerland; (*c*) Elizabeth, wife of François le Venier, sgr. de La Grossetière. By the 2nd marriage of Pierre Tallemand with Marie de Rambouillet, he had a daur. Marie, wife of Henri Massüe de Ruvigny, and two sons, the elder of whom, Gédéon, married his cousin, Elizabeth de Rambouillet, and had three daurs.: Anne Elizabeth, Angélique, who abjured, and Charlotte, who escaped to England (Haag). Both Gédéon Tallemand and his wife abjured. A Mr. Tallemant appears in Dublin, 1702, when he was godfather, 27 July, to Louise Pillier. Members of the family de Rambouillet went to Denmark and England. Anthony and Charles William, sons of Nicolas de Rambouillet and Louise Magdalen Henry, his wife, born in Copenhagen, were naturalised 1 Ap. 1708, in London. They appear, together with Anne, probably their sister, as godparents at the French church of La Savoye, London, 1746–1750. (A full account of the Tallemant, Le Venier, de Ruvigny and De Cosne alliances is in Proceedings, Huguenot Society of London, IX., Pt. 3, page 544.)

(F) There is a fine portrait of the Marquis de Ruvigny, Lord Galway, in the French Protestant Hospital, Victoria Park Road, London.

(G) Among some papers (MSS. Fr. 7052, p. 392, Arch. Nat., Paris) dealing with the affairs of the Protestants, 1685, etc., chiefly reports of spies and secret agents, is the following: " Mr. de Ruvigni, fils (in margin) Les P.R. disent que M. le Marquis de Ruvigni le fils espousera Mlle. de Siret qui est passée en Angleterre avec Madame de Ruvigni, le 4 Sept. 1685."

Mlle. de Siret, or Ciré, was a niece of the old Marquis de Ruvigny and Marie Tallemand, who had suffered much persecution in France for her religion. Madame de Massüe brought her to England, where she died of smallpox at Southampton House (Agnew i, 319). She was probably daur. of René du Culant, Marquis de Ciré.

THE DE RUVIGNY SUCCESSION

(H) Twelve dossiers containing a great mass of papers dealing with the claims to the property of the late Marquis de Ruvigny and the evidence brought forward in support by the various claimants.

The first analysis contains seven " Demandes " made by : (i.) Mlle. le Comte ; (ii.) le sieur de Launay ; (iii.) le sieur de Réaulx (debts) ; (iv.) le Comte de Polignac ; (v.) Madame la Princesse de Conty ; (vi.) les sieurs Carüe and Daule de Mesnil (Biens de la maison de Ruvigny et Lord Galway) ; (vii.) le Comte de Labattüe, Sourdeval et Gastellier, containing 53 pages.

The Le Comte claim was based on the collateral succession of the two daurs. of Antoine d'Ailly and Charlotte Famechon.

That of the sieur de Réaulx affords some idea of the value of the estates. The property of M. de Ruvigny "qu'on peut regarder comme ceux de milord Galloüay, sont chargés de plus de 600,000 livres de debtes et ne sont pas de cette valeur, puisqu'ils ne consistent qu'en trois Terres dont l'une etoit le Marquisat de Rayneval, vandu avec la permission du Roy 1701 : et dont le prix est aux consignacions et est de 25,000 livres, l'autre est une terre en touraine affermée 1,400 livres appellée la terre d'Essus (elsewhere 'Elie')."

"La troisieme est scituée près Calais appelée la terre de La Caillemothe affermée 4,000 livres, ainsi le prix de ces terres n'est pas capable de remplir les sommes deubes : scavoir sur la terre de Rayneval plus de 150,000 livres à des créanciers privilegiez et principaux."

The de Polignac "demande" gives some closer details. "Au mois de Janvier 1686, le Marquis de Ruvigny eut permission du feu Roy de se retirer en Angleterre avec sa femme et ses enfans. La guerre étant subvenüe il porta les armes contre la France. Les Biens scituez dans le Royaume furent saisis reellement par de pretendus créanciers. De pretendus parens voulurent de leur part s'en mettre en possession."

This property was confiscated in July 1694, and given to the sieur de Launay as confiscated on account of the war. In July 1720, however, Milord Galoway, only son of the late Marquis de Ruvigny, claimed that he had been included in the Act of Amnesty, and that these properties, by this time in the possession of Cardinal de Polignac, should not be included in the confiscation. A revocation of the gift to the Polignac family had been made actually, by Letters Patent to Lord Galway. The "demande" goes on to say : "Ce Milord a depuis fait son testament par lequel il a institué sa legataire universelle la Dame Wriotesky (*sic*) veuve de Milord Russel, sa cousine germaine la quelle demeurant en Angleterre, et avoit cependant des lettres de naturalité en France. Ce Milord est depuis decedé" (22 Mai 1724).

"La Dame de Russel a obtenu le 1 Juillet 1721 un brevet et des lettres patentes de Don de ces mêmes biens comme aquis au Roy a titre de desherence et en qualité d'heritière et de parenté du Milord Galway." (This, however, was barred, 26 June 1723.)

She died in England at a great age and left no heir in France, and her property was claimed by the Princesse de Conty.

The situation had by this time been complicated by the steps taken by Lady Russell to get the matter settled in her lifetime. She had entered into an agreement with the Comte de La Battüe, sgr. de Sourdeval, by which she handed over the estates to him, with the exception of, or as it seems, for the consideration of, 600,000 livres. At her death, her daur., the Duchess of Devonshire, took proceedings to recover this sum.

The progress of the claim is clearly shown by two memoirs of 1725 and 1741.

"1725. R.P.R. Memoire au Conseil pour Milord Duc de Vonshir, Pair de La Gde. Bretagne, et Dame Rachel de Wriotesky, sa femme. Contre la dame de Violenne."

This memoir sets forth that Henri de Massüe obtained leave, 19 Jan. 1686, to go to England. While there he still enjoyed his property in France. On his death, in 1689, his wife and children continued to do so without hindrance. The elder son, Lord Galway, even rendered "foi et homage" to the Chambre des Comptes, in 1690, for the lands he held of the king.

These enjoyments continued till the Peace of Ryswick, and had since been suspended by the war. Lord Galway, only son and heir of his father, found himself engaged in the Spanish army, and obliged by fate to follow the regiment he was attached to [La Fabrèque's Dragoons.—Note, Ed.] Afterwards he was amnestied, and obtained a brevet from the king, 17 July 1720, by which he was dispensed from bearing arms and which reinstated him in his property and allowed him to sell or dispose of it to pay his creditors and use the balance for his own needs.

Having deceased two months after the execution of the deed, he could not make use of it. All he could do was to dispose of his property in his will, dated 30 Aug. 1720, in favour of Elizabeth-Rachel, widow of Lord Russell, his cousin, who had been naturalised French by Letters Patent, Aug. 1641.

Lady Russell, by virtue of this will and of her Letters of French Naturalisation, and in her quality as heiress, obtained a brevet from the French King, dated 1 July 1721, confirming the naturalisation, the dispensation from living in France, and to " take up the succession to the Marquis de Ruvigny in France and to dispose of it." This she did, with the results already stated.

The memoir of 1741 relates to this transaction : " Memoire Sommaire, pour Henry De Sales, Chev., Comte Delabattüe au nom et comme etant aux Droits de deffunte Dame Elizabeth-Rachelle de Wriotesky, veuve de Milort Russel, nièce et plus proche héritière du feu sieur Marquis de Ruvigny, son oncle : contre Anne Damoiseau, veuve de Claude Viollainne et consorts."

The matter, however, did not end here, but had been still further complicated by part of the property having been sold and passed into other hands. The seigneurie of Caillemotte had been bought in 1726, by le sieur de Thosse, Président à Calais, sold to him by the Comte de La Battüe de Sourdeval for 110,000 livres ; the date of the contract was actually 25 Aug. 1725. He had apparently been within his rights in selling, for Lady Russell had obtained a brevet 1 July 1721, quoted above, to dispose of her property, and also, more important still, an Arret de Conseil in 1723, by which the King confirmed previous brevets. Meanwhile all the other claimants had been carrying on their suits to dispossess the actual holders of the property, most of them basing their claims on the thinnest of pretexts. Thus, in 1736 we find a request from " Valter Joseph Gédéon, Marquis de Douglas, cy devant capitaine, feu gouverneur en chef, et vice-amiral des iles anglaises de l'Amérique, refugié en France à cause de La Religion Catholique, dont il fait profession : a été obligé d'abandonner des biens considerables qu'il avoit en angleterre, et entre autres un gouvernement de 200,000 livres par an " !

He urges his claims to the grant of the property on the grounds that all the other claimants professing to be the nearest relatives of the Marquis de Ruvigny have not, after 47 years, succeeded in proving their claims!

Among these papers are the Letters of Naturalisation of "Rachelle de Wriotesky (*sic*) à l'effet de pouvoir succèder au Sieur Marquis de Ruvigny des biens etant en France," April 1641 (17 Juillet et Aoust 1720).

A "Brevet de don des dits biens en faveur de Milord Galouay, 1 Juillet 1720," and "Lettres Patentes sur ledit brevet, Aoust 1720," in which Lady Russell and her sister are described as "Elizabeth-Rachel et Magdeleine de Wrioteski, enfants nés du mariage celebré et consommé en ce Royaume de l'année 1634 entre Notre cher et bien aimé thomas de Vrioteski Comte de Southamptont, pair du royaume d'Angleterre et Rachel de Massue auparavant veuve de feu Ezechiel de Beaujeu vivant sr et Baron de La maison fort et fille de Daniel de Massue vivant Gouverneur de notre Château de La Bastille: contenant que les enfants sont nés audite Royaume demeurant en bas âge par le deceds de ladite Massue leur mère, mois de fevrier 1640: à raison de quoy ils pouroient etre estimés comme authaines."

Another claim was put forward by the family de Lespine, descended from the Massue family through Rachel, sister of Daniel Massüe. In this dossier the name of Rachel Wriothesley is written "Variateski."

There is also a memoir by the Marquis de Ruvigny, stating that his late father had obtained a passport to go to England with his wife and children 29 Jan. 1686, and a copy of the brevet by which the King gave back his property: presented by Lord Stair, Feb. 1720.

(Arch. Nat. T.T. 207.)

DE SAINTE-HERMINE

Arms : D'argent, semé de mouchetures d'hermine.

I. Jean de Sainte-Hermine, éc., married Dlle. Marguerite de La Duch, noble Dame du Fa : a widow in 1435. (A deed of 1435, 23 Oct.) (A). He left :

II. Jean de Sainte-Hermine, éc., sgr. du Fa, married 23 Oct. 1435 Dlle. Marguerite Goumard, daur. of Bertrand Goumard, éc., sgr. d'Eschallai, and Anne Bonneau (or Bonnelle). He had :

III. Elie, or Hélie, de Sainte-Hermine, chev., sgr. du Fa, mentioned in a Roll of 28 July 1509, did homage to the Comte d'Angoulême 10 Sept. 1476 for his fief of Marsac, belonging to Gaillardet de La Duch, sgr. de Chaudenac. His son,

IV. Claude de Sainte-Hermine, éc., sgr. du Fa, married Dlle. Cécile Joubert, who was remarried in 1527 to Etienne Forcan, sgr. de Tesson. He left by her

V. Joachim de Sainte-Hermine, chev., sgr. du Fa. He had a distinguished career on the Protestant side in the Wars of the League ; commanded the artillery at Ver, and took part in the siege of Poitiers in the third Civil War, and was Governor of La Rochelle. He married, 10 Feb. 1568, Anne Guibert, daur. of Jean Guibert, Mayor of La Rochelle, and Dlle. Jacquette Foreau, Dame de La Laigne. Their son, Jean, succeeds.

VI. Jean de Sainte-Hermine, éc., sgr. du Fa et de La Laigne, married, 16 March 1560, Dlle. Lucrèce de Lusignan, daur. of Jean de Lusignan, éc., sgr. de Lusignan, and widow of Jean de Lomagne, sgr. de Montagu, and left by her

VII. Joachim de Sainte-Hermine, sgr. du Fa et de La Laigne, gent. ord. de la chambre du Roy, Henri IV. D. in 1597. He married, 10 June 1581, Dlle. Barbe Goumard, daur. of Charles Goumard, éc., sgr. des Ardilliers, and of his wife, Hardouine de Barbezières, and left six children : (*a*) Elie, VIII, who succeeds ; (*b*) Pierre ; (*c*) David, who married, in 1618, Marie Rolland : their daur. Jacquette married Jacques du Vigier, sr. de Chauvin, 12 June 1650 ; (*d*) Leonor ; (*e*) Hardouine, who married in 1615 Isaac de Rogère ; (*f*) Françoise, who was the wife, in 1645, of Isaac de Livennes,(B) sgr. des Brosses et de Merignac.

VIII. Elie de Sainte-Hermine, chev., sgr. du Fa et de La Laigne, married, 9 Oct. 1607, Dlle. Isabeau de Polignac, daur.(C) of François de Polignac, sgr. des Fontaines, de St. Agulain, etc., and of his wife, Louise de Lanes, leaving by her two sons(D) : (*a*) Elie, IX, who continues the Protestant line ; (*b*) Joachim,(E) whose branch is given by d'Hozier, to the exclusion of the descendants of Elie, who is not mentioned by him. Joachim was a Protestant : his children abjured.

IX. Elie de Sainte-Hermine, Marquis de Sainte-Hermine, sgr. de La Laigne (see note (G)). D. in 1677. He married Dlle. Anne Madeleine Levalois de Villette, daur. of Benjamin Levalois de Villette and his wife, Louise Arthémise d'Aubigné, Dame de Murcay. By her he left five children : (*a*) Henri-Louis, who continues, X ; (*b*) Elie, Comte de Sainte-Hermine, who abjured : he became a lieut.-general in the French army ; (*c*) Philippe, lieut. de vaisseau in 1686 ; (*d*) Jean Pharamond, lieut. de vaisseau, and afterwards a priest ; (e) Madeleine-Sylvie,(F) who married Alexandre Dexmier, sgr. d'Olbreuse ; (*f*) Anne-Marie-Françoise, who abjured and became Lady of Honour to the Duchesse de Bourgogne and married, in 1687, the Comte de Mailly.

X. Henri Louis de Sainte-Hermine, Marquis de Sainte-Hermine, known as the Chevalier de Saint-Hermine, was arrested, 10 March 1686, and imprisoned in the Bastille, where he remained for a year, receiving better treatment on account of his relationship to Madame de Maintenon and the family of d'Olbreuse. He was released by order of the King, 17 Ap. 1687, and expelled from France in 1688. He went to Holland and followed William of Orange to England, and held a commission in Schomberg's regiment of Horse. D. in 1715. He had married Dlle. Marie-Genevieve Morel de Putanges, who was imprisoned in 1686 in the Convent of the Miramiones, and showed the same fortitude as her husband. Their five daughters abjured. Madeleine-Silvie, the fifth daur., died 13 Oct. 1725, in her 34th year, wife of Antoine Drummond, Comte de Melfort.

NOTES.

(A) A family belonging to the Pays d'Aunis : Marquis de Sainte-Hermine : seigneurs du Fa, Merignac, Chenon, La Laigne, Cireuil, known by deeds of 1090 (Charts of Tonnay-Charente, Gérard de Sainte-Hermine), 1323, 25 Oct, 1435 (homage to Guillaume, Evêque d'Angoulême : Elie de Ste. Hermine) 1460. Agreement between Elie de Ste. Hermine and the monks of the Abbey of La Couronne, 1471, 1500, etc.

(B) Arms : D'argent, une fasce d'azur, losangée d'argent et d'azur, et accompagnée de 3 etoiles de gueulles. Members of this family took refuge in England at the Revocation. Marianne de Livenne married Samuel Beauchamp, 21 Jan. 1742, at the French Church of St. Patrick, Dublin. The Beauchamp family were living in Dublin in 1787.

(C) A Protestant Branch of this family established in Saintonge and Angoumois.

(D) He probably left daughters, for an Elizabeth de Sainte-Hermine married, 29 March 1667, Daniel de Mazières, éc., sgr. de Voutron, des Fontaines et de Ché (Pr. Reg. La Rochelle). The de Mazière family migrated to Ireland, where it is found in the Registers of the French churches in Dublin. She is godmother, 19 June 1672, to Marie-Françoise, daur. of Messire Charles-Casimir de La Rochefoucauld, chev., sgr. de Fontpastour, etc., and Dame Marie de Mazières (Reg. Dompierre and Bourgneuf).

(E) Joachim de Sainte-Hermine married, 17 June 1635, Dlle. Anne de Polignac, his cousin german, daur. of Haut et Puissant Louis de Polignac, sgr. Baron d'Argence, and of his wife, Susanne Geoffroi, and had (*a*) Elie, who abjured in 1668, sgr du Fa ; (*b*) Louis ; (*c*) Cézar ; (*d*) Léon, d. a captain in the Regiment de la Reine ; (*e*) Isaac, d. a captain in the Regiment de Béarn ; (*f*) Alexandre, sgr. de La Barrière, unmarried ; (*g*) Diane, wife of François Lemouzin, sgr. de La Michellière ; (*h*) Marie, wife of Michel Frellat, sgr. du

Chastenet ; (*i*) Anne Charles Vigier, sgr. de Massac ; (*k*) Susanne.

The marriage contract of " Louis de Ste. Hermine, chevalier, sgr. de Chenon, fils mineur de Haut et Puissant Messire Joachim de Sainte-Hermine, chevalier, sgr. de Cireuil, de Chenon, etc., et de Dame Anne de Pollignac, sa femme, demeurans au lieu noble du Fa, paroisse dudit Cireuil en Angoumois, 15 Août 1661, avec Dlle. Marie de Livennes, fille de Messire Isaac de Livennes, chevalier, sgr. du Brousse et de Merignac, et de feue Françoise de Ste. Hermine, sa femme, demeurant dans la maison noble de Merignac." (d'Hozier, Carrés, 339.)

Louis de Sainte-Hermine made an application at St. Jean d'Angély, 30 Dec. 1672, as guardian of his younger brothers and sisters, heirs of Dame Anne de Polignac, widow of Messire Joachim de Sainte-Hermine.

Susanne Geoffroy, Dame d'Arganse, was godmother, 21 Nov. 1631, to Abraham Menanceau (Pr. Registers of Salles, near La Rochelle), and also, 14 Feb. 1633, to Pharamond, son of Messire Osée Green de Saint-Marsault, chevalier, Baron de Chatelaillon, and of his wife, Dame Madelaine de Polignac ; baptised in the Château of Roullet. She is there named " Haute et Puissante Dame d'Arganse." Her husband, Louis de P., was dead in 1661.

(F) Madeleine-Silvie, sister of Henri-Louis, chevalier de Sainte-Hermine, remained staunchly Protestant, in spite of all efforts to convert her, and married Alexandre Dexmier, sgr. d'Olbreuze, son of Alexandre Dexmier, sgr. d'Olbreuze, and Jacqueline Poussard de Vaudié. Eleonore Dexmier, sister of Alexandre Dexmier d'Olbreuze, the younger, married William of Brunswick, Duke of Zell, in 1665. She d. in 1722. Alexandre Dexmier, father of Alexandre and Eleonor, was imprisoned for his Protestant faith, but released in 1686. His son, Alexandre, and Marie-Silvie de Ste. Hermine, had a daughter Silvie Dexmier d'Olbreuze, wife of Christian von Bulow, Grand Bailli of Zell.

(G) Elie de Sainte-Hermine et de Lalaigne is godfather, 23 July 1673, to Angélique, daur. of Messire Charles-Casimir de La Rochefoucauld, sgr. de Fontpastour, and Dame Marie-Françoise de Mazières. (Reg. Pr. Dompierre et Bourgneuf.)

DE VIÇOSE

Arms : Ecartelé, 1 and 4, d'or, à un aigle deployé de sable : en chef, un soleil d'or, 2 and 3, d'or, sur 3 barres de gueules un saltier de sable.

I. Michel de Viçose, sgr. d'Alteiran, of Montauban, married Dlle. Astrugue d'Arondeau, and had 3 children : (*a*) Marguerite, wife of Pierre de Vaures ; (*b*) Jean, d. 6 Dec. 1620 (will dated 15 Aug. 1619), married Dlle. Marie d'Escorbiac,(A) daur. of Guichard d'Escorbiac, 24 Feb. 1591 ; (*c*) Raymond, II.

II. Raymond de Viçose, Baron de Castelnau et de Casenave (will dated 29 Sept. 1618), Governor of St. Maixent. He married Suzanne Dupin, daur. of — Dupin de Lalier, by whom he left : (*a*) Marguerite, bapt. 8 March 1598, married in 1614 Jacques de Chaussade de Calonges(B) ; (*b*) Henri, b. 22 Aug. 1602, bapt. 1 Jan. 1603, godson of Henry of Navarre. He married Dlle. Marie de Favas, daur. of Jean de Favas, and widow of Jean de Gontaut-Cabrères. Their daur. Marguerite married François Nompar de Caumont, Marquis de Castelmoron, 10 July 1641 ; (*c*) Alphonse ; (*d*) Jean de Viçose, b. about 1616, sgr. de Saubiac, de Genebrières et de Courondes. He married, 1st, Dlle. Anne de Ségur-Cabanac, (C) 4 Aug. 1647. She d. 13 May 1654 ; 2nd, Dlle. Marie de Caumont, in Sept. 1676. He was then 60 and she 40. By his first wife, Anne de Ségur, he left 4 children : (i) a daur., b. 1649 ; (ii) Benjamin, b. 2 April 1650 ; (iii) François, Baron de Viçose, b. March 1653, major-general in the service of the Netherlands (will made at Breda, 17 April 1710, P.C.C. 274, Price. Prob. 29 Oct. 1733). He married Dlle. Anne du Bousquet de Verlhac at Montauban (will P.C.C., 213, Browne). Her sister, Elizabeth du Bousquet de Verlhac, lived and died at Breda (will P.C.C., Browne) ; (iv) another daur., b. 1655-1656) ; (*e*) Jean Jacques ; (*f*) Benjamin, III. ; (*g*) Louise ; (*h*) Anne de Viçose, married (1st) J. du Bourg, sgr. de Cavaignes, de Belvéze, etc., (2nd) François Dupin de Lalier ; (*i*) Catherine de Viçose, who married, 17 Oct. 1637, Jonathan du Bousquet, sgr. d'Ordolhac, de Montgaillard, etc.

DE VIÇOSE

III. Benjamin de Viçose, sgr. Baron de La Cour de St. Pierre, b. about 1622, d. at Montauban, 23 May 1688. He married, 26 Nov. 1643, Dlle. Suzanne de Bar, daur. of Guy de Bar,(D) sgr. Baron de Villemade, and of his wife Jacquette de Cahusac (b. 1627). They had 9 children: (*a*) Isaac de Viçose, b. 13 Nov. 1645; (*b*) Guy de Viçose, IV.; (*c*) Jacques, sgr. de St. Pierre, b. Jan. 1648, lieut. in the Regiment du Dauphin; (*d*) Pierre de Viçose, sgr. de La Mothe, b. 28 March 1649, captain in the Regiment de Navarre; (*e*) Anne, b. Feb. 1650, imprisoned at Montauban for religion, 1686; (*f*) Jean de Viçose, b. 30 March 1654; (*g*) Jeremie de Viçose, b. 19 Aug. 1655; (*h*) Marie, wife of M. de Saint Fauret, or Saint Faust: she emigrated and came to London: her will, dated 29 Jan. 1733–34, was proved 12 Oct. 1736 (P.C.C. 218, Derby); (*i*) Judith, married in London (Lic. 27 June 1696, Faculty), Joseph Dailigues.

IV. Guy de Viçose, sgr. Baron de La Cour, bapt. 6 Feb. 1647. Lieut. in the Regiment de Turenne. Left France at the Revocation.(E) One of the original directors of the French Hospital of La Providence, London, and Governor 1722 to 1728. He married, 9 Jan. 1685, Thomasine, daur. of Abel Garrisson,(F) and Dlle. Jeanne de Noailhan, who d. 1743 (admon. London, 28 Feb.). By this marriage he left: (*a*) François de Viçose, sgr. Baron de La Cour, who remained in France and married Anne Garrisson, his cousin, daur. of Jonathan and Jeanne Garrisson, of Montauban; (*b*) Guy de Viçose, V.

V. Guy de Viçose, of St. Anne's, Westminster, and Hampstead, d. *s.p.* 1753 (Will P.C.C., Searle, 96). He married Marie Magdeleine de La Fontaine, of St. Anne's, Westminster. (Her will was proved by Michael Fountain, 3 Feb. 1769.)

NOTES

(A) This family came originally from Saintonge, and established itself at Montauban at the end of the fifteenth century. Arms: d'argent, au chevron d'azur: acc. en chef de 3 étoiles en fasce, et en pointe d'un lion couronné, de sable, armé et lampassé de gueules. (Bull: Hérald. de France,

1892.) A Marie de Garrison was the wife of M. d'Escorbiac, Conseiller au Parlement de Toulouse, in 1696, daur. of Jonathan de Garrison, sieur de Liesfrac et de Bressols.

Pierre d'Escorbiac, éc., sgr. de St. Gemme, married Marie Cornelia du Peyron, and d. at Amsterdam. Her will, dated Feb. 1728 at Amsterdam, witnessed by Philip de Marolles, notary, was proved in London, 15 Jan. 1729. Her daur. Marie Jeanne du Peyron is mentioned, by her first marriage to Pierre du Peyron.

(B) The family of Chaussade de Calonges was a noted Protestant family of the Agenais. Jacques de La Chaussade, Baron and Marquis de Calonges, was celebrated for his defence of Monpellier in 1602. He left two daurs.: Marie, who married Jean Le Révérend de Bougy in 1654, and Judith-Suzanne, dlle. de Calonges. The young Marquis de Bougy, Jean Jacques Le Révérend, was b. in 1654, and lived in the château of Calonges with his aunt, Judith de Calonges, till both were arrested in 1686. He was imprisoned in the château of Angoulême, but eventually was released and escaped to Holland in 1693. He or his son appears as godfather in 1702, Ap. 2, to a child of M. Bazin de Limeville, at Rotterdam. He had married at Caen, before 1685, and not as stated by Haag, in Holland, " Haute et Puissante Dame Elizabeth de Bar, Dame de Campernault," and left a son, Henri, whose baptism is recorded at Caen, 7 Nov. 1683 : " fils de Mr. Le Reverend de Bougy, sgr. de Bougy, Marquis de Calonges, Baron de Campernault." He left also, according to Haag, two daughters.

His aunt, Judith-Suzanne de La Chaussade, kept up the Protestant service in the temple built in the château of Calonges till 1685, in spite of the attempts made by the clergy to stop her. Jacques de La Chaussade had built the temple and removed the bells of the parish church to it. (Série T.T.) Judith de La Chaussade made her Reconnaissance in London at the French church of the Savoy, 24 May 1686, and d. at the Hague in 1700.

The Le Révérend family of Normandy was ennobled for services in 1594. Arms : écartelé, 1 and 4 de sinople, chargé de 3 mouches d'or : 2 and 3 de gueules, à un aigle déployé d'argent.

DE VIÇOSE

Jean Le Révérend, husband of Marie de La Chaussade de Calonges, was the son of Michel Le Révérend and Judith Le Gabilleur, whom he married in 1597.

(C) This family was an ancient one in the Bordelais, where it is found established in the Entre-deux-Mers district in the thirteenth century. The Branch of Cabanac was Protestant, and several members of it came to England at the Revocation, and are found in the Registers of the Savoy and Glasshouse, Leicester Fields, French churches. Henri de Ségur, chev., Vicomte de Cabanac, son of Eléonor de Ségur and of Dlle. Jeanne de Vincens de Launay, married Marie Gillet, daur. of Joseph Gillet, escuyer, secrétaire du Roi, and of Anne Joly, 7 Jan. 1680. (Prot. Reg. Bordeaux.) Arms: de sable, à une fasce d'argent.

François de Viçose, son of Jean and Anne de Ségur, commanded a regiment of Horse in Piedmont in 1694, under Lord Galway, and also in Spain at the Almanza, where his regiment was on the Dutch establishment (Add. MSS. 22264, Mil. Affairs, 1697–1734).

(D) The family of de Bar belonged to Montauban, seigneurs de La Mothe-d'Ardus, Villemade, La Garde and other places. Arms: écartelé 1 and 4 d'azur, à 2 bandes d'or: 2 and 3 de gueules, au lion d'or.

(E) A Procès-verbal "concernant les biens des Consistoires des ministres fugitifs, Montauban, 1 Ap. 1689," states that Guy de Viçose, Baron de La Cour, possessed a house at Montauban, and some vineyards, which had belonged to the late Benjamin de Viçose, his father, as testified by Abel Garrisson, avocat. Also property belonging to Dlle. Catherine de Viçose, daur. of the late Benjamin de Viçose, sgr. Baron de Genebrières et de Courondes. (Série T.T. 254.)

A claim was made, 4 Aug. 1699, at Bapome by a cousin, the sgr. de Villemade, to the property of Guy de Viçose, sgr. de La Cour, "Religionnaire Fugitif." The memoir states that Guy de Viçose, son of Benjamin de Viçose and of Suzanne de Bar, married, 9 Jan. 1685, Thomase Garrisson, daur. of Abel Garrisson, bourgeois, of Montauban. Shortly after their marriage, Guy and his wife left France, leaving all their property, consisting of money, lands, and the seigneurie of La Cour, a house at Montauban, 4,000 livres of rent in all. Benjamin de Viçose, d. 23 May 1688, leaving as his heir Abel Garrisson, father-in-law of Guy, who had since then always enjoyed this property. (Série T.T. 221 bis.)

(F) Abel Garrisson was ennobled by Letters Patent in May 1701: registered in the Parlement de Toulouse 7 Sept. following, and in the Cour des Aides of Montauban, 17 Feb. 1702. Arms: d'or, au chêne de sinople, fruité d'argent. (Lainé, Nobil.)

Some members of the Garrisson family left France and came to England. Isaac Garisson, son of Isaac and Catherine Garisson, b. at Montauban, was naturalised 19 March 1705–6.

Antoine Garrisson, of St. Anne's, Westminster, married Marie Genais Duchail, of St. Giles', Westminster, by licence 13 Aug. 1707, at the Savoy French church, London. The Genais family was from La Vendée, and bore for arms: d'argent, à 3 gourseaux de genêts de sinople. (Genais du Chail de Sauvré.)

INDEX

INDEX

INDEX

INDEX

INDEX

G

INDEX

INDEX

D

INDEX

INDEX

INDEX

INDEX

INDEX

M

INDEX

INDEX

N

INDEX

INDEX

S

INDEX

INDEX

INDEX

HUGUENOT PEDIGREES

HUGUENOT PEDIGREES

By CHARLES E. LART
FELLOW OF THE ROYAL HISTORICAL SOCIETY
FELLOW OF THE HUGUENOT SOCIETY *of* LONDON
MEMBRE CORRESPONDANT DE LA SOCIÉTÉ DES ARCHIVES DE POITOU

Editor of
"Jacobite Extracts from the Parochial Registers of St. Germain-en-Laye." The "Protestant Registers of Caen: Loudun: Le Rochebeaucourt," etc.

VOL. II

"O Seigneur, Tu as été notre Refuge de l'une génération à l'autre."

CLEARFIELD

PREFACE

THE question of French Noblesse was fully discussed in the first volume of "Huguenot Pedigrees." It may only be necessary to repeat the main points—that there is no analogy between the English nobility of to-day and that of France in the sixteenth and seventeenth centuries. The "noblesse" in France began with the "ecuyer," which rank alone constituted nobility; the titles of Marquis, Comte, Baron being administrative only, and not personal, and appertaining to persons of the rank of "ecuyer" who possessed a certain number of seigneuries constituting a "marquisat," or "comte," or "baronie," and not passing to posterity, of necessity, *i.e.*, if the property was sub-divided and passed into other hands.

Later, in the eighteenth century, the custom of using titles without reference to the older usage, came into being; and those of the Restoration, of course, when the feudal system had been swept away, were all personal.

There remains the vexed question of armorial bearings. Here again, although in theory the system of a College of Arms primarily existed, similar to that in England, in practice it ceased to operate as fully as it has done in this country: owing to various causes which did not exist here.

Territorially France was composed of two kingdoms, France and Navarre, hence certain differences are apparent in coats of arms borne by families in Gascony and in Picardy. Moreover, France was a country always liable to civil war, when a Duchy like Brittany or Normandy was at times at war with the King, whose writ did not always run in a particular province, for the time being, and central authority became impossible. Hence the extraordinary numbers of the same armorial bearings borne by different families.

The theory and rules laid down in books of Heraldry are found to be continually vitiated by local exceptions, so that the dictum of "the rule being proved by the exception" has no force. It is to be borne in mind also that since "noblesse" denoted the "ecuyer," and the French noblesse being equivalent to the English Peerage, Baronetage,

Knightage, and Landed Gentry, it follows that the numbers of persons who bore arms far exceeded those in England, where the question of Visitations and control of Arms was far more easily dealt with; and in addition, the population of France in the reign of Louis XIV was something like three times as large, if not more.

In the beginning the system of Heraldry was controlled by a "Roi d'Armes," whose official name was "Montjoye St. Denis," because it was his duty to cry "St. Denis Montjoye" in his official capacity and presence at tournaments, that being the "cri de guerre" of the Kings of France. He had the pre-eminence over the other Kings of Arms, who presided over the Marches, "Rois d'Armes des Marches." Each King of Arms, of France and the Marches, had two Heralds, and each Herald had two Pursuivants. There were sixteen Kings of Arms of the Marches: Bourgogne, Normandie, Dauphiné, Bretagne, Alençon, Orléans, Anjou, Valois, Berry, Angoulême, Guyenne, Champagne, Picardie, Bourbon, Poitou and Provence.

A Herald had to be a Pursuivant for seven years before being promoted to Herald, and Pursuivants were attached to nobles of high rank and to Chevaliers Banneret, under the authority of a Herald.

They were called by picturesque titles such as "Plein-chemin," "Joli-coeur," "Claire Voye," etc. Their duty was to make Visitations, to enquire into the armorial bearings and pedigrees of families within their jurisdiction.

Not one of their Books or Visitations has survived.

There is no exact record of how soon or when the system began to fall into disorder, but fall into disorder it did, and very few "Recherches"—Visitations—of any kind are in existence before the great "Recherche" of 1666, instituted by Louis XIV in order to regulate the disorder which culminated with the civil wars of the sixteenth century.

Desultory Visitations* were made here and there, such as that of Jean Guilloches, in 1523, for Normandy, of which a manuscript exists in the Public Library at Rouen (published by A. de Tesson, 1898). An earlier one had been made

* They were entrusted to officials, such as Intendants or some other official.

in 1463-64 by Raymond de Monfault, Général des Monnaies, by the orders of Louis XI, on account of the disorder which had arisen during the English occupation (1417-1450). This Visitation however was revoked, since many of the " noblesse," ruined by the struggle against the English, had been obliged to enter into commerce, which vitiated their claim to nobility, or had lost their family papers, which had in many cases been taken to England, or lost, and without which they could not support their claim.

Various attempts had been made to introduce order throughout France generally. Charles VIII had created a Marshal of Arms, who should regulate armorial bearings, apart from questions of " noblesse," and to issue an armorial for princes, ducs, comtes-barons, châtelains, seigneurs and other nobles of the Kingdom. His catalogues and lists survived up to the reign of Henry III and were in constant use, but the disorders and civil wars threw everything into confusion again.

In 1614, the Estates General represented to the King, Louis XIII, the desirability of regulating the use of armorial bearings, then in a state of confusion, and the King appointed a " Conseiller-Juge General d'Armes " and gave him all the prerogatives formerly belonging to Heralds and Pursuivants, but the work was not carried out until the reign of Louis XIV, who appointed Pierre d'Hozier Juge d'Armes, 25 April, 1641.

The great Recherche which Louis XIV ordered to be made by d'Hozier, Juge d'Armes, for the whole of France, begun in 1666, was continued, with many interruptions, till 1727.

The object of this Visitation was to bring back some official order in the regulations for the Noblesse. Deriving as it did from the " terre " or fief, the possession of which by the " ecuyer " alone conferred nobility, the sub-division of seigneuries after the devastating wars of the sixteenth century had led to a multitude of unauthorised claimants to the title of ecuyer, based on the purchase or possession of a parcel of a " terre noble " ; and the King, or his minister, Colbert, saw in this a vista of possible taxation which they proceeded to put into execution.

Those who had usurped the title of " noble ecuyer "

were heavily fined, those who substantiated their claim were taxed, and those—and they were many—whose position was unassailable and who could prove descent for many generations and who deemed it derogatory to appear before the Commissioners, were also fined.

The Visitation of 1666 proved a gold mine to the State.

d'Hozier issued a commission to the Intendants of Provinces to carry this out, and they deputed their task to "Commissaries," mostly men who had recently been ennobled by purchasing some "office" by "Finance" or the "Robe," many of them without knowledge of heraldry, who very often imposed a fantastic coat of arms on some ancient family of the old nobility who failed to appear.

The claims to "noblesse" were supported by family deeds of all kinds, marriage contracts, deeds of partition, wills, and other documents, in which the persons interested had been described as "noble" or "ecuyer," and not by any previous heraldic grants or visitations, which did not exist, generally speaking, except in isolated visitations such as that of Jean Guilloches, de Roissy or de Montfault in Normandy and a few other districts.

The question arises as to who was responsible for the regulation of armorial bearings during the period of comparative anarchy, when the Pursuivants were dying out and were not replaced? It is a question to which the Editor has not been able to get a clear answer even from genealogists of high repute, and it is one which does not appear to have been considered.

The answer seems to be that so far as new nobles were concerned, created either by Letters Patent or by the usual methods of "anoblissement" by Finance, the Legal profession, etc., mentioned in Volume I, armorial bearings were adopted by the person concerned and registered in the local Courts, such as the Cour des Aides, with the title of ennoblement.

To use a coat of arms was not a privilege confined to the "ecuyer"—anyone below that rank could use one—but it was a plain one, without casque or supporters: those who belonged to the newer Noblesse and the Haute Bourgeoisie and rich merchant families probably already had adopted a coat. The " armorial " of 1696 was a purely fiscal one, ordered by an arrêt en Conseil, dated 20 November, 1696, and the fact of a coat of arms being registered therein does not necessarily imply " noblesse." This " armorial " contains something like 50,000 coats of arms for which no grant was ever made, but which provided a source of revenue to the State, which recognized them by official registration.

Contrary to popular belief, the use of the particle " de " does not necessarily denote nobility. In the eighteenth century it became the custom to put it before the family name when the numbers of " anoblis " had become so great, and when so many persons who had acquired wealth thought it the proper thing to do, just as the profiteer of to-day takes the title of Count or Baron, or even Prince, in order to " get into society " ; but previous to the reign of Louis XIV the old noble families never used it before their family name, being known by the name of their seigneury. To take an example from those English families of Huguenot descent still existing : Chevalleau de Boisragon was never " de Chevalleau," and they were known as " de Boisragon," as they are to-day.

There are seeming exceptions to this rule, but where an ancient family of long descent does use the particle it is because the original family name has been forgotten from long disuse, and the seigneurial title has become the accepted family name. The ducal family " de la Rochefoucauld " descends from Foucauld (a christian name), Seigneur de la Roche-Foucauld ; it never was " de Foucauld." Brittany is specially rich in examples of this kind. There are also families who use " de " before their names who have never claimed " noblesse," the particle simply being equivalent to the old English " of "—John of York, etc.

The sole title denoting " noblesse " in legal and official deeds is " noble homme," " ecuier " or " chevalier " (in ancient deeds, " nobilis vir " : scutifer : armiger).

Whatever may be said to the contrary, there seems to be little doubt that the older families of rank managed their armorial affairs themselves, when no other authority was available, with the aid and advice of some clerk from a neighbouring abbey learned in such matters. The greater families probably retained their Pursuivants to a later date than others.

That such was the case is evident from family records which come to light from time to time. The following extract is a case in point and seems to shew that a seigneur sometimes imposed a rule. " Messire Bertrand de Lart, Chevalier, seigneur de Rigoulieres et de Montagnac, permet à Jean de Lart, seigneur de Calignac, son bon parent et notable amy, que tous les biens qu' il possède, en la Seigneurie de Montagnac soient tirés de cadastres, terriers et Liéves de ladite Seigneurie : et pour l'affection qu'il a envers ledit De Lart, il entend et declare que ledit De Lart *porte les armes rustiques et marques dudit Seigneur y mettant une barre de travers tendant sur la main droite, des qeuelles ledit De Lart pourra user*, etc. The particular coat of arms of this branch were quartered, four coats, with the differences mentioned above, a " franc canton de sinople," and " barre de travers " on the first quarter. Jean de Lart de Calignac was the eldest son of Bertrand sgr. de Rigoulières et de Montagnac : the transaction was made before a notary, Dangles, 23 June, 1602, and is a private deed. Other instances shew that differences, at least, were made without recourse to a Herald, who at that date is not known to have been in existence. No records of any Visitations at this date either remain or are known to have been made in this province of Guienne.

Although in theory differences and marks of cadency, the bordure, lambel, etc., existed, they are seldom found in the case of the smaller families ; the greater families, ducal and others of high rank, generally used the lambel. Cadet branches, from the middle of the sixteenth century, sometimes used the brisure.

The usage in quartering arms varies, principally in the North and South. Occasionally, from the middle of the seventeenth to the end of the eighteenth century, a man quartered his arms with those of his mother. From the end of the fifteenth and during the sixteenth century the custom was to impale the husband's coat with that of his wife, but in doing so it was often usual to impale only half of each coat.

PREFACE

In Navarre, though sometimes in other provinces, the custom was common of quartering (1) the arms of the person, (2) those of his mother, (3) of his paternal grandmother, (4) maternal grandmother. Numerous instances are found of a branch using for some generations the coat of an ancestor who had impaled his own with the coat of his wife, which coat was quartered, but where the original male coat had "pals," the number and tinctures have been changed.

The usages and customs of Heraldry changed from century to century and in different parts of France. Only in the case of great families, Pairs de France, does there seem to have been any consistent adhesion to the earlier rules of Heraldry.

The Visitations were not primarily concerned with armorial bearings, but with the claims to "noblesse," *i.e.*, to the rank of "ecuyer."

In publishing the second volume of "Huguenot Pedigrees," the Editor again calls attention to the fact that in France the MS. sources of genealogical information are practically untouched so far as printing is concerned. The object in view is to publish as much unprinted matter as possible, and wherever a pedigree may have been printed in whole or part before, none have been included without additions and corrections, with notes from MS. French sources, and with the object of carrying the pedigree back as far as is possible in France.

The Editor begs to thank all those who have so kindly given their help and advice, whose names are mentioned in the Preface to Volume I, and to express his thanks to the President and Council of the Huguenot Society of London for their kind permission to make use of the collection of pedigrees and notes made by the late Mr. Henry Wagner, as well as to Major F. Kennedy for valuable information relating to the Portales family, and to Dr. Guillemard, of Cambridge, and Mr. R. E. N. Palairet for the long and accurate pedigrees of their families, to which he has been able to add very little.

It is intended to add to this and future volumes all available details of family portraits and heirlooms.

The criticism has been made that there is little or no

interest in publishing the pedigree of a family now extinct. In answer the Editor would point out that most families, though extinct in the male line, are represented in the female line by marriage, either with another family also of Huguenot descent or with one of purely British or American blood, to whom heirlooms and portraits of great interest have passed. Moreover, it very often happens that families which are supposed to be extinct are not always so—in the male line—owing to some cadet in some previous generation having migrated to another country, or part of this country, and who has lost connection with the main stock; and it sometimes happens that the supposed main stock is, in fact, a cadet branch and that the elder branch or line still exists, possibly spelling the name in a different way. There is a special possibility of this kind in Huguenot families, one branch Anglicising its name, and another preserving the French spelling. That this took place can be seen in the registers of the French churches in England.

In conclusion, the Editor wishes to express his most grateful thanks to Miss Ida Layard for her munificent gift of her very large and accurate collection of pedigrees, the work of her lifetime, on which he has drawn largely in compiling this volume.

C.E.L.

Authors' Club,
2, Whitehall Court, S.W. 1.

Abbreviations :—a.e.b. = été baptisé ; b. = born, né ; bapt. = baptisé ; m. = married ; sr. = sieur ; sgr. = seigneur ; daur. = daughter, fille ; d. = died, mort. P.C.C. = Prerogative Court of Canterbury, Wills (Registre des Testaments, Londres).

D'AULNIS DE LA LANDE

Arms : D'azur : à 2 aigles de profil d'or : affrontés et ess : posés sur un rocher de gueules et supp : de leurs becs un casque grillé d'or, doublé de sa. taré de front.

I. Louis D'Aulnis, sr. du Caillaud, of the parish of Breuillet, in Saintonge, m. Judith Chasseloup (B. 579 1663, Sentences, Presidial Court of La Rochelle). They had three sons : (*a*) Pierre, who succeeds II ; (*b*) Louis, sr. de Petit-pré, of the par . of Breuillet, who m. Alouée grand-daur. of Jean Grand, sr. de Claunay and of Rebecca Baudouin (Minutes de Notaire, Gillet) ; (*c*) Charles, chev. sgr. du Vignau, m. Suzanne Boybellaud. He d. in 1722, and was concerned in a suit V. Charles Boybellaud, sr. de La Barrière, guardian of Suzanne Boybellaud his wife, heiress in part of Samuel Boybellaud, avocat, and of Debora Bellet ; and also of her brother Samuel Boybellaud, and of Polyxène Boybellaud, wife of Henri du Bon, sr. de la Gravière. (B. 478. Presidial of La Rochelle.)

II. Pierre D'Aulnis, sr. du Caillaud, a doctor. d. at Portarlington, 23 Nov. 1709. He was a fugitive in 1687, as appears by a claim to his property in France, made in 1738 (Serie TT. 124) by Pierre Martin and Louis, Jean, Denis, and Francois Robin, his nephews and grandsons. A memoir (*idem*) of 21 July 1717, says that Pierre D'Aulnis, medecin, went to a foreign country for Religion without the King's permission in 1687, that he was a son of Louis D'Aulnis, and that it was not possible to get his burial certificate, he having died in a foreign country in 1711 (actually in 1709). He m. Dlle. Henriette Boybellaud de Montacier de L' Isle Marais, sister of General Sir Henry Boybellaud, Kt. She was naturalised at Amsterdam, 18 March 1710 They left (*a*) Henri, who succeeds, III ; (*b*) Marie, bapt. 9 Aug. 1711, at the French Church of Le Carré, London. (*c*) Francois, captain in the British Army, who m. his cousin, Angelique Judith D'Aulnis. Francois D'Aulnis de La Lande D. in 1722 in Ireland (P.C. I) and his wife Angelique Judith D'Aulnis d. in 1752 (P.C. I). She was daur. of Pierre de La Lande, sr. du Caillaud et de Bourouaille, who fled to Holland and m. Angelique Boybellaud.(A) He was probably son of Francois de la Lande, sr. de Bourouille, mentioned in a deed (Not. Gillet) in 1663, and was ancestor of the branch in Holland, Barons du Caillaud et de Bourouille (B). Francois D'Aulnis de La Lande and his wife Angelique Judith left four children surviving out of twelve : (i) Pierre François, b. 3 Jan. 1703, at Portarlington ; (ii) Angelique Henriette, b. 9 Jan. 1709 at Portarlington, m . . . . . d'Hérisson about 1760 ; d. at Portarlington 2 June 1799, aged 90. (iii) Jeanne, b. 4 Nov. 1713 at Portarlington and d. there 7 June 1741 ; (iv) Charles, b. 15 March 1715. The remaining children were born at Portarlington, and died young (see Registers, French Church). The four surviving are mentioned in the will of Angelique Judith D'Aulnis, their mother (made 6 Sept. 1733, pr. 16 July 1752).

III. Henri D'Aulnis, sr. de La Lande et de Lomadé. d. at Dublin 25 Aug. 1737. Captain on half-pay. He m. Mary . . . ., whose surname is not known, but as he is also styled "Lislemarais" it is probable that she was a Boybellaud. She d. at Dublin, 28 Oct. 1763, aged 76 (Dublin Fr. Ch. Reg.). She made her will 31 Jan. 1762, Pr. 10 March 1764 in Dublin (P.C. I). They left (*a*) Henry, who succeeds, IV ; (*b*) John de La Lande, who went to Virginia ; (*c*) Anne Henriette, bapt. 26 Aug. 1714 in the French Church of the Savoy, London. She m. in Dublin, 26 Aug. 1730, Captain Paul Mangin, by whom she left Col. Samuel Henry Mangin, who m. Suzanne Corneille ; (*d*) Jean, bapt. 12 Feb. 1718, who may be the above John (*b*) (Savoy Fr. Ch.) ; (*e*) Angelique, bapt. 24 Sept. 1719 (Savoy Fr. Ch.) ; (*f*) Charles, bapt. 14 Dec. 1720 (*idem*)
IV. Henry de La Lande, or Lalande, of London, left several children, whose names are not known, but who are mentioned in the will of their grandmother, Mary Lalande, of Dublin (P.C.I. 1764). The name of his wife is not known.

Abraham Lalande, b. in 1752, and Carey Lalande, b. 1754, are said to have been sons of Henry Lalande IV, but no proofs can be found. They entered the Honourable East India Company's service. Abraham Lalande d. 13 Feb. 1844 at his house in Sloane Street, Chelsea; and General Carey Lalande d. at Madras, 7 Sept. 1824. Their sister, Catherine Elizabeth Lalande, m. a Mr. Waller. She is mentioned in the will of her brother Abraham, who also left a legacy to his cousins Reuben Menyon and John Silvio Higgs.

NOTES.

The pedigree is complicated by marriages having been made with different members of the Boybellaud family, and by several members of the English and Dutch branches bearing the same christian names. A Pierre D'Aulnis, captain on half-pay, d. at Portarlington, 23 Nov. 1709, but Pierre D'Aulnis de La Lande II is described in the deed 17 July 1717 (serie T.T. 124) as " medecin." It is possible however that he entered the British Army and is identical with Pierre II.

(A) The husband of Angelique Boybellaud is identified as Pierre D'Aulnis by a baptismal entry in the Registers of the French Church, Portarlington, 2 Aug. 1694, of Louis Vidal, whose godmother was Dame Angelique de Boisbleau (Boybellaud), wife of Pierre D'Aulnis, escuyer sr. du Caillaud. He was therefore a cousin of Pierre D'Aulnis II. Angelique Boybellaud has been mentioned as wife by a second marriage of Pierre D'Aulnis, sr. du Caillaud II. This, however, cannot be, as Francois, son of Pierre II, married Angelique Judith, daur. of the other Pierre and of Angelique Boybellaud.

Since Pierre D'Aulnis, husband of Angelique Boybellaud, is the ancestor of the branch in Holland, Barons de Bourouille, it is probable that he was son of Francois D'Aulnis, esc. sr. de Bourrouille, mentioned in a deed of 1663. (Not. Gillet.)

The pedigree given by me in Vol. IX, p. 120, Huguenot Society Proceedings, 1909, must therefore be corrected.

Mr. Wagner is clearly incorrect in his note on this pedigree (p. 125). The Pierre D'Aulnis who m. Henriette Boybellaud de Montacier was ancestor of the English branch, and distinct from the Pierre D'Aulnis, husband of Angelique Boybellaud.

Angelique (D'Aulnis) Boybellaud stood proxy at the baptism of her grandson, Pierre, son of Francois D'Aulnis, sr. de La Lande, and of his wife Angelique Judith D'Aulnis (Portarlington French Church), 3 Jan. 1703, for the godmother, Dlle. Magdelaine Joly du Fié, "grand'-tante paternelle."

The Joly family was a numerous one in Saintonge, and connected by marriage with that of D'Aulnis. Judith Joly was wife of Francois D'Aulnis, living at La Lande, parish of St. Sulpice, near Mornac, mentioned in a notarial acte of 1673 (Minutes de Notaires, Dangibaud). This Francois was almost certainly the François D'Aulnis, mentioned in 1663 as sr. de Bourrouille.

(B) Branch in Holland.

Pierre d'Aulnis, sr. du Caillaud, and Angelique Boybellaud had a son and daur., Angelique Judith, wife of her cousin, Francois D'Aulnis de La Lande, and Pierre, or Peter Louis, Lt.-Col. in the Dutch Army, d. 1739; m. (i) Gurtruda, daur. of Egidius van den Bogaard, Burgomaster of Utrecht, by whom he left issue, and (ii) at the Hague, 25 March 1714, his cousin, Marie, daur. of Francois Boybellaud de Montacier, who d. at Boesburg, 8 July 1782, said to be 104 years of age. (See Vol. I, Boybellaud, Pedigree.)

By his second marriage he left two daughters: (i) Angelica Henrietta, of Nymegen (Will P.C.C., 16 Holman, 1794), and (ii) Aletta Catherina Everardina, who m. at the Hague in 1740, Sir John Baptist Silvester, M.D.

(Note.—I am indebted to the late Mr. Wagner for these notes on the branch in Holland. Vol. IX, p. 125, Hug. Soc. Proc.—Ed.)

BELCASTEL

Arms : Ecartelé, 1 and 4, à une Tour d'argent, surmontée de 3 donjons crenelés, ajourés et maconnés de sable (de Belcastel) ; 2 and 3, à 3 lances d'or posées en pal, la pointe en haut (de Montvaillant).

I. Jean de Belcastel, chev. sgr. de Belcastel en Rouergue, m. Dlle. Christine de Saunhac, and left (*a*) Raimond, who succeeds, II.

II. Raimond de Belcastel, chev. sgr. de Belcastel, Lieut : d'une compagnie d'hommes d'armes. m. 4 Feb. 1526, in Languedoc, Dlle. Jeanne de Montvaillant, heiress of her line (perhaps daur. of Frédal de Montvaillant, conseiller, Cour des Aydes, Monpellier in 1514) (La Roque, armorial de Monpellier), by whom he had (*a*) Jean, who succeeds, III ; (*b*) Robert, author of the branch of Escairac, who m. Dlle Philippe de Boutiers 7 Ap. 1571 ; (*c*) Raimond, author of the branch of Montlauzun in Quercy ; (*d*) Jean, chevalier de Malte, 1580 ; (*e*) Catherine, m. 29 Jan. 1576, François de Ginestoux.

III. Jean de Belcastel, dit de Montvaillant, sgr. de Montvaillant et de Castanet. He presided, with Nicolas de Calvière, sgr. de St. Cosne, at the assembly of Protestants at Anduze, 22 Nov. 1579. M. his cousin, Dlle. Jeanne de Belcastel de la Pradelle (before 4 Jan. 1553), and left by her (*a*) Marguerite ; (*b*) Pierre (v. Haag, La France Protestante), who succeeds, IV.

IV. Pierre de Belcastel de Montvaillant, sgr. de la Pradelle. m. 18 June 1587, Dlle. Louise de Vabre, and left (*a*) Claude, who m. Paul de Vignolles ; (*b*) Marie, m. in 1646, Henri Tremolet-Bucelli, sgr. de Montmoirac ; (*c*) Daniel, who succeeds, V.

V. Daniel de Belcastel, sgr. de Montvaillant et du Mazel, of Montpellier ; d. at Montpellier. M. 10 Ap. 1638, Dlle. Marie de Lignières(A) (probably the daur. of M. de Lignières, Deputy for Haut-Languedoc in the assembly at La Rochelle in 1620). Maintained his noblesse, 19 Jan.

1668, and left (*a*) Pierre, who succeeds, VI; (*b*) Louise-Adelaide, who was the second wife of Samuel Louis Crommelin, d. s.p.; (*c*) Judith, who re-married in France, and died at an advanced age; (*d*) Françoise, mentioned in the will of General de Belcastel.(B)

VI. Pierre de Belcastel, sgr. de Montvaillant, Marquis d'Avèze, Baron de Beaufort, was born at Montpellier, and naturalised in London 4 May 1699. M. Dame Anne Charlotte de Roese, or Roësse(C) (Royce, in Vic. Gen. Marr. Lic. 9 Dec. 1692). He was 44, and she was 21, a spinster, of St. Martin-in-the Fields, by consent of her father; alleged by Louis de Rosset, of St. Anne, Westminster. He was of St. Martin's, and a bachelor. The marriage was to take place at St. Mary Magdalen, Old Fish Street, London.

He was Lieut.-Col. of Caillemotte's Regiment of Foot, raised in Holland in 1689, and became Colonel after the death of the Comte de la Caillemotte at the Boyne; Brigadier-General, 1 June 1696. After the regiment was disbanded in 1698, he commanded a French regiment raised in Holland for the service of the States General, and became Major-General in the Dutch service in 1704 and served in Spain and Portugal, being killed at the battle of Villaviciosa in 1710.

On the 17th May 1701 he was ordered to go with his regiment to Breda, and in 1702 he applied for the post of Major-General of Infantry and was promoted in 1703. In 1704 he requested that his service in the British Army might be counted as service in the Dutch Army.

His will (P.C.C., Young 76) was proved in London. He left to his eldest son (Pierre) two portions of his property if his mother re-married, and appoints Nicolas de L'Etang(D) as guardian. When his eldest son "shall be reinstated in the Marquisate d'Avèze" his share shall go to his brother and sisters. He made his will at the Hague at three o'clock in the afternoon of Sunday, 8 June, 1704, in the presence of Daniel de Belcastel, chev. sgr. de La Menerie, and of Mr. Louis de Senegas, Lieut. in the regiment of Major-General de Belcastel (by Cornelius de Grave, notaire).

The will was proved 14 March 1711 by his widow, who

appeared at the Hague and in London (5 Nov. 1712) and opened in the presence of Dame Anne de Roese, his two sons, "and the gentlewoman, daur. of the said Sr. de Belcastel," with relations and friends hereinafter named, viz., Dame Anna de Roese, Pierre de Belcastel, Marquis d'Avèze, Baron de Beaufort, Joseph Louis Stephen de Belcastel, Anne Charlotte de Belcastel his children, Henri de Montèze, Major-General in the Dutch Army, Dame Martha de Montèze, a relative of General de Belcastel, Nicolas de L'Etang, Major-General (Melonière de l'Etang).

The probate was signed by De Roese Belcastel, Belcastel Beaufort, Anne Charlotte de Belcastel, Henry de Montèze, M. de Montèze, and Nicolas de l'Etang. (D)

Pierre de Belcastel, eldest son, appears to have left France with his father in 1686, and was a captain of cavalry. "Pierre de Belcastel, capitaine de cavalerie à fl. 900: ayant servi dans la cavalerie: officier sorti de France." (Fiches de Belcastel, Bib. Wallonne, Leyde). He was probably the Pierre de Belcastel de Montvaillant, Major-General in Savoy in 1705, in Catalonia 1708, and who applied for promotion to rank of Lieut.-General in 1709. Killed at the battle of Bruega (*idem*). A Pierre Raimond de Belcastel de Montvaillant, son of General de Belcastel, brought back the news (Ap. 1710) of the victory of Almenaar, and received a medal and gold chain. He claimed his expenses of the journey, 80 pistoles. (E)

General Pierre de Belcastel left by his wife, Anne Charlotte de Roese (*a*) Pierre; (*b*) Joseph Louis Stephen; (*c*) Marthe Elizabeth, bapt. at the Hague, in the Grande Eglise, 3 Aug. 1701. Her godmother was Marthe de Montmoyral; (*d*) Jean Karel, or Pieter (10), 28 Aug. 1702. Godfather, Edmond de Belcastel. (The mother's name is spelled "Anne Droes.") (*e*) Charles, "fils de Pierter de Belcastel, et de Anne Desroyes." At the Nouvelle Eglise, 20 Ap. 1704.

One of these sons appears to have left male issue. "Anno 1735, Belcastel, capitaine au regiment de Montèze, autorisé à accepter le commandement sur Philippine." (Bib. Wallonne, Fiches Belcastel.) He was a captain in the regiment de Montèze, 25 Sept. 1710, and major 22 March 1736 (*idem*) (E).

NOTES.

(A) Marie de Lignières suffered great cruelties after her arrest: two of her fingers were cut off, and after many great indignities she and her sister were imprisoned in a convent (Benoit, *Hist. of the Revocation*, vol. v, p. 1020.)

(B) Francoise de Belcastel was a witness to the marriage of Joseph D'Avessein and Marguerite De Villettes at Dublin (French Church, St. Patrick), 23 Aug. 1697, and also to that of Simon Chabert to Francis d'Hours, daur. of Antoine d'Hours, of Mauguio, Languedoc, and of Dame Louise de Belcastel, his wife.

(C) The family of Roese, or Roësse came from the neighbourhood of Rouen, and was connected by marriage with those of Civille and Dericq. Jean de Roësse, chev. sgr. de Beuzevillette, de Beuzeville, du Feuqueray, patron du Mesnil-Pieu. M. in 1669, Elizabeth Chappellier (Reg. Prot. Quévilly). Isaac de Civille, ec. sgr. de St. Mars, Remefville, Cottevrard and other places, m. Genevieve de Roësse de Beuzevillette, and their son, Isaac de Civille m. Jeanne Dericq at Bacqueville, 23 Feb. 1642 as his second wife. (Commission del' hist. du Egl. Wallonnes. Bull, II, serie I (2) 137.) The family became Royce in England.

(D) Nicolas de Monceaux de l'Etang was naturalised 8 July 1697 in London. The family belonged to the generalitè of Alençon.

(E) Peter de Belcastel, major in the regiment of Soute, made his will at Middelburg, 24 March 1735. Pr. 19 Nov. 1739 (P.C.C., Henchman 226). Trans. from Low Dutch. He left £300 to the French Hospital, Hackney; £300 to Miss Nancy Du Roure, daur. of Lt.-Col. Scipio Du Roure; £50 to Widow Dupré, his old nurse; £25 to Mrs. Sally Marple, who lives with his sister Charlotte de Belcastel, his heiress. The exors. were Colonels Scipio and Alexander Du Roure.

Scipio Du Roure, son of François Du Roure, and Catherine de Rieutort, b. in Bremen 15 March 1689. Colonel of the 1st regiment of Foot; mortally wounded at Fontenoy, 1745. M. Marguerite, daur. of Charles de Vignolles and Marthe, daur. of Samson Du Roure de Bonneaux.

Alexandre Du Roure, his brother, was b. in London 3 Sept. 1692 and baptised at Les Grecs French Church. Governor of St. Mawes Castle, Cornwall. Colonel of the 4th Regiment of Foot. D. at Toulouse, 2 Jan. 1765. Buried in south cloister, Westminster Abbey. M. Louise Bruchelles, or Brushell, of Hammersmith (Faculty Lic., 8 Nov. 1748). (See Vol. IX and Vol. X, p. 399, *Proceedings*, Huguenot Society of London.)

The family has no connection with that of Grimouard de Beauvoir, Seigneurs Du Roure.

BOILEAU DE CASTELNAU

Arms: d'azur, au chateau d'argent, maconné de sable, au croissant de même en pointe.

Motto: " de tout mon coeur."

I. Guillaume Boileau, said to be son of Antoine Boileau, b. 1381, d. 1459, Tresorier of the Royal demesnes of Nismes and Beaucaire. B. in 1420, d. in 1494.(A) M. Etienette Bourdin, daur. of Jean Bourdin, Receveur General of Poitou, by whom he left (*a*) Antoine, who succeeds, II; (*b*) Guillaume, protonotaire of the Pope and Prior of St. Nicolas, near Uzès; (*c*) Jean Guillaume, conseiller of Montpellier; (*d*) Madeleine, wife of Pierre de Rollot, Treasurer of Provence in 1491; (*e*) Nicolas, conseiller du Grand-conseil; (*f*) Agnes, m. in 1496 Pierre de Rochemaure; (*g*) Jeanne Catherine, m. in 1525 Jean de Ganay, Chancellor of France under Louis XII and others.

II. Antoine Boileau bought the seigneuries of Castelnau la Garde and Ste. Croix de Boirac, 5 Feb. 1500, in the dioc. of Uzès. First sr. de Castelnau. D. at Nismes in 1530. M. in 1497 Francoise Troussellier, daur. of Jean Troussellier, a doctor of law and Conseiller du roi, Chancellor of the Faculty of Montpellier. He left (*a*) Jean, who succeeds, III; (*b*) Catherine, m. Claude de Marçay; (*c*) Madeleine, m. 1529 Jean de Sauzat; (*d*) Etiennette, m. 1516 Barthelemy Doulon, sr. de Ners.

III. Jean Boileau, sr. de Castelnau, Treasurer of Nismes, was the first of his family to become a Protestant. B. 1500, d. Oct. 1562 (said to have been beheaded). M. Dlle. Anne de Montcalm,(B) 12 Feb. 1538, who d. in 1560. They had (*a*) Jean, who succeeds, IV; (*b*) Claude, m. in 1554 Jean Jacques de Lageret, sgr. de Caissargues, or Caillargues; (*c*) Guillemette Marie, wife of Robert de la Croix; (*d*) Gabrielle, m. 1562 Antoine de Barnière; (*e*) Anne Marie, wife of Guy de Bons.

IV. Jean Boileau, sgr. de Castelnau, First Consul of Nismes in 1605, and Syndic of the Diocese. B. in 1543, d. 10 May 1618. He was summoned by the Constable de Montmorency to join him with his following in the expedition in Haut-Languedoc, and answered the call of Ban and arrière-ban. M. firstly, 15 July 1571, Honorade Blanc, daur. of Robert Blanc, sgr. de la Rouvière ; secondly, Dlle. Rose de Calvière de St. Cosme, daur. Nicolas de Calvière, sgr. de St. Cosme, 15 Oct. 1576. By his second marriage he left thirteen children : (*a*) Nicolas, who succeeds, V ; (*b*) Jacques, doctor of medicine, m. 1614 Dlle. Arnaude de Rossel, author of the branch established at Uzès, and afterwards at Dunkirk, Abbeville and St. Dominique ; (*c*) Guillaume, m. Dlle. Rose de Falcon ; (*d*) Jean, Sergeant-major in Piedmont, d. at Candal ; (*e*) Claude, Captain in the regiment of Monpezat, killed in 1616 at the siege of Cèrissolles ; (*f*) Daniel, killed at Prague in 1620 ; (*g*) another Claude, who m. in 1598 Etiennette de Monteils ; (*h*) Anne, m. in 1593 Daniel Arnaud, sgr. de la Cassagne ; (*i*) Marguerite, bapt. 1589 in the church of S. Chaptes, and others.

V. Nicolas Boileau, sgr. de Castelnau, b. 31 Dec. 1578, travelled in Italy, Germany, England and Holland. On his return he studied Law, in which he gained some reputation. D. 1657. He m. Dlle. Anne de Calviere de Boucoiran, 18 March 1619, and left (*a*) François, Lieut.-Col. of Cavalry, drowned at Naples ; (*b*) Jacques, who succeeds, VI ; (*c*) Charles, sgr. de Vignargues, who entered the army ; (*d*) Marguerite, wife of Gaultier de Pontperdu ; (*e*) Isabeau, wife in 1650 of Jean de Leyris, sgr. d'Esponcher ; (*f*) Anne Marie, wife of Guy d'Airebodouze, sgr. de Casalette ; (*g*) Françoise, m. in 1653 Jean de Galoffre, sgr. de Languissel.

VI. Jacques de Boileau, ec. sgr. de Castelnau, b. 15 Jan. 1626. Served in the company of gentleman cadets, and became head of the family at the death of his brother François. Elected a Councillor of Nismes in 1652. Maintained his nobility at the Visitation of 1668. He was imprisoned in 1685, and remained in the prison of St. Pierre Ancise at Lyons for eleven and a half years, where he died, 17 Jan. 1697, in the 71st year of his age. His portrait was painted by Jeanne Garnier Charpy, of Lyons, dated 15 Ap. 1694.

He had married, 18 Nov. 1664, Dlle. Françoise des Vignolles, who d. 14 Jan. 1700 at Geneva (Thursday, at 1.30 a.m.), daur. of Jacques des Vignolles and of Dlle. Louise Baschi d'Aubais(c) (contract of marriage, 12 Oct. 1660, Daleirac, Notaire). By this marriage he left 22 children: (*a*) François Henri, first cadet-gentilhomme, and then Captain in the grenadiers-à-cheval of Brandenburgh, killed at Tournai, 1709; (*b*) Jean Louis, killed at Hochstett; (*c*) Charles, who succeeds, VII; (*d*) Maurice, who succeeded to the estates of Castelnau, etc., and to whom his brother Charles left his possessions in France, although already confiscated(D); (*e*) Françoise, m. in 1690 Joseph Pandin de Jarriges, father of the Grand Chancellor of Prussia; (*f*) Louise, m. in 1708, Abel de Ligonier de Montcuquet, brother of Field Marshal Lord Ligonier, son of Louis de Ligonier and Louise du Poncet. They left issue (Ligonier Ped., Hug. Soc., vol. VIII, p. 379); (*g*) Jean Jacques, b. at Nismes, 1673. (Arch. Commun.)

VII. Charles Boileau, sgr. de Castelnau, b. 1670. Left France with his brothers and entered the English army as ensign in Farringdon's Regiment, 1698; Lieut., 1703. Naturalised 4 May 1699 (" Charles Castelnau, born at Kismet (*sic*) in Languedoc in France, son of James de Boileau by Frances his wife "). Taken prisoner by the French in 1704, and exchanged at Valenciennes 1 Feb. 1709. Left the army in 1711 and lived at Southampton till 1722, when he went to Ireland, where he became a wine merchant in Bride Street, Dublin. Died in Dublin, 7 Mar. 1733, aged 60. He m., 30 Dec. 1703 (French Church St. Patrick), Dlle. Marie Madeleine Collot d'Escury, daur. of Daniel Collot, sgr. d'Escury, Capt. and Major in Galway's Horse, and of Dame Catherine de la Valette, living formerly at La Touche, near Azay-le-Rideau in Touraine. By this marriage he had 18 children, some of whom died in infancy: (*a*) Marguerite, b. 20 Dec. 1710, d. 6 Jan. 1778, aged 68, m. 22 Ap. 1737 Rev. Jean Pierre Droz (Eg. Fr. Unies., Dublin); (*b*) Charles Daniel, b. at Southampton, 2 Nov. 1711 (French Church Register), lived in the parish of St. Peter-le-Poor, Dublin, died suddenly in London 12 Jan. 1772; (*c*) Henry Charles, b. 28 Sept.

1712, at Southampton (French Church Register); (*d*) Marie Louise, b. 10 Oct. 1713 (*idem*); (*e*) Georgette Magdeleine, b. 31 Oct. 1715 (*idem*). Her godfather was Maurice Boileau de Castelnau, her uncle, by proxy; (*f*) Simeon, who succeeds, VIII; (*g*) Pierre, b. 18 Aug. 1720 (*idem*); (*h*) Jean, b. 22 Aug. 1721 (*idem*), d. in Dublin 2 Feb. 1722 (Vignolles MSS.); (*i*) Marie, b. in 1723, m. Henry Hardy, d. at Cork 7 June 1760.

VIII. Simeon Boileau de Castelnau, b. at Southampton, 10 Oct. 1717 (French Church), d. 15 July, 1767 in Dublin. Merchant. M. in 1741 Dlle. Madeleine Elizabeth Desbrisay (d. 12 Jan. 1786, aged 66), daur. of Théophile de la Cour Desbrisay (E), and of Dame Madeleine de Vergéze d'Aubussargues: she (the latter) was buried in the Nonconformist French Church at Dublin, 13 Dec. 1788, aged 85. They had (*a*) Bonne, who m. Captain Lestock Wilson; (*b*) Madeleine, b. 9 Feb. 1743 (Egl. Unies, Dublin); (*c*) Jean Théophile, b. 25 Jan. 1744, who succeeds, IX; (*d*) Solomon, b. 31 Jan. 1745, who will succeed, IX; (*e*) Simeon, b. 13 Dec. 1745 (Eg. Fr. Unies.); (*f*) Jean Pierre, b. 30 Nov. 1747, d. May 1837, of Madras C.S. and of Castelnau House, Barnes. M. Henrietta Pollen, eldest daur. of the Rev. George Pollen, of Little Bookham, ancestor of the branch created Baronets. His son, J. P. Boileau created a Baronet 1869 (see *Baronetage*) (F); (*g*) Thomas, b. 1746, d. 1806; (*h*) Anne Charlotte, b. 19 Nov. 1748 (Eg. Fr. Unies.), m. Peter Freill; (*i*) Henrietta, m. John Peach; (*j*) Elizabeth, m. Michael Carter.

IX. Jean Théophile Boileau de Castelnau, m. 4 Aug. 1781, Jeanne Wilson, daur. of George Wilson, of Dublin, and of (Jeanne ?) Darquier (Eg. Fr Unies.). They left (*a*) Simeon, bapt. 8 Sept. 1783; (*b*) Madeleine, bapt. 12 Ap. 1785; (*c*) Jeanne, bapt. 21 Feb. 1788, m. Stephen Henry Gaisford, 2 June 1814; (*d*) a son, d. 16 May 1788, aged one year (Fr. Ch. Dublin); (*e*) Elizabeth, bapt. 22 Aug. 1790; (*f*) George Wilson, bapt. at St. Bride's, Dublin, 8 Jan. 1793, who succeeds, X; (*g*) Harriet, bapt. 24 Aug. 1795; (*h*) Jasper Desbrisay, bapt. 16 Sept. 1796, buried 31 Oct. 1834 (St. Bride's, Dublin); (*i*) Henrietta, bapt.

25 Oct. 1798, m. Richard Beverley Usher, 3 Aug. 1822, at St. Peter's, Dublin; (*j*) Samuel Brandram, bapt. 1 July 1801 (*idem*), who follows X; (*k*) John Theophilus, m. Elizabeth Dorothea . . . . . .

X. George Wilson Boileau, d. 1876, m. Anna Phipps, daur. of William Phipps, and had (*a*) Georgiana, bapt. at St. Bride's, Dublin, 15 July 1819; (*b*) George Wilson, bapt. 22 Oct. 1821 (*idem*); (*c*) Harriet, bapt. 13 July 1823 (*idem*); (*d*) Isaac Spencer Barré Phipps, bapt. 29 Nov. 1825 (*idem*); (*e*) John George, b. 10 Dec. 1826, bapt. 10 Jan. 1827 (*idem*); (*f*) Simeon, b. 19 March, bapt. 11 Ap. 1828 (*idem*); (*g*) William Phipps, b. 13 Sept. 1830, privately bapt. 30 Sept. 1830, publicly bapt. 25 March 1833; (*h*) John Theophilus, b. 15 Jan. 1833, bapt. 25 March 1833, buried 29 Aug. 1833 (*idem*).

X. Samuel Brandram Boileau, fifth son of Jean Theophile Boileau and Jeanne Wilson, m. Frances . . . . and had: (*a*) Jane, bapt. at St. Bride's, Dublin, 15 Aug. 1824; (*b*) Samuel Brandram, buried 4 Nov. 1834, aged 2 years (St. Bride's).

IX. Solomon Boileau, b. 31 Jan. 1745, second son of Simeon Boileau de Castelnau and Madeleine Elizabeth Desbrisay, m. Dorothy Gladwell in 1766, d. 1810. They had: (*a*) Henrietta, b. 1773, d. 1853, m. S. Davis, Bengal C.S.; (*b*) John Boileau, b. 1787, d. 1858, Colonel, who left posterity; (*c*) Simeon Peter, b. 1772, d. 1842, m. Hannah, daur. of Annesley De Renzy, co. Wicklow, widow of Mr. Ribton (G); (*d*) Lestock F. Boileau, b. 1785, d. 1849, left posterity; (*e*) Dorothy, who married M. E. Jones; (*f*) Anne, m. John Reid, B.C.S.; (*g*) Frances, m. A. Franco, B.C.S.; (*h*) Alicia, m. C. Elliott, B.C.S.; (*i*) Maria, m. S. Goad, B.C.S.

NOTES.

(A) A pedigree has been given which gives a descent from Etienne Boileau, Grand Provost of Paris in 1250. No proofs of descent are produced, or marriages given.

The name is a common one, and many distinct families exist of the same name, quite unconnected. From the fact that Guillaume I was Tresorier of the royal domains at Nismes, it is evident that his family was ennobled " par finance " ; his sons also bought legal office, entitling them to " noblesse."

(B) The Montcalm family had many Protestant members who occur in the Protestant Register of Montpellier.

(C) Baschi d'Aubais. Arms : de gueules à l'écu d'argent, à une couronne de comte cousue. Originally from Italy. Guichard de Baschi, co-seigneur de Vittozio, settled in Provence (Test. 7 Sept. 1425). Balthasar de Baschi m. Dlle. Marguerite du Faur, daur. of Charles du Faur, sgr. Baron d'Aubais et du Caylar, in Bas-Languedoc, and became seigneur baron of these two seigneuries by right of his wife, whom he m. 18 June 1591 (Test. 1 Mai 1609). His son, Louis de Baschi, m. Dlle. Anne de Rochemaure, daur. of Louis de Rochemaure, juge du presidial de Nismes, and of Dlle. Anne de Barrière his wife. Their daur. Louise was the wife of Jacques des Vignolles.

(D) Maurice Boileau, b. 25 Ap. 1678, d. in 1741, m. Dlle. Eva de Guiran, 11 Dec. 1709, daur. of the President of the Parlement d'Orange. Their son, Charles, captain in the regiment of Normandy, b. 1715, d. 1783, m. in 1745 Dlle. Catherine Vergèze d'Aubussargues.

(E) Théophile de la Cour des Brisay, b. circ. 1721, a captain in the King's Carabineers, m. Dlle. Magdelaine Vergèze d'Aubussargnes 6 Aug. 1741. He was son of Samuel Théophile Desbrisay, b. 1694, who d. 5 July 1772 at Dublin. (Non. Con. Fr. Ch.)

Samuel Théophile was son of Théophile de la Cour des Brisay, or Desbrisay, captain in Lord Lifford's regiment, and of Dlle. Magdelaine Boisrond de St. Leger.

(F) John Peter Boileau, by his marriage with Henrietta Pollen (b. 1772, d. 1817), daur. of the Rev. George Pollen, Rector of Little Bookham (d. 1812), and of Mary, daur. of William Goode, co. Worcester, left two sons : (i) the Rev. George Pollen Boileau, b. 1798, d. 1817, who assumed the name of Pollen on succeeding to the manor of Little Bookham, Surrey. He m. Elizabeth, daur. of Sir James

Hall, Bart., and left a son, John D. Boileau-Pollen. (ii) Major Charles Lestock Boileau, of Castelnau, Barnes, b. 1800, d. 1889, m. Margaret Stirling, daur. of William Stirling, of Brompton, Middlesex, and had Mary Elizabeth Boileau, b. 1838, who m. Henry Davis Wilcocks, Bengal Civil Service.

(G) Simeon Peter Boileau and Hannah (née de Renzy) are believed to have left a son, General F. P. Boileau, b. 1806, d. 1888, who left a son, Colonel F. W. Boileau, C.B., b. in 1835, whose son Frank Boileau was b. 1867 (of Kensington).

"Boileau de Castelnau et la Dame de Montcugnet demandent permission de vendre les biens qu'ils possèdent par indivis à Languedoc, 15 Mai 1723" (Série T.T. 106, 3).

A letter from Louis Daniel Boileau, of Uzès, Nouveau Converti, formerly a captain in the regiment d'Anjou, demanding seisin of the property of Roze Boileau, his aunt, wife of David Perrotat, a fugitive (1704-1714). He says that Jacques de Boileau, R.P.R., left two children, Jean, brother of the suppliant, and Roze, wife of David Perrotat, both R.P.R., that David Perrotat left five children: two sons, who fled from France and were killed in arms against the King, and three daughters who with their mother fled to Lausanne, where two are married, and where Roze Boileau was living at the date of this application, helped by her husband with moneys part and parcel of his, the suppliant's own, which he enjoys by reason of the King's Edict of 1689 according to the custom of Languedoc, now (in 1704) abrogated (*idem*).

(*Note.*—This Edict gave an extension of time to all fugitives to return to France before their property was finally confiscated.)

The Perrotat family came from Orange (d'azur à 3 griffons d'or, 2 and 1).

Further information about the Perrotat family is to be found in the will of "Rose Boyleau de Perrotat, refugee in the Country of Switzerland for the sake of my religion." (P.C.C., 26 Leeds.)

Her will was proved in London, 12 May 1736, by Philippe de Perrotat, spinster, her daughter and heiress; the administration granted to John Narbonne, attorney for the said Philippe de Perrotat, during her absence, having expired by reason of his death.

Rose Boileau de Perrotat left 400 livres French to the poor refugees at Lauzanne. She confirms the settlement given to her daughter Francoise at the time of her marriage to Mr. de Bercher, also that given to her daughter Rose at the time of her marriage to Mr. de Corselles. She makes her eldest daughter Philippe her universal and general heiress. She makes the following proviso "in case my dear husband happen to leave the Kingdom of France to pass the remainder of his days in this country he shall enjoy my said goods which he shall remit at his death to my said daur. Philippe de Perrotat."

4 Nov. 1701. Certificate of Burgomaster and Council of Lauzanne, 9 Sept. 1712.

The will of Henri Boileau de Castelnau (P.C.C., Smith 62, Pts. French will), 1710, is probably that of François Henri Boileau, eldest son of Jacques Boileau, VI, and of his wife, Françoise des Vignolles, killed at Tournai in 1709. The will was made at Berlin in 1702. He was a captain in the Prussian service, and leaves 100 Rix dollars to François Auguste de Pandin de Jarriges, his nephew, "when he is 15." Mentions his brother Maurice and sister Louise "still in France," Jean Louis, and Charles Boileau, his brothers, "out of France." To Alphonse and Louise, his uncle and aunt, and Magdalene des Vignolles, brother and sisters of "his dear dead mother." The will was made in presence of Mr. François Gaultier, one of the French Ministers at Berlin (20 Jan. 1702); Sir Louis de Montolieu de St. Hypolite; St. John de Seyvargues, captain in the regiment of Darennes; Annibal de Vergèze, sgr. de Daubesarane (D'aubussargues); Captain Claude Gaultier, "proposant en Theologie"; Pierre Gaultier, ditto; Charles Galbert; Etienne Sevin, wyne merchant, living at Berlin, who sign their names. Pr. in London, 19 March 1709, by Charles Boileau de Castelnau, heir and exor.

CHARDIN

Arms : A chevron between 2 roses in chief gules, and a dove in base az.

I. Daniel Chardin, a jeweller, of Paris, son of Francois Chardin and of Marie Thierry, daur. of Pierre Thierry, m. in May 1635, at Charenton, Jeanne Ghiselin, of Rouen, daur. of Jean Ghiselin, merchant, and of Marie Dressant (or Diessart). They had (*a*) Jean Chardin, who succeeds, II ; (*b*) Jacques, b. 1646, d. same year ; (*c*) Daniel Chardin, bapt. 19 March 1649, d. at Madras in Sept. 1709, diamond merchant; will dated at Fort St. George 19 May 1709, admon. 11 Ap. 1723 to his two sons-in-law (P.C.C. Richmond, 71). He m. Marie Madeleine . . . ., of Leicester Fields, a widow, and left two daurs., (i) Marie Louise, m. in 1707 at Fort St. George, Henry Davenport, Deputy Governor of Fort St. David, his first wife. She d. at Fort St. George, Dec. 1712. (ii) Jeanne, bapt. at Fort St. George, 29 Nov. 1687. She m. firstly, at Fort St. George, Joseph Lister, merchant, 13 March 1704. He d. at Madras, 14 March 1707. She married secondly, at Fort St. George, 5 June 1709, Charles Boone, Governor of Bombay, 1716-20, M.P. for Ludgershall, Wilts. She d. 28 Nov. 1710, leaving a son, Daniel Boone, bapt. at Fort St. George, 11 Dec. 1710. (*d*) Antoine, bapt. 22 Sept. 1650 ; (*e*) Guillaume, bapt. 14 Aug. 1653 ; (*f*) Jeanne, m. in 1602, as his first wife, Jean Girardot de Chancourt, b. 1634, who married secondly Jeanne Girardot, daur. of Paul Girardot, of Chateau Chinon (naturalised 11 Mar. 1700) (A) ; (*g*) Charlotte Marie, m. Jean de Laat, sr. du Fresne, and left Jean Pierre de Laat, of Rouen, settled at Maestricht, Colonel in Dutch Army.

II. John Chardin, b. in Paris 26 Nov. 1643. He left France in 1664 and travelled abroad, returning in 1670. He then travelled in Persia, 1671-1677, and in India till 1680, when he returned and came to London, where he was knighted, 24 Aug. 1681. Made Denizen in Feb. 1682, and naturalized 27 June 1685 ("John Chardin, Kt., b. in

Paris, son of John Chardin by Jenny Ghiselin, his wife." He was elected a Fellow of the Royal Society in 1682, and was employed on several diplomatic missions. Evelyn mentions him in his Diary. He had a house at Turnham Green, where he d. on Christmas Day, 1712; buried at Chiswick. His will was pr. 29 Dec. 1712, by Charles Parry, with power reserved to the Marquis de Ruvigny, Lord Galway, and Dr. John Wickart (P.C.C. Barnes, 231). He m. in London, 24 Aug. 1681, Esther, daur. of Israel Peigné, or Le Pigné, sr. de Lardinierès, of Rouen, conseiller au Parlement de Normandie, and of Madeleine Jourdain, of Dieppe. His wife d. in London, 1691.

They had two sons and four daurs.: (*a*) Jeanne Emilie, m. at St. James, Piccadilly, Aug. 1703, Henri Le Coq de St. Leger,(B) of Trunkwell, Shinfield, Berks (will pr. 9 Nov. 1747, P.C.C. Potter, 285), by whom he had several children; (*b*) Marie Charlotte, d. 18 Dec. 1735 (will, P.C.C., 12 Mar. 1736), m. Charles Parry, b. at Lisbon, 15 Oct. 1679, of Oakfield, Berks, son of Francis Parry, British Envoy to Portugal, by Catherine, daur. of Charles Peirse. He d. 1730. Their daur. m. Henry, fourth Duke of Bolton. (Admon., 22 May, P.C.C., to his relict.). (*c* Elizabeth, b. at Holland House and bapt. at Kensington, 19 Sept. 1685. Will dated at Winchester, 20 Oct. 1741, pr. 16 Jan. 1742 (P.C.C., Trenley 7); (*d*) Julie, m. Sir Christopher Musgrave, 5th Bart., of Edenhall, Cumberland, 21 June 1711, at Mortimer, Berks; (*e*) Sir John Chardin, 1st Bart., bapt. at Greenwich, 6 Oct. 1687. Barrister of the Inner Temple. Cr. Baronet, 28 May 1720. He purchased the Kempton Park Estate, near Hampton Court, from Grantham Andrews, of Sunbury. He appears to have lived at Sunbury, where there was a small Huguenot colony. An entry in the Sunbury Registers records the marriage of his servant, Hannah Moythen, 3 Jan. 1720. In 1746 he gave Kempton Park to his nephew, Sir Philip Musgrave, and d. unmarried in 1755, 26 Ap., and was buried in Westminster Abbey, 10 May. (Will dated 18 July 1747, pr. 28 Ap. 1755, P.C.C.). (*f*) George Chardin, bapt. at St. Martin-in-the-Fields, 11 Oct. 1691. (Will dated 27 May 1764, pr. with five codicils 1 Ap. 1769. Exor. and heir, Henry Lumley, of Nacton, Suffolk. (P.C.C., Bogg 115.)

NOTES.

(A) Jean Girardot de Chancourt and Jeanne Chardin left a son and a daur., (*a*) Andrew Girardot, who married Marguerite Stample, and left posterity. She d. in London, 18 Jan. 1720. His will, dated at the Hague, 26 March 1735, was pr. in London 19 May 1735 (P.C.C., Ducie 19); (*b*) Jeanne, who m. Godfrey Otho de Sabrine de Cressewithe, Brigadier in the Dutch Army, d. s.p. 1725. Her will, dated at the Hague, 13 July 1721, was proved by her brother Andrew, 1 May 1725 (P.C.C., Romney 112).

Paul Girardot, Andrèe his wife, and four or five small children, le sr. Girardot de Chancourt, and his sister-in-law appear in a list of Protestants in the Parish of St. Nicolas de Chardonet in 1686 who had left Paris. (MSS. Francais, 7051, Bib. Nat.).

The family of Girardot was from Burgundy, and Paris, seigneurs de Chancourt, de Tillieux and du Perron.

Jeanne Girardot de Chancourt, wife of Godfrey Otho de Sabrine de Cressewithe, made her will at the Hague, 13 July 1721. Her brother Andrew and Robert Peter Chitton, sgr. de la Davière, were her executors. She confirms her husband's previous will and makes her brother Andrew her heir, and leaves a legacy of 2,000 florins to Mr. de Laat (Jean Pierre), father of her god-daughter: he was son of her aunt du Fresne. His father's will (P.C.C., Barrett, 6) was made in Holland, 30 June 1707, and opened at the summons of Charlotte Marie Chardin, his widow, "signed with his seal." He makes his only son, Jean Pierre de Laat, universal heir, and speaks of a possible return to France. The aunt du Fresne mentioned in the will of Jeanne Girardot is the Charlotte Marie above.

(B) Henry Le Coq de St. Leger was the son of Theodore Le Coq de St. Leger, sgr. des Moulins and Jousserans, m. Madeleine Muysson, daur. of Henri Muysson, sgr. de Toillon and de Rieux. Theodore Le Coq was "ancien" of the church of Charenton, and d. in London. His will was pr. 29 July 1712 by his wife (Barnes, 137), dated 13 May 1712. He describes himself as "well stricken in yeers," and makes his son Henry his universal heir. Wife Madeleine Muysson. His daurs. Charlotte, who m. her cousin, Philip

Muysson, of the Hague, son of Jacques Muysson and Anne de Rambouillet, in 1698 at St. James, Piccadilly; Madeleine Le Coq, widow of Capt. Henry David de la Croix, whom she married in 1696 at the French chapel in Swallow Street; the heirs and assigns of his daur., Dorothy, widow of Louis de Saumaize, whom she married 1 Jan. 1702 (Swallow Street). To each of these daurs. he left £4,000. He mentions a debt of 12,000 livres Tournois on the estate of the late Mr. de Louvigny d'Orgemont, and a debt owing by his brother, Charles Le Coq, sgr. du Port de la Sablière (who had succeeded to the property of his brothers in France). For Muysson family, see Rambouillet Pedigree.

Arms: On a field az. a cock argent, beaked and combed gules. Motto: " Semper Vigilans."

Henry Le Coq de St. Leger and Jeanne Emilie Chardin had six daurs: (i) Emilie Margaretta, (ii) Henrietta, (iii) Elizabeth, b. 1708, bur. at Shinfield, Berks, 27 Ap. 1752, m. Major Solomon de Blosset, bur. at Shinfield, 24 March 1796; (iv) Mary; (v) Caroline; (vi) Jeanne, m. in 1739 John Dodd, b. 1717, d. 1782, M.P. for Reading, of Swallowfield Park, Berks, leaving posterity.

Two portraits of Sir John Chardin, 1st Baronet, are in the possession of the Musgrave family at Edenhall. A portrait of Marc Antoine du Crozat de la Bastide, by Lilley, was left by him in his will (Ash, 68), dated 25 Feb. 1704, to Sir John Chardin. Marc Antoine de Crozat died at Chiswick; his daur., Jeanne Suzanne, m. Col. Paul de Blosset in 1714; their son was Solomon Stephen de Blosset, above. Paul de Blosset d. in 1719, was son of Solomon de Blosset and Catherine Hodes de Beugnot, of Clelles, in Dauphiné, d. in Dublin, 20 Oct. 1721 (Peter Street Fr. Ch.). Another son, Solomon de Blosset, m. 26 June 1722, Jeanne Marie Chateigner de Cramahé, daur. of Captain Hector Francois de Cramahé and Mariannè de Belrieu de Virazel. (Dublin Fr. Ch.)

Additional information will be found in *The Genealogist* (N.S., Vol. XXXI, 1914).

CHATEIGNER DE CRAMAHÉ

Arms: De sinople, aux rochers, d'argent sans nombre, un chef, consu de gueulles.

I. Pierre de Chateigner, ec. sgr. du Treuil-Bonnet,(A) Maire de la Rochelle, 1504. He obtained permission, 14 Ap. 1518, from Jeanne, Duchesse de Longueville, Vicomtesse de Chatelaillon, to erect his chateau of Cramahé in the par. of Salles d'Aytré, into a fief with High, Middle and Low Justice, near la Treil Bonnet in the same parish. He was one of the Council of la Rochelle who received the King, François I in 1519, and bore the Queen's dais. M. Dlle. Françoise de Donnes, and had (*a*) François, who succeeds, II; (*b*) Françoise, who appears in a deed of partition with her brother, 29 July 1546, in succession to their father.

II. François de Chateigner, ec. sgr. de Cramahé, échevin of la Rochelle, d. in 1555; m. Marie Mervault, and left (*a*) Pierre, who succeeds, III; (*b*) François, author of the Branch of Bergerion; (*c*) Marie, mentioned with her mother and sister in an "aveu" dated 16 March 1555; (*d*) Marguerite, m. 21 May 1576, Pierre de Nourrigier, ec. sgr. de Moulidars: she was then the widow of Geoffroy de Lynières, sgr. de Laumont, whom she had married 5 Dec. 1563, at La Rochelle (Reg. Pr. La Rochelle).

III. Pierre de Chateigner, ec. sgr. de Cramahé, joined with his brother in the succession of his father and mother. M. Marie le Roy, 10 Oct. 1560, who was named guardian of his children by an acte dated 10 Oct. 1578. (*a*) Rachel, b. 12 Oct. 1563, m. Noé Nouveau, ec. sgr. du Breuil de Rouillac, 22 Nov. 1594; (*b*) Saul, b. 1569; (*c*) Jean, sgr. du Péré, or Peyray, and la Mothe, m. Anne Gentilz, who, at his death, married again with Lenar, or Leonard, de Remigieux, sgr. de la Fuye, Lieut.-particulier of la Rochelle; (*d*) Benjamin, sgr. de Boisfontaine, de la Pierre-Levée and other places. d. in 1620; (*e*) Roch, who succeeds, IV;

(*f*) Etienne, sgr. de l'Isleau, m. Charlotte Grisy in 1603; (*g*) François, sgr. de la Linaudière; (*h*) Hector, chevalier, sgr. de Péré, or Perray, m. Dlle. Elizabeth Isle, daur. of Isaac Isle, sgr. de Louze and of his wife Lydie Palet; (*i*) Françoise, wife, in 1632, of Pierre Charrieu, sgr. du Fief Lambert.

IV. Roch Chateigner, ec. sgr. de Cramahé and Luigny, m. before 1609 Dlle. Françoise de Conan, sister of Nicolas de Conan, sgr. du Roc,(B) and maintained his "noblesse" 18 March 1606. He left Roch, who succeeds, V.

V. Roch Chateigner, ec. sgr. de Cramahé,(C) inherited property from his uncle Benjamin de Chateigner, in 1620. M. Elizabeth Gendrault, 20 July 1620, who was his widow in 1647. They had (*a*) Roch, who succeeded in France, VI; (*b*) Henri Auguste, who was made Denizen in London, 9 Ap. 1687, and naturalised by Oath Roll 11 Nov. 1698. He had married, 21 March 1651, Dlle. Louise de Cumont, daur. of Benjamin de Cumont, sgr. de Vausey; (*c*) Alexandre-Thesée, sgr. de l'Isle, VI; (*d*) Hector-François, who succeeds in his line, VI; (*e*) Jean Herbert; (*f*) Marie-Henriette, wife of Samuel Pynyot,(D) or Piniot, ec. sgr. de la Largère. Their son, Henri Piniot, was bapt. 7 Aug. 1695, at the Fr. Ch. of le Temple Neuve, London; (*g*) Reneé-Charlotte, m. Louis Hortax de Béjarry. All the above children of Roch Chateigner and his wife, Elizabeth Gendrault, appear in an "Acte de partition," dated 15 March 1681.

VI. Roch Chateigner, ec. sgr. de Cramahé, m. by contract passed at Thouars, 12 May 1649, Dlle. Jeanne Herbert, daur. of Francois Herbert, el. sgr. de Bellefont, and of his wife, Jeanne de Maulay. They left (*a*) Roch, d. s.p. 18 Feb. 1677; (*b*) Cézar, d. s.p. in 1659.

VI. Hector François Chateigner, ec. sgr. de Cramahé et des Rochers, left France with his brothers Henri-Auguste and Alexandre-Thesée and entered the British Army. D. at Dublin, 13 Feb. 1725, and was buried in the cemetery of the Fr. Ch. of St. Patrick. M. Dlle. Marie Anne de

Belrieu, daur. of Jacques de Belrieu, sgr. baron de Virazel(E) They had (*a*) Charlotte, b. in 1700, d. 13 Nov. 1765, aged 65 (St. Patrick Fr. Ch. Reg.); (*b*) Jeanne, b. in 1700, m. Captain Solomon Blosset de Loche(F) at Dublin, 26 June 1722 (Eg. Fr. Unies.), and d. 19 Ap. 1783, aged 82 (St. Patrick Fr. Ch. Reg.); (*c*) Marie Charlotte, b. 1 Aug. 1702, d. eight days old; (*d*) Jean Thomas, b. Aug. 1703, d. 29 Nov. 1703; (*e*) another son, buried Dec. 1703, an infant; (*f*) Henri, b. 1 Nov. 1706, d. 25 March 1717; (*g*) Marie Anne, b. 11 June 1709; (*h*) Alexandre, b. 14 Dec. 1710, bapt. 4 Jan. 1711 (St. Marie, Dublin). His godfathers were "son cousin (*sic*) de Cramahais qui est en Caroline, nommé Alexandre Chateigner, et Mr. François de Le Larger un de les cousins" (François Pynyot, sgr. de la Largerè); (*i*) Jacques, b. 10 May 1713; (*j*) Another Henri, b. 3 Feb. 1716; (*k*) Théophile Hector, b. 1 Oct. 1720 (Eg. Fr. Unies).

VI. Alexandre Thesée Chateigner de Cramahé, went to Carolina, where he m. Suzanne Le Noble, daur. of Henri Le Noble and Catherine Le Serrurier: their daur. Catherine m. firstly Paul Mazyck, secondly René Louis Ravenel of Pooshee (see Ravenel Pedigree, Vol. I).

NOTES.

(A) This family had no connection with that of Chataigner, seigneurs de la Grolliere, another notable Protestant family of Poitou.

(B) The Conan, or de Conant family was of Poitou. Elizabeth de Conan, wife of Paul Charles le Vasseur, sgr. de Cougné, was godmother to Charles Desbordes, son of Vincent Desbordes, notaire, and of Louise Lambert, of Vérines, 11 Nov. 1668. The godfather was Charles Casimir de la Rochefoucauld. (Reg. Prot. Dompierre et Bourgneuf.)

Members of this family came to England, and the name is common in the West of England.

The family of le Vasseur, Marquis de Thouars et de Puisar, also emigrated to England. Jean, or Jacques, Louis le Vasseur de Cougné, son of George, Marquis de Thouars, was first Colonel of the 24th Regiment, commonly known as the Marquis de Puisar's. He m. Katherine Villiers, daur. of Sir Edward Villiers, Kt. Marshal, 30 July 1685 (Westminster Abbey Registers). His will is dated 7 May 1697, pr. 1701.

(C) Roch de Chateigner and Eliz. Gendrault had a daur., Françoise, bapt. 29 March 1626, by Mr. Coutant. Her godfather was Haut et Puissant Daniel Green de St. Marsault, chev. sgr. baron de Chatellaillon ; godmother, Françoise Chateigner (Reg. Prot. La Rochelle).

(D) Several members of the Pyniot family came to England. Moïse, son of Moïse Pyniot and Suzanne de Plasset, was bapt. 21 Aug. 1689 (Leicester Fields Fr. Ch.) ; godfather. Samuel Pynyot, and godmother, Dame Anne de Menou, Henri, son of Samuel Pynyot, sr. de la Largere and of Dame Marie Henriette de Chatagne (*sic*), bapt. 30 Oct. 1698. His godfather was Jacques Gendreau, sr. de Charmon (Leicester Fields). Another Henri, bapt. at le Temple Neuve Fr. Ch., London, had probably died.

Two other children of Samuel Pynyot, Jacques Auguste and Hector Françoise, were naturalised 12 June 1701, both born in Poitou. Jacques Auguste Pynyot states in his petition that he was born of Protestant parents in Normandy, but not brought up in France, and had resided 10 years in England.

By a judgement of the Presidial Court of La Rochelle (B. 747) this property of Auguste Hector (*sic*) de Chateigner was granted to " le sieur Pinion " (Pyniot).

In a list of fugitives and their property (Arch. Presid. Saintes) the property of the Chateigner family is given as 45,000 livres. " Le sieur Chasteigner, sgr. de Cramahé fils ayné, et les deux frerès, sont hors le royaume (45,000 ll.) Charles Auguste de Chasteigner, frerè dudit Chasteigner."

In his will, dated 11 Ap. 1699 (Pett, 100), in St. James' Parish, London, Samuel Piniott, alias De la Largère, armiger, sgr. de la Largère, gent., of Poitou, " a Refugee for the cause of the gospel," after thanking God for the gift of " his wife, Marie Henriette Chatayner," leaves all to her and her three children in France, in the event of their coming to England. He mentions Mr. de Cramahé, his brother-in-law, papers which are to be restored to

Mr. D'Escury. Exors.: René de Royrand, sgr. des Clouseaux. Witnesses: Louis Barraud, De la Noue, Louis Royrand, Louis Duplessis (or Duplessy).

(E) The family of Belrieu de Virazel was from the neighbourhood of Bordeaux. Jacques de Belrieu, sgr. de Virazel, conseiller à la Cour, came to England and d. at Dublin. He m. Marie de Gamont, who was dead in 1706. Their daur., Marie Anne, was the wife of Hector François de Chateigner. Charles de Belrieu, their son, Baron de Virazel, Conseiller au Parlement de Bordeaux, continued the line in France. Their eldest son, Daniel de Belrieu, married, 11 March 1706, at Dublin (Ste. Marie Nouvelle Eglise) Dlle. Catherine Vatable, daur. of Pierre Vatable and Marie Brevet.

Arms: d'azur, à 3 étoiles d'argent, rangées en chef, et en pointe une rivierè ondée de même, chargée d'une croissant de gueules.

Originally from Perigord, Comtes de Cleyrans, Barons de Virazel et Beaumont, seigneurs de Virazel, Tiregant, St. Didier, la Grace, and other places.

(F) Solomon Blosset was the son of Solomon Blosset, sgr. de Loches, who d. 28 Oct. 1721 at Dublin, and of Catherine Hodes de Beugnot, of Dauphiné. His brother, Paul Blosset, Colonel of Blosset's Foot Regiment, married Jeanne Suzanne de Crozat de Creissel.

(G) A grant of land in Carolina was made to Alexandre Thesée Chastaigner, sgr. de l'Isle, and Henri Auguste Chastaigner, sgr. de Cramahé, Signed, Craven and P. Colleton, Thos. Amy (Col. Office, 5, 286). " 1,000 acres sold to above by the undersigned for £50: with frontage to a navigable river or creek, and 2,000 more at 1d. per acre Rent. The said 3,000 acres to be made a manor if they soe desire," 4 Sept. 1686.

Idem. A letter signed by Craven, Lord Palatine, A. Ashley, P. Colleton, Tho. Amy. To Mr. Trouillard, minister, Mr. Buretell, ancien, Mr. Jacques Serrurier, ancien, Mr. Courrau, ancien, Mr. Vervart, Mr. de Lisle Cramahé, and Mr. Duqué, in Carolina, who had complained of some hardships.

CHATEIGNER DE CRAMAHÉ

In some accounts at the end of this book is the sum of £50, received from Mr. de Cramahé and Mr. de Lisle, for 1,000 acres.

Mr. de Vervart also paid £75 for 3,000 acres. Mr. James le Maire £5 for 100 acres. Mr. Isaac Le Grand £5 for 100 " akers." Mr. Petitbois paid £10 for 200 a. Bartholomew Le Keux £17 10s. 0d. for 350 a. Nicolas de Longuemare £5 for 100 a. James Le Bas £90 for 3,000 a. in part.

CHAUVIN DE LA MUCE

Arms: De gueules, à 9 bésants d'argent, 3, 3, 3.

I. Jean Chauvin, of Pont Hus, Brittany, m. Dlle. Françoise Hus, or Hux, dame de la Muce, or Musse.(A) They had: (*a*) Bonaventure, who succeeds, II; (*b*) Gui, sgr. de Limarand, m. Dlle. Catherine de Quatrebarbes, daur. of François de Quatrebarbes, sgr. de la Volué, and of Dame Olive de Brie (5 March 1561).(B)

II. Bonaventure Chauvin, sgr. de Ponthus, was the first of his family to become a protestant. Governor of Vitré and Chamberlain to Henri IV. He was granted leave to assume the name of his mother's property by deed dated 2 Aug. 1572. D. at Vitré, 3 March 1591, and was buried in the choir of the Temple de la Madeleine by permission of Anne d'Alégre. He m. Dlle. Françoise Pansion de la Hamelière, and left three sons, of whom one was killed at Brouage in 1577, and the other d. at Vendôme after the Siege of Paris. The third, David, succeeds, III.

III. David de la Muce, sgr. de Ponthus, m. firstly at Vitré, 8 March 1591, Dlle. Philippe, or Philipote, de Gouyon, Dame de Pommerit, daur. of Charles de Gouyon, sgr., Baron de la Moussaye. She d. soon after, and he m. secondly, 28 Nov. 1593, Dame Sara de Bois de Baulac. He d. soon after his second marriage,(C) leaving a posthumous son, David, who succeeds, IV.

IV. David de la Muce, born at Vitré 1 Dec. 1594, bapt. 15 Ap. 1595, "David fils de noble David de la Muce et de Sara Duboys." M. in 1618 Dlle. Anne de la Noue, daur. of the famous soldier, La Noue. He was Deputy at the Assembly of La Rochelle, and presided twice at the last assembly of Huguenots, 25 Jan. and 26 Sept. 1622. His seigneury was erected into a marquisate in 1622 by Louis XIII. By his marriage with Anne La Noue he left: (*a*) César, who succeeds, V; (*b*) Marguerite, wife of Ollivier de St. Georges, sgr. de Vérac.(D)

V. César de la Muce, b. circ. 1620, m. 2 June 1646, Dlle. Ursuline de Champagné de la Suze, sixth daur. of Louis de Champagné, Comte de la Suze, Marquis de Normanville, Lieut.-Gen. des armeés du Roi, and of Dame Charlotte de Roye de la Rochefoucauld.(E) He d. 7 Sept. 1676 at his chateau of Ponthus, aged 55 (Reg. Sucé), leaving: (*a*) Ollivier Marquis de la Muce, who succeeds, VI; (*b*) Claude Henriette, m. 19 May 1687 to Claude Charles de Gouyon, sgr. Baron de Marcé, Vicomte de Terchant(F); he was 45 years of age, she was 27 (Reg. Sucé); (*c*) Marguerite, d. 9 May 1681, aged 24 (Reg. Sucé); (*d*) Elizabeth Charlotte; (*e*) Henrietta Marie, Dlle. de Chavaigne.(G)

VI. Olivier de la Muce, chevalier banneret, Marquis de la Muce, sgr. de Villeneuve, was imprisoned in 1685 and expelled from France; took refuge in England, where he conducted negotiations with the English Government for the establishment of a Huguenot colony in Virginia, at Manakin Town, afterwards called King William's Town, on the St. James river. A grant of land in Norfolk County was made by the Government, to be taken over by M. de Sailly, the chief agent, and the Marquis de la Muce on their arrival (March, 1700). This land was part of an original grant to Lord Matravers in 1627, and later was the property of Mr. Coxe. M. de Sailly and the Marquis de la Muce left England in April 1700, and a list of the refugees who came with them is to be found in the State Papers, Record Office (America, Colonial Office, Board of Trade, Virginia, vol. xi, p. 681, No. 56), 108 men, 59 women, 38 children, beside M. de la Muce and M. de Sailly.

He appears to have returned to England soon after, and d. in London in 1708, in the parish of St. Anne, Westminster. Administration was granted to Lucretia (Lucrèce) his wife, 28 Sept.(H) No children are mentioned. He was on the Irish Huguenot pension list in 1702: "Comte de la Musse, R. captain, served in Ireland and Flanders ten years, sickly, disbanded March 1699," and appears on the Bounty List, 1702, as drawing £150.

NOTES.

(A) The Chauvin family belonged to La Vendée. Bonaventure Chauvin obtained leave to adopt the name of the seigneury of la Musse, to which his father had succeeded by right of his wife Françoise de la Musse, at her death. The primitive name of his mother's family was Hux de la Musse. In 1250, a seigneur of that name built a bridge over the river near the chateau, called " le pont de Hux." By a deed, dated 1478, a chateau was built, called Pont de Hux, or later, Ponthus, which became the seat of the La Muce family (Vaugiraud, iii, 181). The seigneurie of La Muce, or Musse, is in the parish of Ligné, near Nantes.

(B) The existence of Gui Chauvin, sgr. de Limarand, is known by his contract of marriage : " Gui Chauvin, sgr. de Limarand et Caterine de Quatrebarbes, ff. de feus nobles personnes François de Quatrebarbes, sgr. de la Volué, et de Dame Olive de Brie, 5 Mars. 1561. Reçu par Marceul, notaire en lieu seigneurial de Saucé en pr'ce de nobles hommes François de Sesmaisons, sgr. de la Sauzinières : de Jacques Ridouet, sgr. de Saucè ; et de Jean Quatre Barbes, sgr. de la Bonnadiere : demeurant à Angers. Devoit ètre ratifié par noble homme Bonnaventure Chauvin, sgr. de la Musse et de Ponthus, frère dudit Gui."

The family de Quatrebarbes, sgrs. de la Volué, de la Rongère and other places, was originally from Anjou, and descends from Foulques de Quatrebarbes, whose arms are shewn in the Salle des Croisades, Versailles : de sable à la bande d'argent, accostée de 2 filets de même.

(C) The Gouyon, or Goyon, family was one of the most illustrious in Brittany : Seigneurs de Matignon, la Moussaye, la Roche-Gouyon, Plevenon, Maupertuis, and other places. Arms : D'argent, à la croix pleine de sable. *alias* Gouyon-Matignon, écartelé, 1 and 4 d'argent, au lion de gueules, armé, lampassé et Couronné d'or (Gouyon). 2 and 3, d'or, à 2 fasces noués de gueules, acc. de 9 merlettes du même poseés en orle, 4 en chef, 2 en flancs entre les fasces, et 3 en pointe (Matignon.)

Philippe de Gouyon, daur. of H. et P. Charles, Baron de la Moussaye, and of Claude du Chastel. Charles de Gouyon was grandfather of Claude Charles de Gouyon, Baron de Marcé, who married Claude Henriette de la Muce, sister of Olivier de la Muce (see after V).

(D) Several members of the St. George de Vérac family came to England from Poitou.

(E) " Contrat de Mariage, 1646, 2 Juin (Lecatet, notaire), de Messire Cézard de la Musse, chevalier, baron dudit lieu, de Limarand, Villeneufve, le Moulin, Rieux-en-Nort, et autres lieux, demeurant en son chateau de Pont-Hus en Bretagne, fils de feu messire David de la Musse, chev : seigneur baron desdits lieux, et de Anne de la Noue ; et de damlle. Urseline de Champagné, fille de deffunt messire Louis de Champagné, Comte de la Suze, et de feue dame Charlotte de Roye de la Rochefoucauld. (Arch. Dép : Loire, Inférieure, E. 1071.)

This family de Champagné is not to be confounded with that of Robillard de Champagné, of Saintonge, one of which, Josias de Robillard, sgr. de Champagné, m. Marie de la Rochefoucauld, and went to Dublin (see Vol. I, *Huguenot Pedigrees*.) This Marie de la Rochefoucauld has been identified as being a daur. of Charles Casimir de la Rochefoucauld, sgr. de Fontpastour.

Another branch of the la Rochefoucauld family, Seigneurs de Roye et de Roussy, emigrated to England. Frederic Charles de Roye et de la Rochefoucauld, Comte de Roye et de Roussy, Lt.-Gen. of the Armies of the King of France in 1676, paid homage for his fief Comté of Roussy, 6 June 1681 ; went to Denmark, by permission, in 1683. Became Grand Marshal of the Danish Army. Migrated to Hamburg, 1686, and in 1688 to England, and was created Earl of Lifford. He d. at Bath in 1690, 9 June, aged 57. His wife, Elizabeth de Durfort, his cousin-german, m. 3 June 1656, d. in London 14 Jan. 1715, aged 82. She was daur. of Guy Alphonse de Durfort, Marquis de Duras et de Lorges, and of Elizabeth de la Tour-Bouillon.

They left twelve children, of whom Frederic Guillaume, fourth son, Comte de Champagné-Mouton and de Marthon, followed his father to Denmark and thence to England, where he commanded a French Refugee regiment in Ireland ; second Earl of Lifford; d. unmarried. His sister, Charlotte de Roye-Roussy, eighth child, accompanied her mother, the Comtesse de Roye in 1688, and was governess of Prince William and the Princess Mary, children of George II, in March 1734.

She d. 1742. Admon. granted 1743. Her sister, Henriette de Roye, m. William, Earl of Strafford, K.G., and d. s.p.

Another member of the branch of Montandre, François de la Rochefoucauld, son of Charles Louis, second Marquis de Montandre, was b. in Sept. 1672; m. Marie Anne, daur. of Ezechiel, Baron Spanheim, and who d. in London, 18 Feb. 1772. François de la Rochefoucauld was married at St. James, Westminster, 21 Ap. 1710, and buried in Westminster Abbey, 15 Aug. 1739. He commanded the French Refugee regiment of Montandre.

Charlotte de Roye was niece of Louis de Duras, Earl of Faversham, who mentions her in his will (P.C.C., Lane 3). He was the youngest son of Guy Alphonse de Durfort, above, Marquis de Duras, and brother of the Duc de Duras. He married Mary, eldest daur. and coheir of Sir George Sondes, of Lees Court, Kent, Bart., created Earl of Faversham, 8 Ap. 1676, and succeeded to the title, under the Patent, on the death of his father-in-law. His sister, Elizabeth de Durfort, married the Comte de Roye.

Louis de Duras d. 8 Ap. 1709 in the 69th year of his age, and was buried first, 28 Ap. 1709, in the French church of the Savoy, and afterwards in Westminster Abbey. His sister, Henriette de Durfort, m. Louis de Bourbon, second Marquis de Malause, as his second wife, and their second son, Armand de Bourbon, Marquis de Miremont, was Lieut.-General in the British Army, Jan. 1703-4. He d. and was buried in the French church of the Savoy in 1732.

Charlotte de Bourbon-Malause, sister of the Marquis de Miremont, also died in London, 15 Oct. 1732, aged 73, unmarried, and was buried at the Savoy French church. By her will she desired her remains to be re-interred, with those of her brother, in Westminster Abbey.

(F) Claude-Charles Gouyon de Marcé was son of Jacques, Baron de Marcé et de Beauregard and Dlle. Elizabeth du Matz, and grandson of Charles Baron de la Moussage (see above). His wife, Claude-Henriette de la Musse, Comtesse de Marcé, abjured, and in 1703, as a Nouvelle Convertie, petitioned for the ratification of a contract of sale of two small fiefs, Malorais, or Marolais, and Baquaire, near Nantes, belonging to her by succession from her brother (Olivier), a fugitive for religion: she speaks of him as " un de mes frères." She is described in the procès as widow of Claude Charles Gouyon, Chev. Comte de Marcé, " soeur d'Olivier de la Musse, son frère ainé, sorty du Royaume pour cause de Religion." A certificate is attached, from the Rector of Petit Mars, to the effect that Me. la Comtesse de Marcé has attended Easter Mass, and her behaviour is good. (Série T.T., 165, xxiii). In the year 1715, however, she was still recalcitrant (" aged over 60 "). (Vaugiraud.)

(G) Henriette-Marie fled with, or joined, her brother in England. She was on the Pensions List in 1703 and drew a pension of £30 0s. 0d. in 1715, 1726 and 1731, 25 March (Hug. Soc. Proc., vol. IV, p. 344). P.C.C., Boycott 205.

(H) Lucrece de la Musse is called in the administration act " Marquise Douairière," which is somewhat of a riddle, as no children are recorded, and they appear to have left no son, in which case only Urseline de Champagné, mother of the Marquis de la Musse, could be " Marquise Douairière," unless her daughter-in-law assumed the style. The male line in France was extinct.

Quicke says in his *Synodicon*, quoted by Agnew (*French Protestant Exiles*, Vol. II, p. 297), that a Peter de la Musse, a Deputy at the 19th Synod of Loudun in 1659, was in London in 1692, the date of the " Synodicon."

" Here is a Marquess of that name in London, a faithful confessor of Christ, having forsaken his estate and embraced the Cross, rather than part with his religion and his God, and I think, the same Deputy."

He, however, according to Agnew, was Pierre de la Musse, sieur des Roquettes, an elder of the church at Caen, and not a member of the family of Chauvin de la Musse.

COLLOT D'ESCURY

Arms: D'azur, au chef d'arg: chargé d'une molette de sable.

I. Jean Collot, chev., was living in 1531. M. Dame de Chaumont, and left a son, Louis, who follows, II.(A)

II. Louis Collot, sgr. d'Escury et de Drouilly, m. firstly Dlle. Adelaide de Drouilly, through whom he became sgr., secondly Charlotte de Lattre. By his first marriage he had: (*a*) David, who succeeds, III; (*b*) Louis.

III. David Collot, ec. sgr. d'Escury, m. in 1560 Dlle. Renée d'Avrout, daur. of Georges d'Avrout, sgr. de Hergny, massacred at Vassy in 1560, by whom he left two sons: (*a*) David, who succeeds, IV; (*b*) Jean, d. unmarried in 1603.

IV. David Collot, ec. sgr. d'Escury et de Landauran near Vitré in Brittany, m. firstly, in 1583, Dlle. Philippe de Villorio, who d. childless in 1601; secondly, 9 July 1606, Dlle. Marie le Noir, daur. of Christophe, sr. de Landauran, valet de chambre de Monsieur de Laval, orig. of Orléans, and of Esther de Couaisnon (who was b. 31 Oct. 1563 at Vitre, d. 9 July 1626). Marie Le Noir(B) was b. 3 Nov. 1583, and after the death of David Collot d'Escury at Landauran, 8 Dec. 1611, she married Amaury de Mardeaux, who d. before 1666. She d. 13 Jan. 1666. By his marriage with Marie Le Noir, David Collot left: (*a*) Philippe, b. 28 Aug. 1607, at Vitré, sgr. de Landauran, which seigneury he inherited from his uncle André in 1685. He abjured, and married, in 1638, as a Roman Catholic, Marie Lecocq, and left issue: (*b*) Marguerite, b. 4 Nov. 1608, d. in Normandy as Lady Abbess of the Abbey of Stranches; (*c*) André, who succeeds, V; (*d*) Guy, b. 23 May 1612 (Vitré): his godfather was Guy Lenoir, his uncle, sr. de Crevain, pastor of La Rochebernard and Croisic.(C)

V. André Collot, sgr. d'Escury et de Landauran, b.

21 Ap. 1610, at Vitré, Governor of St. Quintin in Brittany in 1650. Maintained his noblesse in 1666; fled from France at the Revolution, and d. at Nymeguen in Holland. He m. Dlle. Marguerite de la Primaudaye(D) in 1640. She d. 26 June 1649 at Vitré. By this marriage André Collot left eight children: (*a*) Henri, b. 25 Feb. 1641; (*b*) André, b. 18 Feb. 1642; (*c*) Daniel, who succeeds, VI; (*d*) Anne, b. 29 July 1644. Her godmother was Anne de la Primaudaye, Dame de la Motte. (*e*) Suzanne, b. 27 Sept. 1645. She abjured, but took refuge in Jersey, where she again abjured at St. Heliers, 27 March 1686. She was godmother to her niece, Anne Collot d'Escury, at Nymeguen, in 1688. (*f*) Simeon, b. 13 Jan. 1647, Lieut. in the Auvergne Regt., wounded at the battle of Seneffe, and d. soon afterwards; (*g*) Charlotte, b. 11 March 1648; (*h*) Marie, b. 11 March 1649, d. 23 Jan. 1653. (All at Vitré.)

VI. Daniel Collot d'Escury, sgr. de Landauran, b. 27 June 1643, at Vitré. He left France in 1685 with his father, André Collot d'Escury. M. in France, 19 May 1677, Dlle. Anne Catherine de la Valette, youngest daur. of Pierre de la Valette, chev. governor of the Chateau Stenay, sgr. of la Touche in Touraine.(E) She d. in Dublin, 1 July 1699, aged 46 years and 10 months: "femme de Mr. Daniel Descury, cappne major cy-devant dans le regiment de Gallway" (Egl. Fr. St. Patrick). Daniel d'Escury was Major and Lt.-Col. in Lord Galway's regiment of Horse. On Pensions List, Civil Establishment in Ireland, 1702. "Served in King William's Irish Regiment in Holland, Ireland and Flanders 13 years: seven children & sister." He appears on the List of Oath Roll Naturalisation, 17 Nov. 1698.

By his marriage with Anne Catherine de la Valette he had: (*a*) Marie Madeleine, b. in France 12 Nov. 1679, m. Charles Boileau de Castelnau, 30 Dec. 1703 (see Boileau Ped., Vol. II); (*b*) Daniel, b. in France, 26 Feb. 1681, Captain in the Dragoons of Waleffe, d. unmarried 1709; (*c*) Henri, b. in France at the chateau of la Touche in 1682, d. in 1733, at Zwolle, in Holland, Major of Cavalry in the Dutch Army. He was godfather to Henry Maret de la Rive, his nephew, at Dublin, 8 May 1724 (Egl. Unies.)

He appears to have been baptised again, 20 Oct. 1691, at the Fr. Ch. of Le Carré, London : " Henri, f. de Daniel, gentilhomme de la province de Bretagne, refugié, Major au Regiment de Cavalerie de Ruvigny (Lord Galway) et de Dame Anne Catherine de la Vallette." He was probably only " ondoyé " in France. He m. 23 Oct. 1716 Johanna Martina Gertruid, Baroness Sweerts de Landas, who d. in 1744 at S. Hertogenbosch, aged 56. Henri Collot d'Escury was the ancestor of the branch in Holland, Barons d'Escury, existing in 1895. (*d*) Simeon, b. at Tours (la Touche), 21 March 1684. Naturalised 16 July 1713 in London, " officers lately from Spain," Colonel in British Army. He m. firstly Dame N. Sulyaard de Leefdaal, 29 Jan. 1719, she d. in same year ; secondly, Elizabeth Baron. By his second wife he had two sons, Henri Collot d'Escury and Simeon Collot d'Escury, both captains in British service, of whom nothing is known. (*e*) Anne, b. 28 July 1688 at Nymeguen, m. at St. Patrick's, Dublin, 3 Nov. 1721, to Captain Jean Maret de la Rive, son of Mr. de la Rive, of St. Anthonin, Rouergue. She d. in Jan. 1768, at Castle Comer, Kilkenny, Ireland, aged 80 years. He d. in 1763, aged 91, and was buried at Castle Comer, leaving issue; posterity living in 1895.(F) (*f*) Jeanne Gabrielle, bapt. 9 Ap. 1690 at Leicester Fields Fr. Ch., London. Her godfather was Gabriel Philiponneau de Montargier ; (*g*) Lucresse Elizabeth, b. 28 Mai, bapt. 2 June 1695, at Le Carré Fr. Ch., London. Her godfather was Louis de St. Denis, Marquis de Heucourt ; godmothers, Dame Lucresse, Dame de Chavernay, and Dame Elizabeth Addée, wife of Mr. de Cherres. (*h*) Marie Jeanne, b. in Dublin, 1699, m. at St. Patrick's Fr. Ch., Dublin, 20 June 1715, Jean Corneille. (See Corneille Ped., Vol. II.)

NOTES.

(A) According to a printed pedigree, Jean Collot I was the son of Guyon Collot, alive in 1411. No proof is given, and the name of his wife is not known. As he was alive in 1411, and his son Jean was living in 1531, or 102 years later, it is probable that another generation intervened.

(B) The seigneury of Landavran came into the Collot

family by this marriage. Esther de Couaisnon, wife of Christophe Le Noir, was daur. of André de Couaisnon, ec. Seneschal of Vitré, and of his wife Jeanne de Trélan.

(C) Guy Le Noir, brother of Marie Le Noir, was the father of Philippe Le Noir, sr. de Crévain, pastor of Blain, who so often appears in the Vitré Protestant Register, author of "*l'Histoire du Protestantisme en Bretagne*" in MSS. His wife was Anne Henriet, who d. at the birth of his daur. Suzanne. Their marriage is given in the Registers of Blain, 26 May 1652, "le dimanche de la Trinité," and was celebrated by Mr. Gautron, pastor of the Rennes Pr. church. He is described as son of Guy Le Noir and Anne de la Haye. His wife was daur. of Pierre Henriet and Gabrielle Fournier; she d. 27 Ap. 1656. Ph. Le Noir continued to sign entries at Blain till the demolition of the Temple in 1682, after which date the entries are at the "Maison seigneuriale" of Pontpiétin.

(D) The family of Primaudaye was from Touraine, and bore for Arms: Semé de France, à l'écu d'or en abîme, chargé d'un tourteau de sable traversé d'une patte de griffon d'or. Gabriel de la Primaudaye, ec. sgr. de La Ripaudière, and his sons Daniel, Eleazar or César, and Gabriel, maintained their noblesse in 1667, together with Maurice, sgr. de Goullau, Philippe, Pierre and Jacques de la Primaudaye, nephews of Gabriel above, with descent from Nicolas de la Primaudaye, conseiller and secretaire du Roy, in 1540, grandfather of Gabriel above.

Maurice de la Primaudaye went to Ireland, and a Daniel de la Primaudaye was m. to Charlotte Primaudaye 16 Oct. 1717 at the Fr. Ch. of Les Grecs in London (by Lic., Archbp. of Canterbury).

(E) This family came originally from the Bourbonnais. Arms: D'azur, à la fasce d'or surmontée de 3 etoiles de même. Pierre de la Valette, or Vallet, ec. sgr. de la Touche, lived in the parish of Chillé, near Chinon. He and his brother, René de La Valette, ec. sgr. de La Brosse, living at St. Laurent-du-Lin, near Angers, maintained their noblesse since the year 1532, commencing with their grandfather, in 1668.

(F) Capt. Jean Maret de la Rive and Anne Collot d'Escury

left: (i) Henry Maret de la Rive, b. in Dublin 1724, m. Bridget Talbot, of Mount Talbot (d. 1799), buried at Castle Comer, and left issue; (ii) Marguerite Suzanne Maret de la Rive, b. in Dublin 1726, buried at Castle Comer in 1809 aged 83, m. the Rev. Thos. Wilkinson, of Corballis, Dublin, son of James Wilkinson; d. abroad, and left issue.

Elizabeth Catherine d'Escury, daur. of Charles d'Escury, was baptised at the Cape of Good Hope, 20 Dec. 1817.

CORNEILLE

I. Rodolphe Corneille, son of Rodolphe Gedéon Corneille and Anne his wife, was born at Medemblick in North Holland, and was a member of the Dutch Church at Nimeguen in 1688. Naturalised in London, 4 May 1699, and was Captain in the Royal Engineers (Rodolph Corneille, 2d engineer in 1692, Commission Bk. 4 Ap. 1692). He appears on half-pay in Ireland in 1701 on a pension of 3s. a day. "Captain Rodolp Cornolle (*sic*) of Sir John Hanmores regt. disbanded." The family appears to have come originally from Denis in Flanders. By his wife, Jeanne, surname unknown, he left a son, Jean, who follows, II.

II. Jean Corneille, said to have been born in Switzerland, Capt. R.E., m. firstly, Jeanne Charlotte Renée Ravenel, born in Carolina, daur. of René Ravenel, at the Fr. Ch. of St. Marie, Dublin, 20 Feb. 1710. (See Ravenel Ped., Vol. I.) Secondly, Marie Jeanne Magdeleine Collot d'Escury, daur. of Daniel Collot d'Escury, Major in Lord Galway's Horse, and of Anne Catherine de la Valette, at St. Patrick's Fr. Ch., Dublin, 20 June 1718.

By his first marriage he left: (*a*) Edouard, b. in 1710, d. at Dublin 7 Feb. 1772, aged 61, buried at St. Peter's Fr. Ch., Captain 18th Royal Irish Regt. He m. Marguerite Caillaud, sister of General John Caillaud.(A) She d. in Dublin, 20 Aug. 1790. Their daur., Suzanne Corneille, m. at St. Anne's, Dublin, 26 Sept. 1769, Lt.-Col. S. H. Mangin, 12th Dragoons (b. 1731, d. 1778); (*b*) Barthélémy, b. 14 Feb. 1712, at Dublin (St. Marie Fr. Ch.), Major in the 91st Regt. He m. Miss Thompson, of York, where he died. (*c*) Jean, b. in 1713, Captain in the 39th Foot in 1762; (*d*) Jeanne, b. 8 Oct. 1713, bapt. 17th at St. Marie, Dublin. Her godfather was Paul de St. Julien de Malecare, represented by Pierre Coudier, proxy; godmother, Dame Jeanne Renée d'Arabin.

By his second marriage, with Marie Jeanne Magdeleine Collot d'Escury, he left: (*e*) Sackville, b. 1716, Captain d. unmarried; (*f*) Magdeleine Rodolphe, b. 9 Oct. 1717 (St. Marie), d. 20 Feb. 1786, aged 70 (*sic*) (Non. Con.

Fr. Ch., Dublin). She m. in Dublin, 2 July 1741 (Egl. Fr. Unies.), Gaspard Erck, of Bremen. Their son, Gaspard Erck, m. his cousin, Marie Collot d'Escury (see Collot Pedigree, Vol. II); (*g*) Marguerite, b. 10 Sept. 1723 (Non. Con. Fr. Ch., Dublin); (*h*) Benigne, b. 25 Ap. 1728, m. in Dublin, 20 March 1755 (St. Anne), Jean Lescure. She d. 14 May 1812, aged 84 (Non. Con. Fr. Ch.). (*i*) Marie Marguerite, b. 17 June 1729 (Eg. Fr. Unies.), d. unmarried 8 March 1803, aged 74 (Eg. Fr. Unies.); (*j*) Daniel, b. 7 Dec. 1731, Governor of St. Helena, m. Mary Thwaites, who d. 25 Nov. 1813, in Dublin, aged 69. He d. suddenly at Portarlington, 17 Ap. 1792. They had (i) Jean Corneille, who m. Charlotte Ormsby, and left issue living in France, of whom a daur., Selina Benigne, was bapt. 2 Feb. 1813 at St. Anne's, Dublin, and a son d. an infant (Non. Con. Fr. Ch.); (ii) Jeanne, bapt. at St. Anne, Dublin, 25 Ap. 1799; (iii) Daniel Barthemy, Capt. 30th Regt., d. 12 Aug. 1825, aged 52 (Non. Con. Fr. Ch., Dublin), who m. Elizabeth Stewart. Their children, Suzanne, bapt. 25 July 1804, and Charles Sackville, bapt. 21 Ap. 1806, were baptised in St. Anne, Dublin (posterity living in 1906). (*k*) Jeanne, b. 18 July 1733, d. 22 Nov. 1801, aged 69; (*l*) Elizabeth, b. 11 Aug. 1734; (*m*) Emilie, b. 3 Ap. 1738; (*n*) Jean Henri, b. 14 Jan. 1741, Major 39th Regt., d. unmarried; (*o*) Anne, b. 9 Feb. 1742 (Eg. Fr. Unies., Dublin).

NOTE.

(A) The Caillaud family was from Saintonge. Ruben Caillaud, born at Charente in Saintonge, son of Daniel Cailleau (*sic*) and Susan his wife, was naturalised 4 May 1699; commission as Captain, Aug. 1698 (Comm. Bk.). Daniel Caillaud, his father or brother, had been made a Denizen in 1681. General John Caillaud was son of Reuben and Marguerite Caillaud, born 5 Feb. 1726 (Non. Con. Fr. Ch., Peter St., Dublin). Marguerite, wife of Edward Corneille, was born 15 Feb. 1723 (*idem.*).

GOUICQUET DE ST. ELOY

Arms: d'Azur, à la Croix engreslée d'argent, cantonnée de 4 roses de même.

I. Isaac Gouicquet, sr. de Tertre, of Plémy(A) in Brittany, m. Jeanne Doudart before 1663, and had (*a*) Isaac, who succeeds, II; (*b*) Suzanne, bapt. at Cleusné, Rennes, 1 Jan. 1664. She m. Antoine Hullin d'Orval at Hungerford Fr. Ch., London (by Lic. dated 29 Nov.), 2 Dec. 1703; buried at Portarlington, 10 Nov. 1743. Their daur., Françoise, m. Jean Daniel de Gennes (see De Gennes Ped., Vol. I). Antoine d'Orval d. 14 March 1739, at Portarlington (B); (*c*) Esther, who m. Charles Le Blanc by Lic. dated 29 Jan. 1700.(C) Her will was dated 5 Nov. 1735, pr. 23 Oct. 1747 (P.C.C., Potter 288). Her husband, Charles Le Blanc, made his will at Sunbury-on-Thames, 13 June 1707, pr. 29 Aug. 1735 (P.C.C., Ducie 173).

The will of Esther Le Blanc (née de St. Eloy) was witnessed by the Rev. Balthasar Regis, Rector of Adisham, in Kent, and by the Rev. John Metcalfe, Vicar of Sunbury. She left most of her property to her husband's relations, and mentions her sister-in-law, Mary Le Blanc, her sister Darène, Elizabeth the second sister of her husband, her nieces Chauvet and Croyé, her nephew Moses St. Eloy, her niece d'Orval, Samuel St. Eloy, and the son of her nephew John St. Eloy (a minor), the son of Mary St. Eloy, her nephew Charles St. Eloy, her niece De Gennes, the children of her nephew de Bienassy, the children of her nephew Abraham de Villepierre. She left £20 to her servant, Betty Oude, and her diamond ring to her great-nephew, Peter Tenison St. Eloy, and to Peter St. Eloy, her great-nephew, her silver ewer.

II. Isaac Gouicquet, sgr. de St. Eloy, was b. at Plémy in Brittany. Naturalised 24 March 1698. On leaving France he entered the British Army and served some years in the Low Countries. He was a Captain in the regiment of the Earl of Bath in 1689, but does not appear again in the Army Lists. He bought the manor of Sunbury-on-Thames in

1703, and resold it to Sir Roger Hudson in 1718; d. in June 1728. His will was dated 16 Dec. 1727, pr. 1 June 1728 (P.C.C., Brook 193).

He m. at Rennes, before 1685, Dlle. Marguerite Le Blanc, sister of Charles Le Blanc above, and daur. of Pierre Le Blanc de Beaulieu, Elder and Councillor of Sedan, who abjured after twelve years at the galleys. A daur., Jeanne-Marguerite, was bapt. at Rennes, 24 June 1685; her godfather was Henri de St. Eloy, ecuyer, her uncle. They also left four sons: (*a*) Pierre, b. in Flanders, and naturalised (under six years of age) in 1698; (*b*) Jean or John, living in 1762, in Broad Street, London. He m. Mary, daur. of Isaac Houssaye, and left a son, living in 1735; (*c*) Charles, Notary Public, Proctor in the Commons, and Clerk of the Prerogative Court of Canterbury; d. 29 May 1755. He m. Marie Arnaud, at St. George's Chapel, Hyde Park Corner, 17 Sept. 1742. (*d*) Moses St. Eloy, Vicar of Langford, Beds, where he is buried (31 March 1746). His will is dated 18 March 1742, and pr. 18 Ap. 1746 (P.C.C. Edmunds, 132). He m. firstly, Esther Andrewes, 30 Ap. 1724, at St. Benet. Pauls Wharf, London, and left no issue; secondly, Catherine . . . . ., no issue.

III. Pierre, or Peter St. Eloy, Proctor of Doctors Commons, and of Mitcham, d. at Collier's Wood, and left directions to be buried with his three wives at Merton. His will is dated 21 Sept. 1760, pr. 19 May 1762 (P.C.C., St. Eloy, 219). Peter St. Eloy m. firstly Judith Sayer, who d. 22 March 1733, buried at Merton, by whom he left: (*a*) a daur., buried at Merton 12 March 1741; (*b*) Esther Ann, buried at Merton 18 June 1742. Secondly, Mary, daur. of Samuel Whitaker, Flag-Captain to Admiral Sir Cloudesley Shovel, and drowned with him 23 Oct. 1707; marriage, 12 Oct. 1736; she d. before 26 July 1738, when administration was granted to her husband. Thirdly, a third wife who is only known by her burial entry: "Mrs. St. Eloy, wife of Peter St. Eloy of Mitcham," 2 Aug. 1751. He had a son(*d*) Peter, by this marriage, b. in 1750, buried at Merton, 15 March 1758. Fourthly, Henrietta (Margaret), daur. of the Rt. Rev. Edward Tenison, Bishop of Ossory, 1731-1735, and nephew of Archbishop Tenison, bapt. at Sundridge,

Kent, 11 Aug. 1714, m. after 1736. (She must have married after 1751.—Note, Ed.) She is stated to have been living in 1753. By this marriage he left: (*e*) Edward Tenison St. Eloy; (*f*) the Rev. Henry St. Eloy, Rector of Edermine, co. Wexford. Will dated 11 June 1825, pr. 8 Dec. 1832 (P.C.C., Tenterden, 780). M. firstly, Miss Stopford, secondly, Susanna, daur. of John Nunn, of Gorey, circ. 1790. She was living in 1832. (*f*) Sophia, living not married in 1774; (*g*) Judith, who was executrix in 1780 to her cousin's wife, Mrs. Trevigar, of Hurstmonceux,(D) she being of Chichester; (*h*) Henrietta Tenison, m. at Rockall, co. Kilkenny, 11 Feb. 1768, to William Hayden, of Crose, co. Kilkenny, and left issue.

NOTES.

(A) This pedigree was communicated to " Misc. Gen. et Her.," March, 1905, by the late Mr. Henry Wagner, F.S.A., as a tentative pedigree. The difficulty of apportioning the children among the different wives is solved by internal evidence. The third wife, " Mrs. St. Eloy," d. in 1751, and as Peter has been found to have been b. in 1750, the remaining children must have been by Henrietta Tenison. Some errors in the pedigree have been corrected, and many additions made.

The place of origin in Brittany is Plémy, and not Plumy, near Loudeac. The Doudart family were seigneurs de la Haye, du Parc, de Plessis, and other places. Arms: D'argent, à la bande de gueules chargée de 3 coquilles d'or. The Gouicquet family were vassals of the des Goyon de la Moussaye. The parish registers of la Moussaye are in private hands. Jacques Gouicquet, sgr. du Tertre, m. Jeanne du Hardas before 1618, when their daur. Marie was born, 20 July 1618; Isaac, b. 21 Oct. 1619; Amaury, 22 Feb. 1621; Catherine, 8 Jan. 1625. This Isaac Gouicquet was probably Isaac, sr. du Tertre, who m. Jeanne Doudart. A Catherine Gouicquet abjured, 3 May 1665; she had abjured in 1648, but had rejoined the R.P.R. (Arch. Côtes du Nord, G. 4). Denis Gouicquet, sr. de Ville-en-Marques, son of Luc Gouicquet, was bapt. as a Catholic, became a Protestant, and abjured 3 May 1665, probably a brother of above.

Vaugiraud has some references to this family, Vol. II, pp. 37-42.

Isaac Gouicquet de St. Eloy, de l'Evêché de St. Brieux, abjured in Guernsey, 2 Jan. 1689.

(B) Hullin d'Orval, see note (B), De Gennes Pedigree (Vol. I).

(C) The Le Blanc family, though originally of Sedan, appear at Vitré, probably owing to the fact that Madame Gouyon de la Moussaye, Dame de Quintin, " grande protectrice des églises protestantes " of this locality, was a daughter of the House of La Tour d'Auvergne, and was Princesse de Sedan, and brought servants and officials from that town. The Poulce family was one of these, and were legal officials at Moussaye. It is probable that Mr. Le Blanc, minister at Sunbury, came from Vitré as chaplain to the colony.

Pierre Le Blanc m. Suzanne de Moranvilliers, who retired to Berlin, with her four daughters ; the three sisters of Marguerite and Charles Le Blanc were Elizabeth Darène (Darennes), Suzanne Barratt (or de Baret), and Rachel Croyé ; the husband of the last, Captain de Croyé, of Sedan, settled in Brandenburg. A Thomas Le Blanc was Overseer of Mitcham in 1763. (See Note to Pedigree by Mr. H. Wagner, " Misc. Gen. et Herald.," March, 1905.)

(D) The Trevigar family were also from Brittany. Luc Doudart Trevigar, M.D., was made Denizen, 8 May 1697, and Mary Trevigar, 24 June 1703.

Henri de Saunières m. secondly, Suzanne Trevigar, 20 Dec. 1730. Thirdly, Magdalen, daur. of John Francis Portal, of Poitiers (P.C.C., 13 March 1775, Alexander 118). His first wife was Marthe Marie Moreau, whom he m. in 1723 (see Trevigar Pedigree, *The Genealogist*, N.S., Vol. XXX, p. 188).

A Mary Trevigar, child, was buried in St. James Parish, Piccadilly, 7 Ap. 1701, probably a daur. of Luke Trevigar, of that parish. He also practised in Islington.

GUILLEMARD

Arms: Arg: 3 bars gules, on a chief 3 trefoils, within a bordure az., charged with 8 mullets or, *alias* d'or, au chevron d'azur: acc. de 3 têtes de renard, de gueules, 2 and 1.

I. Daniel Guillemard, sr. d'Ablon et de Soussigny in Poitou, Procureur of the Chambre des Comptes 1618, b. 156..(?); d. 1645; m. Magdeleine Gobelin,(A) second daur. of Francois Gobelin, Teinturier at St. Marcel, Head of the House of Gobelin, and of his wife, Générviéve Canaye, b. 1567, d. 1645, buried at Paris.(A) They had six children: (*a*) Pierre, b. June 1601, d. young; (*b*) Pierre, who succeeds, II; (*c*) Magdeleine, b. March 1609; (*d*) Daniel, b. Oct. 1615; (*e*) Marie, m. Pierre Petit, sr. du Chesnoy, avocat au Parlement, became a Catholic in 1680; (*f*) Suzanne, m. in Nov. 1642, Louis de Bérard, Trésorier des Regiments de Languedoc, son of Jean de Bérard, avocat, and his wife, Isabeau du Portal.

II. Pierre Guillemard, sr. de Mélamare, near Bolbec, b. June 1603, bapt. at Charenton, Paris, m. Madelaine Lemanicher, b. 1627, living 1699, a widow. They left: (*a*) Pierre, who succeeds, III; (*b*) Jean, b. 1653, d. 31 July 1671, at Rouen.

III. Pierre Guillemard, sr. de Mélamare, or Millemare, b. 1649. "Nouveau Converti" in 1699. He m. twice. The name of his first wife is not entered in the Protestant Registers of Quévilly, near Rouen, 18 Dec. 1677. His second wife was Judith Heuzé, b. 1662. He left by his first marriage: (*a*) Pierre, b. 1679; (*b*) Suzanne, b. 1681. By the second marriage to Judith Heuzé he had six children: (*a*) Marie Guillemard, b. 2 March, bapt. 11 March 1690. She married Jacques de Beuzeville, of Bolbec, and came to England. He was b. before 1685, and d. in 1745. Their children were baptised in the Walloon church of Threadneedle Street, between 1728 and 1733. (*b*) Madelaine, b. 1692; (*c*) Louis, b. 9 April 1693, buried 22 Aug. 1697;

(*d*) Pierre Guillemard, bapt. 19 May 1695; (*e*) Jean Guillemard, IV; (*f*) Louis, b. 3 June 1703, bapt. 4 June, came to England.

IV. Jean Guillemard, b. at Mélamare, Bolbec, bapt. 26 May 1698 at Bolbec; came to England circ. 1699; d. 24 Feb. 1782, buried in Spitalfields; of Tottenham High Cross; described in his will, dated 14 Ap. 1779, pr. 11 Mar. 1782, as of the Liberty of the Tower. M. Magdelaine Le Play, daur. and coheir of Isaac Le Play and of Magdelaine his wife. Her sister Marie married Jacques Martel. They left four sons: (*a*) Jean, author of the elder branch, V (A); (*b*) Pierre, of the Old Artillery Ground, London, b. 15 June 1731, bapt. at Threadneedle Street Fr. Ch. 26 June 1731, d. unmarried in March 1764. Admon. granted 11 Ap. 1764 to his brother Jean Guillemard. (*c*) Isaac, author of Branch B; (*d*) Jacques, b. 26 Nov., bapt. 13 Dec. 1747 at Threadneedle Street Fr. Ch. A miniature of him is in the possession of J. H. H. Guillemard.

V. (Branch A). Jean Guillemard, of Tottenham High Cross, b. 1 Nov., bapt. 22 Nov. 1729 in the Threadneedle Street Fr. Ch.; m. Françoise Pilon, daur. of Daniel Pilon and of Jeanne Bourdon, daur. of Pierre Bourdon and Francoise Pilon, d. 26 May 1798, and was buried in the Paroissien Vault, Spitalfields. Daniel Pilon, her father, b. in 1692, was buried 24 Ap. 1762, at Dagenham, in Essex. His wife, Jeanne Bourdon, bapt. at the Fr. Ch. of La Patente, Spitalfields, 3 March 1701, was also buried at Dagenham, 15 Feb. 1783. Jean Guillemard and Francoise Pilon left: (*a*) Jean Louis, who continues (B); (*b*) Jeanne (Jane), b. 18 Sept., bapt. 21 Sept. 1765, at St. Jean Fr. Ch., Spitalfields. She m., 13 Ap. 1786, John Griffin, of 21 Bedford Place, of the Goldsmiths' Company, eldest son of William Griffin, of a Huguenot family, and of his wife, Elizabeth Bodenham, of Ludlow, Salop, b. 17 Oct. 1757, d. 2 May 1852. Jane Guillemard d. 3 June 1795, buried at Spitalfields. John Griffin left by his wife, Jane Guillemard, several children, one of whom, Jane, married Sir John Franklin, the explorer.

V (Branch B). Isaac Guillemard, of Waltham Cross,

b. 6 April, bapt. at Threadneedle Street Fr. Ch. 22 Ap. 1744, d. 22 Dec. 1816. His portrait by Burnell is in the possession of Doctor Guillemard, of Trumpington, Camb. M., 5 Ap. 1770, at St. Matthew's, Bethnal Green, Anne Le Maistre, daur. of Daniel Le Maistre and Magdalen, daur. of Matthieu Paroissien, bapt. at La Patente Fr. Ch., London, 4 Nov. 1746, d. 26 May 1784, buried at Christ Church, Spitalfields, in the Paroissien vault. She was first wife of Daniel Le Maistre, who married secondly Judith Hochecorne. Isaac Guillemard and Anne Le Maistre had five children: (*a*) Pierre, or Peter, who continues, VI; (*b*) Daniel, who continues Branch B i, VI; (*c*) Anne, b. 11 July 1773, d. young; (*d*) Anne, b. 1 July, d. 22 July 1775; (*e*) Isaac, b. 12 July, d. 7 Nov. 1777.

VI. Pierre, or Peter, Guillemard, of Tottenham, and afterwards of South Hill House, Reading, b. 4 Jan. 1771, bapt. at St. Jean, Spitalfields, 27 Jan. 1771, d. 13 Ap. 1828. His portrait by Burnell is in possession of Dr. John Guillemard at Trumpington. He m. 11 Jan. 1802 at Holy Trinity, Exeter, Tamazine Venn, fifth daur. of Henry Venn, of Payhembury, Devon, and of Mary Cooke his wife. Tamazine his wife d. at Tottenham 27 Jan. 1818 and was buried in Spitalfields Churchyard.

They had eight children: (*a*) Anne, b. 27 Nov., bapt. 25 Dec. 1802 at Christchurch, Spitalfields. M. at Hackney, 17 Sept. 1839, William Dean Bath and his wife Dorothy Venn, of Payhembury; (*b*) Mary Tamazine, b. 6 March 1804, bapt. 3 Ap. 1804 at Christ Church, Spitalfields, d. unmarried 26 May 1830, buried at Spitalfields; (*c*) Jane Louisa, b. 1 May, bapt. 28th, 1805, at Christ Church, Spitalfields, d. 7 June 1806; (*d*) Jane Sadler, b. 18 Nov. 1806, bapt. 23 Dec. 1806 at Christ Church, Spitalfields, d. unmarried at Bath 5 Ap. 1905; (*e*) Susan, b. 13 March, bapt. 9 Ap. 1808, at Christ Church, Spitalfields; (*f*) Peter, b. 29 Nov., bapt. 25 Dec. 1809, at Christ Church, Spitalfields, d. 4 Feb. 1811; (*g*) Henry Peter, b. 29 Sept. 1812, bapt. 26 Dec. 1812 at Christ Church, Spitalfields, d. 24 Ap. 1857 and was buried at Barton. Fellow of Trinity Coll., Oxford, and Rector of Barton-on-the-Heath, Glos. He m., 24 Oct. 1848, at Henwick, Worcester, Julia Hulme, fifth daur. of the Rev. G. Hulme, of Shinfield, Berks, and of his wife, Elizabeth, eldest daur. of the Rev. John Symonds Breedon, D.D., of Bere Court, Berks ; (*h*) Elizabeth Venn, b. 8 Feb. 1815 at Tottenham, d. 18 May 1837, buried in Spitalfields Churchyard. The succession is continued by—

VI. B i. Daniel Guillemard, brother of Pierre (Peter) Guillemard. He was b. 7 Feb. 1772, bapt. at St. Jean, Spitalfields, 7 March 1772, d. 7 Aug. 1822, buried at Spitalfields. He married, 27 May 1806, at Payhembury, Devon, Susanna, third daur. of Henry Venn and Mary Cooke, and left by this his second marriage the posterity reported hereafter.* By his first marriage to Jeanne, daur. of Jean-Baptiste Hèbert, and of Rachel his wife, b. in 1776, m. 15 Aug. 1796 at St. Botolph's, Bishopsgate, he left : (*a*) John Guillemard, of the Stock Exchange, b. 14 Nov. 1797, bapt. 13 Dec. 1797 in the Fr. Ch. of Threadneedle Street. He d. 30 Jan. 1873, having married, Ap. 1843, at St. Paul's, Finsbury, Amelia Gullick, daur. of Joseph Gullick, of Guernsey. John Guillemard and Amelia Gullick left : (i) Emily, b. 1844, d. May 1893 unm., b. at the Hague, Holland ; (ii) Harvey Milne, b. 1847, m. 1 Jan. 1868, at St. Dunstan's-in-the-West, Julia Mary Hatt, and had one son, Charles Harvey Milne Guillemard, b. 5 Dec. 1868. Harvey Milne Guillemard, his father, d. 13 Nov. 1887 ; (iii) Mary Frances, b. 1852 or 1853, m. firstly Charles Henry Hatt, secondly George Claridge, and had no children by either marriage ; (iv) Ellen, b. 1856, living in 1918 unmarried.

*Daniel Guillemard left by his second marriage, with Susanna Venn, six children : (*a*) James Guillemard, Fellow of St. John's, College, Oxford, Vicar of St. Giles, Oxford, 1836, and of Kirtlington, 1838, b. 24 July and bapt. 7 Dec. 1807 at St. John's, Hackney ; d. 11 Jan. 1858, buried at Tenby. He m. firstly Louisa, only daur. of George Tyser, M.D., 30 Ap. 1839, in London, buried at Kirtlington March 1840 ; secondly, Elizabeth Louisa, second daur. of Henry Watson, of Brandon House, Barnes, 27 June 1843, author of Branch B ii, VII. (*b*) Frances, b. 23 June 1809, bapt. 17 Jan. 1810 at St. John's, Hackney, d. s.p. 9 Feb. 1877, at Tenby, m. 28 May 1833 at St. Lawrence, Isle of

Wight, Frederick Daniel Dyster, M.D., of Madeira, who d. 4 Mar. 1893 at Tenby; (*c*) Isaac, author of Branch B iii; (*d*) William Henry, author of Branch B iv, VII; (*e*) George, M.R.C.S., b. 29 Jan. 1817, bapt. 20 May 1817, at St. John's, Hackney, d. 6 Ap. 1844 at Madeira unmarried; (*f*) Harriet Louisa, b. 10 Dec. 1820, bapt. 4 Feb. 1821, d. 17 Aug. 1842, unmarried, at St. Leonard's, and buried at Hackney.

VII (Branch B ii). James Guillemard, left by his second marriage to Elizabeth Louisa Watson, seven children: (*a*) Fanny Marion, b. 10 July 1844 at Kirtlington, m. 23 Jan. 1879, at St. James, Piccadilly, Percy Swan Wilford, youngest son of Major-Gen. Edmund Ernest Wilford, R.A., Governor of Woolwich Academy, and left one son and two daughters; (*b*) Edith Harriet, b. 19 Ap. 1846, in Madeira, m. 21 Ap. 1870 at St. Thomas', Winchester, Frederick Dobrée Teesdale, Canon of Chichester, and left Kenneth John Marmaduke Teesdale, b. 25 Jan. 1871; (*c*) Walter George, of Malverleys, Hants, b. 20 Nov. 1847, bapt. 19 Dec. 1847, at Kirtlington, d. 8 May 1816, buried at East Woodhay. He m. 8 Aug. 1888, at Sydenham, Agnes Olive, eldest daur. of Charles Cotton, of Audley House, Cork, and left by her: (i) Ruth Antoinette, b. 3 Aug. 1889 at Harrow, m. 21 Oct. 1920 at St. Columba's Church, Nairn, Hugh Rose, of Kilravock, C.M.G., 24th Baron, and left a son, Hugh Rose, b. 26 Nov. 1921 at Kilravock; (ii) Phyllis Louise, b. 29 Sept. 1891 at Harrow, d. unm. 28 Nov. 1916 at Queen Mary's Hospital, Whalley, Lancs, while serving as a V.A.D., buried at St. Martin's, East Woodhay, Hants; (iii) Eleanor Frances, b. 1 Nov. 1893 at Harrow, m. 28 Oct. 1919 at East Woodhay, Duncan Gordon Davidson, of Tillychetty, Aberdeenshire, Captain Queen's Own Cameron Highlanders, and has two daurs., Janet Eleanor, b. 31 July 1920, at Nairn, and Grisel Frances, b. 14 June 1922 at City Park, St. Andrews, Fife. (*d*) Agnes Louisa, b. 11 June 1849 at Kirtlington, Oxon, m. 4 Sept. 1873 at St. Thomas, Winchester, the Rev. John Henry Wilkinson, of Waynfleet, Clifton, second son of the Rev. Matthew Wilkinson, D.D., Headmaster of Marlborough, and left posterity; (*e*) Arthur Franklin, C.E. Scholar of Winchester, b. 14 July 1851 at Kirtlington, m. Esther Theodora, second daur. of the Rev. Walter Gilden, Canon of Salisbury, 14 March 1899, at St. Paul's, Valparaiso; (*f*) Ada Madeleine, b. 20 Jan. 1853, bapt. at Kirtlington, m. 10 Aug. 1875 at St. Thomas, Winchester, the Rev. John Neal, M.A., of Kingsdon Manor, Somerset. She d. 10 Aug. 1909 at Kingsdon Manor, leaving posterity; (*g*) Bernard James, M.D., Edin., b. 5 Oct. 1854, bapt. at St. Peter's, Bournemouth, m. 12 Ap. 1888 at Christ Church, St. Leonard's, Beatrice Elizabeth, fourth daur. of the Rev. George F. Childe, M.A., of Christchurch, Oxford, Assist. Astronomer Royal, Cape Town; their children are: (i) Brian James Childe Guillemard, b. 14 Feb. 1889; (ii) Irene Beatrice, b. 30 July 1891, m. 8 June 1914 Francis Le Geyt Worsley, Lieut. R.N., third son of Godfrey Thomas Worsley, of Evelyns, Hillingdon, Mdx. Children: Rosalind Frances, b. 27 March 1915 at Nairobi; John Godfrey Bernard, b. 16 Feb. 1919 at Liverpool, bapt. in the private chapel at Evelyns 12 Ap. 1919. (iii) Mary Joyce, b. 23 Oct. 1895 at Aliwal North, S.A.

VII. (Branch B iii). Isaac Guillemard, M.D. (of Berlin), of Eltham, Kent, b. 24 June 1811, bapt. 22 Jan. 1812 at St. John's, Hackney, d. at Eltham 18 Oct. 1852, buried there. M. Anne Pierce, only daur. of John Upham, of 19 Guilford Place, Russell Square, 8 June 1839 at St. Leonard's, Exeter, and left by her six children: (*a*) Caroline Ann, b. 1 May 1840 at Eltham, bapt. 9 July 1840, d. unmarried at Eltham 22 July 1903; (*b*) Frederick, b. 14 July 1841, bapt. 29 June 1843 at Eltham, d. 2 June 1847 at Eltham; (*c*) Charles Edward, of Foxden Plantation, Amelia County, Virginia, b. 30 Jan. 1843 at Eltham, bapt. 29 June, d. 27 March 1918, at Eastbourne; (*d*) Arthur George, of Passey House, Eltham, afterwards of 3 Arlington Street, St. James, solicitor, b. 18 Dec. 1845 at Eltham, bapt. 3 Sept. 1846, d. 7 Aug. 1909, unmarried, at Eltham; (*e*) William Mountrich, b. 19 Feb. 1848, bapt. 3 Aug. 1848, d. 25 Dec. 1865, unmarried, at Eltham; (*f*) Francis Henry Hill Guillemard, M.A., M.D., F.L.S., of Gonville and Caius College, Cambridge, and the Old Mill House, Trumpington. B. 12 Sept. 1852 at Eltham, bapt. 11 Dec. 1853 at St. Paul's, Exeter. Writer, naturalist and explorer; author of "The Cruise of the

Marchesa," "Life of Magellan," etc.; Reader in Geography at the University of Cambridge; Council of the Royal Geographical Society, Hakluyt and Walpole Societies, etc. M., 25 June 1890, at St. Martin's, Dorking, Katharine Stephanie, fourth daur. of the Rev. William H. Guillemard, D.D.

VII (Branch B iv). William Henry Guillemard, D.D., Fellow of Pembroke College, Cambridge, b. 23 Nov. 1815, bapt. 13 Jan. 1816 at St. John, Hackney, d. 2 Sept. 1887 at Waterbeach, buried at Cambridge. Headmaster of the Royal School, Armagh, 1848-69, and afterwards Vicar of St. Mary-the-Less, Cambridge. M. Elizabeth Susanna, second daur. of William Hammond Turner, of Severndroog Lodge, Kent, and left by her six children: (*a*) Elizabeth Susanna, b. 23 May 1850 at Armagh, d. 25 Nov. 1873, unmarried, at Cambridge; (*b*) Rosamond Harriet, b. 20 Nov. 1853 at Armagh, d. 25 Nov. 1895, unmarried, at Costebelle, Hyères, France; (*c*) Mary Frances, b. 8 June 1855 at Armagh; (*d*) Katharine Stéphanie, b. 26 Dec. 1859, at Armagh, m. 25 June 1890 to Dr. Henry H. Guillemard, M.D., of the Old Mill House, Trumpington, Cambs.; (*e*) Sir Laurence Nunns Guillemard, M.A., and scholar of Trinity Coll., Cambs., Governor of the Straits Settlements, b. 7 June 1862 at Armagh; entered the Treasury, 1888; m. Ellen, eldest daur. of Thomas Spencer Walker, of Berry Hall, Walsingham, 2 July 1902. (*f*) Lucy Jane, b. 3 March 1866 at Armagh.

NOTES.

(A) Magdeline Gobelin had four brothers and four sisters. Of the latter, three married Huguenots: Claud Chrestien, Matthieu Langlois, and Paul Chenevix.

François Gobelin was fourth in descent from Jean Gobelin and Perrette his wife, founder of the house established at St. Marcel in 1450, who d. in 1475.

(B) Jean Louis Guillemard (son of Jean Guillemard and Françoise Pilon), M.A., F.R.S., of St. John's College, Oxford; of Clavering Hall, Essex. Commissioner appointed on behalf of England to adjudicate on the Treaty of amity with America. B. 31 Aug. 1764, bapt. 4 Sept. 1764 at the Fr. Ch. of St. Jean, Spitalfields, d. 22 Nov. 1844, buried in the Pilon vault at Dagenham, Essex. A portrait of him by Beechey is in the possession of Dr. Guillemard at Trumpington, Cambridge. He. m. Mary Philippa Davies Giddy, only daur. of the Rev. Edward Giddy (afterwards Gilbert) by Catherine Davies his wife, coheir of the barony of Sandys-of-the-Vine, of Tredrea. Her portrait by Opie is in the possession of Dr. Guillemard.

I am indebted to Dr. H. H. Guillemard for the above pedigree which he has kindly allowed me to reprint.

ST. JULIEN DE MALACARE

I. Pierre de St. Julien,(A) sieur de Malacare, b. 1635, m. Jeanne Lefebvre, daur. of Daniel Lefebvre, sieur de Fougeray, and of Marie Berault. He d. in Dublin 20 Oct. 1705, aged 70. They had nine children, all bapt. at Vitré, in Brittany: (*a*) Aimée, b. 7 March 1667, m. Jean Trapaud, an officer in the regiment de Loches in 1685, afterwards Major and Colonel of Trapaud's Foot, raised in 1706 by the English Government for service in Spain. She d. 22 Jan. 1706 aged 38 (Nouv. Egl. Fr., Dublin). They left posterity. (*b*) Charlotte, b. 15 May 1668, at Vitré, m. 24 Oct. 1687 at Charleston, S. Carolina, René Ravenel, sieur de la Masseais, son of Daniel Ravenel, sieur de Cohigny, and of Marie Guerineau (Ravenel Ped., Vol. I); (*c*) Pierre, who succeeds, II; (*d*) Louis, b. 5 Aug. 1670; (*e*) Marguerite, b. 19 Dec. 1671; (*f*) Paul, b. 4 Oct. 1673. He m. 5 May 1709 (by lic., Vic. Gen.), Catherine de Senlecque, of St. Anne, Westm., at the Fr. Ch. of Spring Garden. He was of St. Anne's Parish. He was godfather, 17 Oct. 1713, to Jeanne Corneille (Nouv. Egl. St. Marie, Dublin). (*g*) Emilie, b. 30 Jan. 1675, whose godmother was Emilie de Hesse, Princesse de Tarente, bapt. 3 Feb. Her godfather was Claude Charles de Gouyon, Baron de Marcé. She m. at St. Martin's in the Fields, London, 17 Jan. 1705, Pierre du Foissac (or du Foussat), son of Daniel and Suzanne de Foissac, b. at Rosan in Guienne (Nat. List), Capt. of Dragoons (Lic. Vic. Gen.). She d. in Dublin, 17 Feb. 1707. He d. at Portarlington 5 June 1711. (*h*) Jeanne Réneé, b. 6 May 1678, m. Bartholomew Arabin, or d'Arabin, son of Alexander and of Marguerite his wife, b. at Ricz in Provence (Nat. List, 1699). (*i*) Marie Esther, b. 14 Dec. 1679, m. Jean Adlercorn, and d. in Dublin 8 Feb. 1707 aged about 71. She was a widow 18 Nov. 1697, when she was godmother to Jean Chamier in London (Leicester Fields Fr. Ch.).

II. Pierre de St. Julien de Malacare, b. 4 July 1669, was made Denizen in London 9 Ap. 1687. M. Damaris Elizabeth Le Serrurier, who was b. at St. Quentin, Picardy, daur.

of James Le Serrurier. His will was made in S. Carolina, 12 June 1718 (Prob. Office, Charleston), in French. He describes himself as of Berkeley Co., Province of S. Carolina. Pierre de St. Julien left nine children: (*a*) Pierre, who succeeds, III; (*b*) James; (*c*) Paul, m. firstly Marie Aimée Ravenel, daur. of René Ravenel and of Charlotte de St. Julien de Malacare, secondly Marie Verditty (she m. secondly, in 1744, Thomas Monck: her daur. by this second marriage, Elizabeth Monck, m. Job Marion (Ravenel Records); (*d*) Henry; (*e*) Joseph, d. in 1746, m. Miss Mayrant; (*f*) Alexander; (*g*) Daniel; (*h*) Elizabeth Damaris, m. Daniel Ravenel, of Somerton; (*i*) Jeanne Marie, m. Isaac Mazyck.

III. Pierre de St. Julien de Malacare, mentioned in the will of his father as being engaged to Judith Giraud against his father's wishes, m. Sarah Godin, 1 June 1727, and left posterity, among whom a daur., Damaris Elizabeth, m., 10 Dec. 1749, General William Moultrie. The sixth child, Sarah de St. Julien, m. Daniel Ravenel, of Wantoot. She d. 17 Nov. 1757, and her husband, Daniel Ravenel, m. secondly Charlotte Mazyck, daur. of Paul Mazyck, and Catherine de Chateigner, 12 Nov. 1759 (Ravenel Records).

NOTES.

(A) The family of St. Julien do not appear at Vitré at an earlier date than that of the baptism of their first child. The name does not appear in the Parish (R.C.) registers. There were several families of the same name in different parts of France, and Malecare was the name of a fief near Castres.

Pierre de St. Julien, sieur de Malacare, must not be confounded with Pierre Malacare, of Castres, who m. Lydie, daur. of Jean Auriol of that city, whose son, Pierre Malacare, sr. de Lagayé, m. Marguerite Debeille and had a son Jean de Lagayé, who appears in Carolina in 1742. (See "Malacare de Pratviel," *The Genealogist*, N.S., Vol. XXV, 1909, by Henry Wagner, F.S.A.)

The family of St. Julien, sieurs de Malacare, who appear as Protestants in the Vitré Registers, were of the Haute

Bourgeoisie and do not appear in any Recherche de la Noblesse or in d'Hozier. They did not bear any Arms or attain the rank of " ecuyer."

Pierre de St. Julien left behind him in France property in the parish of St. Julien valued at 3,400 livres, at a rental of 170 livres, and 700 livres by the sale of his furniture and belongings. This was confiscated as the property of an emigré and given to the hospital (Vaugiraud, III). He was made Denizen, in London, with his wife and children (with the exception of Jeanne Renée and Marie Esther), 9 Ap. 1689. Paul de St. Julien was naturalised 23 Mar. 1709, and Catherine de St. Julien, possibly a sister of Pierre, was naturalised by Oath Roll, 1710.

NICOLAS

I. Jean Nicolas, b. at Jonsac, in Saintonge, came to England and received a commission as Cornet, then Lieutenant, in Lord Galway's Horse. He m. Anne Raulin at Jonsac before 1685. She was b. in 1670, and d. in Dublin 13 July 1756, aged 86, and was buried at the Fr. Ch., St. Patrick and Ste. Marie, 14 July 1756, "veuve de Capitaine Nicolas."(A) They had (*a*) Charles, who succeeds, II; (*b*) Henriette, bapt. at the Fr. Ch. of Le Temple, London, 25 Dec. 1691, born 12 Dec.; her godfather was Lord Galway, and her godmother Pauline Nicolas,(B) wife of Mr. Benjamin de Daillon, pastor of the Fr. Ch. at Portarlington. Henriette Nicolas m. at Dublin, 4 Jan. 1719, Paul Martin de Cloussy, at which marriage Jean Nicolas and Anne Nicolas, her father and mother, were present (St. Patrick). (*c*) Pierre, bapt. at Le Temple, London. His godfather was the Rev. Pierre Fontaine, and his godmother Dame Marie Caillard.

II. Charles Nicolas, was bapt. at Le Temple in 1690, His godfather was Charles de Daillon, ec. sgr. de Glatigny. and his godmother Marie Drilhon, Dame de Montassier, in Saintonge (see Boybellaud Ped., Vol. I). He married firstly, Marie Pill, by whom he had (*a*) Anne, d. at Dublin, 8 Jan. 1703, aged 15 months; (*b*) Michel, b. Sept. 1703, d. 10 Feb. 1705 (St. Patrick); secondly, Charlotte des Vignolles, daur. of Charles des Vignolles, of Nismes, and Gabrielle de Sperandieu, of Castres. In the marriage entry (Nouvelle Egl. de Ste. Marie, Dublin) he is described as son of Jean Nicolas, " ec. capitaine refugié," et de Madame Anne Raulin, cy devant habitants de Jonsac, et à present de Clunegon (Clonegaun) dans le Comté du Roy en Irlande." Charles Nicolas d. in Dublin 27 Feb. 1726, and his wife Charlotte des Vignolles d. there, 16 Oct. 1730. By his second marriage he left: (*c*) Henri, b. 9 June, bapt. 27 June 1716 (St. Patrick). His godfather was Lord Galway, his godmother Gabrielle des Vignolles. He d. in Dublin 24 March 1717. (*c*) Charles, b. 26 July, bapt. 10 Aug. 1718 (*idem.*). His godfather was Charles des Vignolles, his grandfather, and his godmother Dame Anne Raulin Nicolas, grandmother; (*d*) Marguerite, b. 7, bapt. 23 Feb. 1721. Her godfather was Jean Nicolas, her grandfather; her godmother, Dame Marguerite des Vignolles de Vendargue(c). (*e*) Louis, who succeeds, III.

III. Louis Nicolas, b. 1724, went to Philadelphia. M. firstly, Christian Doyle, who d. Aug. 1759; secondly, Jane Bishop. By his first marriage he had Captain John Nicolas, b. 1742, served in Portugal, d. 1789, and was buried at Southampton. By his wife whose name is not known he left thirteen children. Charles, b. 1747 at Portarlington (Vignolles MSS.), d. 1751. John Nicolas had a twin brother, who d. at birth (*idem.*). By his second marriage with Jane Bishop he had (*a*) Margaret, b. 12 March 1764, m. . . . . . Bigham, and had a daur., Jane Bigham, b. 18 Dec. 1783; (*b*) Jane, b. 28 Feb. 1765, m. Talmage Hall, by whom she left (i) Lewis, b. 13 May 1783, (ii) Hannah, b. 20 Jan, 1786, (*c*) Mary, b. 14 Ap. 1766, m. Captain Thomas Nack, or Slack (Vignolles MSS.).

NOTES.

(A) Pierre Nicolas was recommended, as a person of note, for a commission in La Melonières Regiment, 1698 (Muster Rolls, Agnew, *French Prot. Exiles*, Vol. II, p. 87). He d. at Dublin, aged 50, 11 Oct. 1702. Probably a brother of Jean Nicolas.

A Laurence Nicolas and his wife Ester had a child baptised at the Non. Con. Fr. Ch., Dublin, 17 May 1702. Nothing more is known of them.

(B) Pauline Nicolas, wife of Benjamin Daillon. Their daur., Anne, m. Jean Grosvenor, cornet in the regiment of Dragoons of Lord Essex. Their son Henri was born in the house of Mr. Daillon, 18 Jan. 1699, at Portarlington. The Daillon family came from Saintonge. Benjamin Daillon, Pastor at La Rochefoucauld, came to England and preached a sermon in favour of James II and was deprived of his benefice; afterwards Minister at Portarlington. Pauline de Daillon his daur. m. Jean Pasquet de Rochebertier, 21, a bachelor in 1693, in London. She was

18. By her parents' consent, attested by her aunt, Anne de Royère. At St. Giles, or elsewhere (Vic. Gen. Marr. Lic. 1693).

(c) Marguerite de Vignolles was b. in 1652, m. Pierre Richard, sgr. de Vendargues in 1683, and d. in Ireland in 1730. Daur. of Jacques de Vignolles and Louise de Baschi d'Aubais.

Abraham Nicolas, Major and Adjutant-General, of Virginia, who d. there in 1738, may have been of this family.

The last generation, III, is from the MSS. of the late Mr. Wagner, who appears to have made notes from the Vignolles MSS. Some of the statements given are obviously incorrect and have been omitted in this pedigree here given. The remainder (III) is on the authority of Mr. Wagner's notes, and no doubt can be extended or corrected from sources in America.

NICOLAS

(Of East Looe, Cornwall.)

It was intended to publish the pedigree of this family, which appears in Vivian's *Visitation of Cornwall*, and is printed by Gilbert, *Historical Survey of Cornwall* (Vol. II, p. 209), and Burke, *Landed Gentry*. On examination of original manuscripts and authorities for the parentage of Abel Nicolas, the first of the family in England, no proof can be found for the statement that he was the son of Jean Nicolas, sgr. de Champsgerault, and Marie Renée de Rosmadec.

The name of Abel is almost *prima facie* evidence that his parents were Protestants, as the Catholic noblesse very rarely used Old Testament christian names. The family of Nicolas de Champsgerault were Catholics and had no Protestant members. Neither is any son Abel to be found. Finally and conclusively, Abel Nicolas arrived with his wife in East Looe in 1685 ; he must therefore have been at least twenty years of age. Jean Nicolas, his reputed father, did not marry Marie Renée de Rosmadec till that year.

Abel Nicolas must have been born circ. 1665. Jean Nicolas de Champsgerault maintained his nobility 20 May 1669, together with his brother Germain, at which date he was unmarried. Germain m. Renée Chenu, Dame de Clermont, and had one son. The family became extinct in male line in 1725 by the marriage of the heiress to the sgr. de la Bourdonnaye.

The name is a common one in Brittany and elsewhere, and doubtless Abel Nicolas was connected with one or other of Breton families bearing the name.

OLIVIER

I. Pierre d'Olivier, son of Bernard d'Olivier, was born 1575, and m. Judith de Brun. They left: (*a*) Isabeau, b. circ. 1623, m. in 1641 Jordain de Vignau; (*b*) Isaac Pierre, who succeeds, II; (*c*) Philemon, bapt. 1625 at Nay in Béarn, m. 2 Dec. 1670 at Salies de Béarn, Sara de Laffitte-Maria, daur. of Jean de Laffitte-Maria, sr. de Cassaber, and of Jeanne du Faur. He d. s.p. 1675; (*d*) Esther, bapt. in 1628 at Nay.

II. Isaac Pierre d'Olivier, b. circ. 1620, d. Oct. 1671, m. Isabeau de Masselin (d. 1654), daur. of Pierre de Masselin and of Marie de Bonnecaze de Ste. Suzanne. They left: (*a*) a daur., b. in 1638, m. 1682, David Perier, of Nay, son of Jean Perier and Marie Day (who d. 1689); (*b*) Judith, bapt. at Nay 22 March 1640; (*c*) Nathaniel, bapt. 4 July 1641 at Nay; (*d*) Jordain, who succeeds, III; (*e*) Esther, bapt. 28 Jan. 1646; (*f*) Jean, bapt. 15 Jan. 1647; (*g*) Isaac, bapt. 1 Nov. 1649; (*h*) Jeanne, bapt. 24 March 1653; (*i*) Theophile, bapt. 10 May 1654, d. at Paris circ. 1683.

III. Jordain Olivier, b. 16 Sept., bapt. 24 Sept. 1643 at Nay, m. Dec. 1677 Anne de Day (b. 1660) at Nay, daur. of Daniel de Day,(A) of Pau, and of Suzanne de Mirassor. Jordain Olivier was a Refugee Pastor in 1686, and d. Aug. 1709. By his marriage with Anne de Day he left eight children: (*a*) Daniel, b. 28 Nov. 1684 at Pau, d. 4 Ap. 1692 in Holland; (*b*) Jerome Olivier, who succeeds, IV; (*c*) Marthe, b. 1689; (*d*) Isaac, b. 1 Oct. 1690; (*e*) Suzanne, b. 17 Ap. 1693; (*f*) Daniel, who m. 2 Sept. 1724 at the Fr. Ch. of Spring Gardens, London, Elizabeth Durand, of St. Margaret's, Westminster, and left (i) Françoise Julie, b. 7 June 1726, bapt. 19th at the Fr. Ch. of the Savoy; (ii) Elizabeth Suzanne Marie, b. 12 May 1727, bapt. 25th (*idem*); (iii) Suzanne, b. 30 March, bapt. 16 Ap. 1728 (*idem*); (iv) Marie, b. 19 Ap., bapt. 7 May 1730 (*idem*); (v) Elizabeth, b. 11 July, bapt. 16 July 1731 (*idem*); Marie Marguerite, b. 25 March, bapt. 30 March 1733 (*idem*). (Daniel Olivier was Minister of the Savoy French Church.) (*g*) Elizabeth, b. 10 Feb. 1698; (*h*) Jourdain, b. 2 Ap. 1703.

OLIVIER

IV. Jerome Olivier, b. 4 March 1687, m. 21 Sept. 1721 Julie de la Motte (b. 16 Sept. 1697, d. 30 Nov. 1770), daur. of Joseph de la Motte and of Sybille Matthieu. Jerome Olivier was chaplain to the Prince of Orange; d. 30 Oct. 1724. By his wife Julie de la Motte he left one son and two daurs.: (*a*) Daniel Josias, who succeeds, V; (*b*) Esther Henriette, b. 27 Nov. 1723, bapt. 18 Dec. at the Savoy Fr. Ch. She m. in 1773 Jean Rocque, of Uzès. (*c*) Marguerite, b. 24 Feb. 1725, bapt. 28 March (*idem*). (Jerome Olivier was Pastor of the Savoy Fr. Ch.)

V. Daniel Josias Olivier, b. 19 July 1722, bapt. 8 Aug. at the Savoy Fr. Ch., m. 30 June 1750, Suzanne Massé (b. 1725, d. 17 Jan. 1803), daur. of Jacques Massé(B) and of Marie Magdeleine Berchere. They had six children: (*a*) a son b. 3 March, d. 15 March 1751; (*b*) Jacques Josias, b. 14 March 1752, d. 22 June 1762; (*c*) Julie Elizabeth, b. 6 March 1753, m. firstly, General Eyre, in June 1779, secondly General Sir William Congreve 3 Jan. 1803. She d. 6 Dec. 1831, s.p. (*d*) Marguerite Esther, b. 8 May 1754, m. in 1778 the Rev. William Conybeare, Rector of St. Botolph, Bishopsgate, son of the Bishop of Bristol(C); (*e*) Daniel Stephen, who succeeds, VI.

VI. Daniel Stephen, Olivier, b. 16 June 1755, Rector of Clifton, Beds, d. 28 Dec. 1826, m. firstly Margaret Arnold, daur. of the Rev. Henry Arnold, D.D., 30 March 1786; secondly, Susan Enderby, 12 May 1821, who d. 7 June 1830 s.p. By his first marriage with Margaret Arnold he left six children: (*a*) Harriet Suzanne, b. 1788, d. 1790; (*b*) Daniel Josias, who succeeds, VII; (*c*) a son, b. and d. 1790; (*d*) Harriet Elizabeth, b. 1791, d. 1818; (*e*) Anna Awdry, b. 1792, m. in 1808 the Rev. Richard Etough, Rector of Claydon, Suffolk; (*f*) Henry Stephen, who will follow, VII.

VII. Daniel Josias Olivier, b. in 1789, d. 1858, m. in 1815 Sarah Elizabeth Chambers, and had twelve children, of whom only three survived: (*a*) John Josias Olivier, b. 1825, father of Major W. Olivier, R.A.; (*b*) Ellen, b. 1829; (*c*) Frances, b. 1834.

VII. Henry Stephen Olivier, of Potterne Manor, J.P., High Sheriff, 1843, d. 1866, m. 11 Dec. 1823 Mary Milligen, second daur. of Rear Admiral Sir Richard Dacres, G.C.B., by whom he left six children : (*a*) Julia, b. 1824 ; (*b*) Henry Arnold, who follows, VIII ; (*c*) Mary Ann, b. 1827 ; (*d*) Mary Harriet, b. 1829 ; (*e*) Dacres, b. 1831 ; (*f*) Alfred, b. 1833.

VIII. The Rev. Henry Arnold Olivier, b. 18 Feb. 1826, Rector of Poulshott, Wilts ; of Shapley Hill, Winchfield, Hants ; Fellow of the Huguenot Society of London. M. Anne Elizabeth, who d. in 1912, youngest daur. of the late Dr. Arnould, of Whitecross, Wallingford, Berks, and d. in 1912, leaving six daughters and four sons, of whom : (*a*) Henry Dacres, who succeeds, IX ; (*b*) Sydney Haldane, b. 1859, cr. Baron Olivier, 1824 ; (*c*) Henry Arnould, b. 9 Sept. 1861, m. 16 Ap. 1913 Margaret Barclay, daur. of Sir William Barclay Peat, Bart. ; (*d*) The Rev. Gerald Keir Olivier, Rector of Addington, Winslow, Bucks.

IX. Henry Dacres Olivier, b. 22 Oct. 1850, Lieut.-Colonel R.E., of Shapley Hill, Winchfield, Hants.

NOTES.

(A) The family of de Day intermarried twice with the Mirassor family. Daniel Day, apothecary, of Pau, m. in 1629 Catherine de Mirassor, daur. of Jean de Mirassor, greffier, and Jeanne de Tisnées, sister of Jeremie de Mirassor, avocat. Jérémie de Mirassor m. Jacquemine de Balagué, 6 Sept. 1625, at Pau.

Daniel de Day, who m. Suzanne Mirassor, was son of the Daniel de Day above and of Catherine Mirassor. Besides Anne de Day, wife of Jourdain Olivier, there were four other children : (i) Daniel, Conseiller du parlement de Navarre in 1689 ; (ii) Jerome, refugee in Amsterdam ; (iii) a son, b. 1663 at Pau ; (iv) a son, b. 1664, Ensign in Caillemottes Regiment in Ireland.

(B) Jacques Massé, a diamond merchant, was b. in 1690, son of Jacob or Jacques Massé, of Chateaudun, and of Suzanne Lancement, daur. of Pierre Lancement, sr. de Pinprenant. His brother, Jean-Baptiste Massé, b. in 1687, was miniature painter to King Louis XV of France. Jacques Massé, of St. Peter le Poor parish, m. in London at the Fr. Ch. of St. Martin Orgars, 21 July 1720, Marie Magdeleine Berchère, daur. of Jacques Louis Berchère, who was the son of Louis Berchère and Madeleine Loyseau, of Paris. Jacques Louis Berchère was a merchant jeweller and banker of Paris, and afterwards of Broad Street, London, and m. 15 Aug. 1700 at St. Martin Ongars, Magdalen Regnier, a widow ; he was then a widower. He was buried in the church of St. Helen's, Bishopsgate, beneath a black marble slab on which are engraved his wife's Arms.

Some portraits of the Olivier family passed into the possession of the Conybeare family.

Miniatures by J. B. Massé, in the possession of Lieut-Col. H. D. Olivier. (Descriptions written on paper on the backs by the Painter) :—

1. No inscription. This is in all probability his grandfather, Eliezard Massé, merchant jeweller at Chateaudun.

2. " Portrait de mon ilustre (*sic*) pere, honorable homme Jacob Massé, orfevre jouaillier a Paris, aussi aimable qu'il etoit respectable a tous egard, fils d'honorable homme Eliezard Massé, marchand orfevre a Chateaudun et . . . . . Bruneau, ses pere et mere. Peint avec zele par son fils J. B. Massé."

3. " Portrait de ma charmante mere Damoiselle Suzanne Lancement aussi bien faisante et noble dans tous ses procedes qu'elle etoit en origine, femme bien aimee de Jacob Massé, et fille de Pierre Lancement, Sieur de Pinprenant, peint avec l'amour le plus respectueux et le plus tendre par son fils J. B. Massé." Buff gloves, stone green bodice, black muff.

4. " Portrait de mon tres respectable, bienfaisant, bon ami, bon frere Etienne."

5. " Portrait de ma tres chere sœur Marie Anne Massé, douee par la divine Providence de toutes les graces et les charmes qui ont . . . droit de plaire dans la societe, mais a laquelle les bienfaits sont totallement inutile etant . . . malheureusement par un gout de singularite qui l'a retenue dans la retraite la plus austere sans que les peines les plus vives de ma part puissent l'en arracher."

6. " Portrait de mon bien aime Frere Jacques Massé, mon camarade des la plus tendre enfance, ayant l'air des plus grave et l'ame gaye, mais cependant prenant autant de plaisir a amasser des Richesses qu'il estimoit beaucoup au dessus de leur valeur que j'en ay toujours goute a lui repandre dans les occasions . . . ou de . . . agrements."

7. " Portrait de Marie Madeleine Berchère. Il me fit autant d'honneur dans le tems qu'on en peut attendre de ses sortes de production, moyennant le secours de la tres spirituelle Me Godfrey, elle l'aimoit de tout son cœur, l'avoit beaucoup vue a Londre (*sic*) et elle . . . si bien sur la noblesse de ses sentimens et de son maintien . . . et de ses descriptions. Elle me le . . . beaucoup mieux que ce mechant portrait qu'on m'avoit envoye."

8. " Portrait de mon tres aime Pierre Massé, brave, tray (*sic*) simple, loyal, . . . sans aucune sorte d'artifice, aimant sa famille et ses amis."

9. " Portrait de ma belle sœur Massé qui eut le bonheur de plaire par la douceur de son . . . a son epoux, ses enfans, et a tous ses amis."

10. " Jean Baptiste Massé. Il n'a plus actuellement qu'un ombre obscur et fletri de ce portrait qu'il n'a peine se faire peindre sous ses yeux que pour completter (*sic*) la collection de son aimable belle sœur d'apres son Portrait fait en son jeune age que l'on trouvoit ressemblable, Tel est le sort de notre hu(manite)."

11. " Je retrouve avec plaisir ces portraits de Massé et de son epouse que je . . . les traits si fidelles (*sic*) des bons amis qui font actuellement les charmes de ma vie qui . . . asse vous exprimer la douleur que je ressens de mes peines quoique tres volontairement."

PALAIRET

I. Antoine Palairet, b. circ. 1475, d. before 1542, m. Florite Tabaries, by whom he had two sons: (*a*) Jean, (*b*) Antoine. They divided their father's property in 1542.

II. Antoine Palayret m. before 1542 Thomasse Dauthrelle and left: (*a*) Jean, who follows, III; (*b*) Antoine, m. in 1574 Marguerite Vernèze.

III. Jean Palayret m. circ. 1560 Marguerite Vidalet and left Denis, IV.

IV. Denis Palayret, m. at Montauban in 1581 Jeanne Delhoste, and left by her Jean, V.

V. Jean Palayret, b. at Montauban 1583, m. there in 1611 Anne de Mourets, by whom he had: (*a*) Pierre, who succeeds, VI; (*b*) Marie, b. 1616; (*c*) Marthe, b. 1619; (*d*) Suzanne, b. 1620; (*e*) another Pierre, b. 1623; (*f*) Daniel, b. 1627; (*g*) Anne, b. 1629; (*h*) Anne, b. 1634; (*i*) Marie, b. 1637.

VI. Pierre Palayret, b. 1613 at Montauban, m. in 1642 Marie de Costes, d. before 1663, leaving: (*a*) Valentia, b. at Montauban, 1643; (*b*) Abel, b. at Montauban, 1645, m. and had a son, Jean Palayret, who m. Catherine Rabosc and had a son, Abel Palayret, b. at Hanau in 1689; (*c*) Judith, b. at Montauban, 1650, m. 1672, Elie Durade, d. s.p. (Elie Durade m., secondly, Catherine Dufoure, and had a son, Abel Durade, b. at Montauban in 1685. Elie Durade left France, and is found in Berlin in 1700.) (*d*) David, b. at Montauban, 1651; (*e*) Dominique, who succeeds, VII.

VII. Dominique Palairet, b. at Montauban 1654, m. in 1679 Marie Lacaze (? daur. of Blaise Lacaze and Isabeau Teissédre, b. at Montauban 1658), by whom he left six children: (*a*) Marie, b. at Montauban 1680, m. Pierre Coustet in 1713, and left a daur., Marie Anne Coustet (who m. Mr. du Croissi); (*b*) Elie, b. at Montauban in 1683, went to Amsterdam, 1701, thence to the Hague and to Rotterdam in 1720, where he d. in 1749. He m.

firstly, Marie Pinset, by whom he had: (i) Jeanne, b. at the Hague, 1705, d. in London, 1789; (ii) Isaac Elie, b. in London, in St. Anne's Parish, bapt. 19 Dec. 1708 (his godmother was Suzanne Ramsey), d. before 1719; (iii) Elie Auguste, b. at the Hague in 1711, d. there 1712. Elie Palairet m. secondly, at the Hague in 1714, Marie Emilie Du Chaine (b. at the Hague in 1692, d. in Rotterdam, 1759), and left by her seventeen more children, one of whom, the Rev. Elie Palairet (iv), was minister at Aardenburg, Tournai and Greenwich: he was b. at the Hague in 1714 and d. in London, 1765. He m. firstly, in 1742, Jeanne Bellesaigne, who was b. at Amsterdam in 1721, d. before 1765 (by whom he left a daur., Jeanne Emilie, b. at Aardenburg in 1744). The Rev. Elie Palairet m. secondly, Marguerite Le Febure, who d. s.p. in London, 1804. (v) Abraham Palairet, brother of the Rev. Elie Palairet and second child of Elie Palairet and of Marie Emilie Du Chaine, Governor and Recorder of Dieren for the Prince of Orange, b. 1715 at the Hague, d. 1776 at Dieren, m. firstly Marie Palairet, his cousin, daur. of his uncle, Dominique Palairet and Marie Anne Housel, and secondly Barbara Agnes Rouse (b. at Deventer in 1727, d. at Dieren in 1818), by whom he left: A, Wilhelmina Carolina, god-daughter of the Prince of Orange and Princess Caroline, b. at Ellecom in 1753, d. at Doesburg in 1807. She m. firstly, in 1788, the Rev. Wilhelmus Hooglandt, who was born at Barneveldt, 1756, d. at Spankeren, 1791. By this marriage she left a daur., Christina Elizabeth Hooglandt, b. at Spankeren in 1788, d. at Oosterbeck in 1824. She m. firstly, in 1815, Dr. John Aleid Nijhoff (b. at Arnheim 1791, d. there 1819), and secondly, in 1821, the Rev. Derk Jacob Wolterbeck (b. 1791, d. 1840). Wilhelmina Carolina Palairet m. secondly, in 1800, Gerhardus Christoffer Fels, who d. at Kampen in 1828. B, Elias Emilius Palairet, second child of Abraham Elie Palairet above, was b. at Ellecom in 1755, d. at Dieren in 1782. C, Maria Louis, god-daughter of the Princess Dowager of Orange, b. at Ellecom, 1757, d. at Rhynberg, 1834, m. Jan Reinier ten Behen Wentholt (b. at Arnheim in 1744). D, Christina Elizabeth, b. at Ellecom, 1758, d. at Spankeren, 1824. E, Maria Emilia, b. at Ellecom, 1761, d. at Leidschendam, 1848, m. 1785, at Ellecom,

Karel Theodoor Godfrid Scheidt. F, Susanna Gertruyd, b. at Ellecom, 1762, d. at Xanten, 1842. G, Wilhelmina, god-daughter of the Prince of Orange, b. at Ellecom, 1765, d. at Dieren in 1856, m. Jan Daniel Hooglandt in 1791, merchant, of Amsterdam (b. at Barneveldt, 1762, d. at Amsterdam, 1817), younger brother of the Rev. Wilhelmus Hooglandt, husband of Wilhelmina Carolina Palairet, and had issue, H, William Frederick Rouse Palairet, Land Agent and Recorder of Dieren, b. at Ellecom in 1768, m. Johanna Arnolda Rasch in 1798 (she was b. near Doesberg in 1772). (vi) Marie Emilie, b. at the Hague in 1717, m. Marcus Symons. (vii) Emilie, b. at the Hague in 1718, d. in London in 1794, m. in 1760 Peter Hervé, by whom she left a son, Pierre Daniel, who also left by his wife Margaret two sons, Pierre and Henri. (viii) Isaac Elie Palairet, b. at the Hague in 1719, d. at Amsterdam in 1760, m. in 1742, firstly, Dorothea Boom, by whom he had three sons: A, Elie, b. at Breda, 1743, d. at Amsterdam, 1745; B, Isaac Elie, b. at Amsterdam, 1744, d. there 1748; C, Theodore, b. at Amsterdam, 1747, d. there 1802. Theodore Palairet m. firstly, 1777, Maria Van Atten (née Akker), secondly, 1798, Catherine Elizabeth Kleynenberg. Isaac Elie Palairet, m. secondly, in 1750, Johanna Biben, and had by her three children: D, Marie Emilie, b. at Amsterdam, 1752, d. there 1788; E, Clara, b. at Amsterdam 1755, d. 1756; F, Jean Jacques, merchant, of Amsterdam, b. there in 1759, m. in 1785 Maria Catherina Loofs, and had two children, Petronella Palairet, b. at Amsterdam, 1787, m. G. Verschuur, and Isaac Elie Palairet, b. at Amsterdam 1789, d. 1790. (ix) Jacob Elie, b. at Rotterdam, 1720, d. before 1730; (x) Jeanne Emilie, b. at Rotterdam, 1722; (xi) Marie Marguerite, b. (*idem*) 1723; (xii) Marie Anne, b. (*idem*) 1724, d. in London 1759; (xiii) Marguerite Emilie, b. (*idem*) 1724, d. there 1757; (xiv) Judith Emilie, b. (*idem*) 1727, m. in 1756 Johannes Adrianus Simons (b. 1728 at the Hague, d. in 1771 at Rosendaal; (xv) Elizabeth Emilie, b. 1728; (xvi) Charlotte Emilie, b. (*idem*) 1729, d. at the Hague 1731; (xvii) Jacob Elie, b. (*idem*) 1730, d. 1731; (xviii) Jacob Elie, b. (*idem*) 1731; (xix) Jean Jacob, b. (*idem*) 1733, m. in 1785 Marie Catherine Lesp; (xx) Marie Emilie, b. (*idem*) 1735, d. there 1802.

(*c*) Dominique (son of Dominique Palairet (VII) and Marie Lacaze), wine merchant, was b. at Montauban, d. at the Hague in 1751. M. firstly, at the Hague, in 1707, Marianne Housel (b. at Villers-le-Bel), and left by her five children: (i) Marie Anne, b. at the Hague in 1708, d. before 1791, who m. firstly in 1741, at the Hague, Dr. Pieter Paupié (b. at Tonnerre in Burgundy, and who d. before 1755), and secondly, at Rotterdam in 1755, Pierre Rossignol, of Paris (b. 1716, d. before 1791), and left issue; (ii) Dominique, b. at the Hague 1710, d. 1710; (iii) Denise, b. at the Hague 1711, d. there in 1741; (iv) Marie, b. at the Hague 1713, d. s.p. there 1743. She m. in 1739, Abraham Elie Palairet, son of Elie Palairet and Marie Emilie Du Chaine (VII), b. at the Hague in 1715, d. at Dieren in 1776; (v) Dominique, b. at the Hague and d. there in 1715. Dominique Palairet m. secondly, in 1717, at the Hague, Marie Marguerite de Monceaux (b. at the Hague, d. there 1736), and left by her seven more children: (vi) Charles, b. at the Hague 1718, went to Bordeaux in 1737; (vii) Marie Marguerite, b. at the Hague in 1720, d. before 1775; (viii) Dominique, b. at the Hague in 1721, d. there in 1738; (ix) Emilie Marguerite, b. at the Hague in 1723, d. before 1775, m. in 1744 Dirk Boom, and left issue; (x) Jean François, a wine merchant at the Hague, b. at the Hague in 1728, d. at Voorburg in 1805. M. Marghereta Buschmann (b. at Gellicum, d. at the Hague in 1765, by whom he had four children (Dominique, a wine merchant at the Hague, b. there 1757, m. Maria Gerard Schmolck; Godefrid, b. at the Hague in 1759, d. after 1805; Anna Gurtruid, b. at the Hague in 1761, d. same year; also a child which d. unbaptised, buried at the Hague in 1762); (xi) Louise Charlotte, b. in 1731 at the Hague, d. before 1775; (xii) Elizabeth, b. at the Hague in 1733, d. there 1736.

(*d*) Pierre Palairet (third son of Dominique and Marie Lacaze), b. at Montauban in 1692, d. in London 1776, m. a wife whose name is not known and had two sons: (i) Dominique, who d. at Greenwich in 1768, m. at Falmouth in 1752, Mary Gregor, and had two daughters, the eldest of whom, Susanna Elizabeth, Palairet, was b. at Falmouth in 1753, d. in London in 1786, having m.

Samuel Thorpe. The second daur., Mary Gregor Palairet, was b. at Falmouth in 1756. (ii) John, who d. after 1809, m. Martha Frances Vias (b. 1721, d. 1814).

(*e*) John (fourth son of Dominique Palairet and Marie Lacaze) was the ancestor of the English Branch, VIII.

(*f*) David (fifth son of Dominique Palairet and Marie Lacaze), b. at Amsterdam 1699, d. s.p. at Southampton in 1778, having married twice, firstly in 1732, Suzanne Daubuz (b. before 1710, d. at Southampton, 1765), and, secondly, in 1766, Elizabeth Despaignol (b. before 1745, d. at Bath, 1787).

VIII. John Palairet, Agent in London for the Dutch States-General, Tutor to the children of George II, b. at Montauban in 1697, d. in London, 1774. M. firstly, in 1727, Elizabeth Dorsan, by which marriage he had: (*a*) Elizabeth, b. in London, 1731, d. after 1790, m. Thomas Burgess in 1775; (*b*) Elias John, who follows, IX; (*c*) Anne, b. in London, 1734, d. in London in 1773, m. Anthony Parquot (b. in London 1744, d. 1774), and had John Peter, Anthoine Jacques, and Elizabeth-Anne Parquot. John Palairet m. secondly, Marthe Dorrée (b. at Rotterdam in 1712, d. in London 1766), by whom he had five more children: (*d*) Suzanne, b. at Rotterdam in 1738, d. in London in 1809; (*e*) David, also b. in Rotterdam, in 1739, d. in London 1789; (*f*) Suzanne Marianne, b. in London 9 July 1744, bapt. at the Fr. Ch. of the Savoy 25 July, d. in London 1770; (*g*) Emilie, born 1 Dec. 1749, bapt. at the Savoy Fr. Ch. 24 Dec., d. in London in 1766; (*h*) Henri, b. 9 March 1752, bapt. 29th at the Savoy Fr. Ch. His godparents were Henry Egerton and Abraham Palairet. D. in London, 1756.

IX. Elias John Palairet, son of John Palairet by his first marriage with Elizabeth Dorsan, was b. in London in 1734, d. in Barbadoes in 1773. M. in 1764, Ellen Boranskill (b. 1738, d. 1824), and left a son, John Gwalter, who succeeds, X.

X. John Gwalter Palairet, b. in London 1765, d. at Reading in 1824, m. in 1795 Catherine Pistor (b. 1774, d. at

Clifton in 1854), by whom he had six children: (*a*) John Gwalter, b. at Reading in 1797, d. at Christchurch, New Zealand, in 1878. M. in 1836 Jane Bateman, by whom he had four children: (i) Gwalter Palairet, b. at Bristol, 1837, m. 1868 Emma Little (b. 19 Feb. 1849), by whom he had seven children, as follows: A, Mary, b. in 1869, m. in 1895 William Branson, and has issue: Norman Palairet Branson, b. at Gisburne, N.Z., in 1896; Mary Vivienne, b. at Wharikui, N.Z., in 1898; Mabel Palairet Branson, b. at Kaiti, N.Z., in 1899, and Ada Lissel Branson, b. at Gisburne, N.Z., in 1909. B, John Gwalter, b. in 1870, m. in 1899 Alice Sandes (b. 4 Jan. 1872), and has issue: Norah, b. in 1900. C, Charles Rowland, b. 1872, m. in 1903, Louise Beszant (b. in 1875), and has issue: Rowland Gwalter Wilbur Palairet, b. 1904, at Clifton, and Mary Winifred Palairet, b. 1908 at Clifton. D, Frederick Bateman, b. in 1874, m. in 1906 Lena Noble-Campbell (b. 8 Dec. 1878), and has issue: Allan Frederick Gwalter Palairet, b. 16 June 1910, and Gordon Hamilton Palairet, b. 9 Jan. 1912. E, Ellen, b. 1875, d. 1901. F, Arthur Henry, b. 1877, m. in 1907 Nellie McVay (b. 3 May 1879), and has issue: Joan Barbara, b. 1908, at Auckland, N.Z., and John Denkir, b. 1909 at Napier, N.Z. G, Ada Clara, b. in 1879, m. 1899, Mainland Lewis Mouat Foster, b. 1 Feb. 1870, and has issue.

(ii) Colthurst Palairet, second son of John Gwalter Palairet and Jane Bateman, b. 1838, d. 1917 at Christchurch, N.Z. M. in 1870, Louisa Slater (b. 1841, d. 1909), by whom he had three children: Clara Jane, b. 1871, d. 1871; Alice Mary, b. 1874, m. in 1900; Wilfrid Godfrey (b. 1871); Ethel Louisa, b. 1879, m. Thomas Henry Jackson (b. Nov. 1861, d. July 1916). (iii) Rowland Palairet, third son of John Gwalter Palairet and Jane Bateman, b. 1840 at Bath, d. 1909 at Westcliffe-on-Sea. M. 1899, Esther Davenport. (iv) Ellen Palairet, b. 1843, m. 1868 Henry Slater (b. 4 Aug. 1839), and left issue.

(*b*) Mary Ellen, b. 1802, d. at Bath 1898; (*c*) Charles, b. 1804, d. at Norton St. Philip, 1890, Clerk in Holy Orders; (*d*) Richard Thomas, b. 1805, d. at Bath, 1890, Clerk in Holy Orders, m. Emily Cameron (b. 1816, d. 1882); (*e*) Septimus Henry, who succeeds, XI; (*f*) Katherine Elizabeth, b. 1808, d. 1883, m. 1837 the Rev. Thomas Girardot, by whom she had ten children. (See Girardot Pedigree, to be published later.)

XI. Septimus Henry Palairet, b. 1807, d. at Edinburgh, 1854. Married, firstly, in 1843, Mary Ann Hamilton (b. in London, 1822, d. in Philadelphia, 1851), by whom he had seven children: (*a*) Mary Ann, b. at Stanmore, 1844, m. 1863, Adolphus Halkett Versturme, by which marriage she had twelve children (Versturme-Bunbury); (*b*) Henry Hamilton, b. at Bradford-on-Avon, 1845, m. firstly in 1869, Elizabeth Anne Bigg (b. 1844, at Cattistock), by whom he had five children: (i) Lionel Charles Hamilton, b. 1870 at Grange-over-Sands, m. 1894 Caroline Mabel Laverton (b. 1871, at Westbury), and had Evelyn Mabel Hamilton (b. 1895 at Kingston, Taunton), and Henry Edward Hamilton (b. 1896 at Hestercombe, Taunton); (ii) Richard Cameron North, b. 1871, at Grange-over-Sands, m. 1899, Emily Katherine Scobell (b. 1875), by whom he has issue: Edward John Palairet, b. 1901 at Taunton; Richard Scobell Palairet, b. 1903 at Taunton; Elizabeth Palairet, b. 1908 in London, and Cyril Hamilton Palairet, b. 1915 at Budleigh Salterton, Devon. (iii) Evelyn Mary Kuhn, b. 1872, at Grange over-Sands. (iv) Edith Veronica, b. 1874, at Cattistock, m. 1913, Edward Hargrave Booth (b. in Jersey, 1856). (v) Rose Eleanor, b. 1879 at Holcombe, Devon, d. 1880 at Cattistock.

Henry Hamilton Palairet m. secondly, in 1882, Charlotte Ellen Rooke (b. 1854).

(*c*) Laura Katherine, b. at Bradford-on-Avon, 1846; (*d*) Charles Harvey, who succeeds, XII; (*e*) Eleanor, b. at Bradford-on-Avon, 1848, d. at Hove, 1913, m. firstly, in 1867, Henry Hodges, of Bolney Court, co. Oxford, and secondly, in 1911, the Hon. James Terence Fitzmaurice. (*f*) Edith, b. at Bradford-on-Avon, 1849, m. in 1871 Sanford George Treweeke Scobell (b. 1839, d. at Ashchurch, 1912), by which marriage she left issue, amongst whom Emily Katharine Scobell, wife of Richard Cameron North Palairet. (*g*) Herman, b. at Philadelphia, 1851, d. there 1851.

Septimus Henry Palairet m. secondly, in 1853, Lydia Bradney (b. at Bath, 1833, d. 1887).

XII. Charles Harvey Palairet, b. at Bradford-on-Avon in 1847, d. in London 1905, m. firstly, at St. Mary's, Dymock, 19 Aug. 1873, Emily Henry (b. 13 Ap. 1851, at Hatfield, Ledbury, d. at Berkeley 14 June 1884), by whom he left three children: (*a*) Charles Harvey, b. and d. at Berkeley, 1875; (*b*) Charles Andrew Hamilton, b. at Berkeley in 1877, m. in 1915 Mabel Lilias Jean Calvert, by whom he has issue: (i) John Hamilton Palairet, b. at Ledbury 23 Jan. 1917; (*c*) Charles Michael Palairet, b. at Berkeley 1882, m. 1915, Mary de Vere Studd, by whom he has issue: (i) Anne Mary Celestine, b. at Paris 14 Nov. 1916.

Charles Harvey Palairet, above, XII, m. secondly, in 1888, Nora Hamilton Martin, by whom he had issue: (*d*) Margaret Nancie Hamilton Palairet, b. in London, 1892.

NOTES.

I am indebted to the Palairet family for this pedigree, who kindly allowed me to reprint it.

Pierre Palairet, marchand à Montauban, né de parents Nouveaux Convertis, demande permission de vendre une maison, 1721 (Serée T.T., 187 bis).

Dominique Palairet, marchand à Montauban, Nouveau Converti, demande permission de vendre une proprieté à Négrepelisse, 1725 (Serée T.T., 187 bis).

John Palairet, of Pall Mall, St. James, gent. Roll of Citizens, Westminster, 1749 (B. Museum, 884, i, 24). He had a correspondence with Count Bentinck, 1750-1758, 1761 (Egerton MSS., No. 1727, 1729, 1741).

The earlier portraits of the family were destroyed by a fire in New Zealand. A copy of a portrait by Romney, of John Gwalter Palairet, X (1765-1824) exists.

PORTALÉS

Arms: De gueules, à une tour maconnée de sable, sur une colline verte: acc. de 2 lions, rampant et affrontés, d'arg.: à un chef d'arg: une arbre verte entre 2 etoiles de gueules.

I. Charles de Portalés, of Vigan in the Cevennes (son of Etienne de Portalés, notaire), was a surgeon of that town. A note in the archives of Vigan (G.G. 9) reports his removal from the post of surgeon to the hospital in Sept. 1683, on account of being a Protestant, all professions being forbidden to those of the R.P.R. at that date. He was, however, reinstated shortly afterwards, probably because no other could be found, the Roman Catholic Seguin having left the country. He fled from Vigan shortly before or after 1685, having m. Marguerite Villaret. Their two young sons are said, from family documents, to have been "conveyed by a faithful domestic concealed in the panniers of an ass to Holland, where they were educated by a relation and entered the service of the Prince of Orange." They left the service when the French regiments were disbanded. Charles de Portalés was employed by Queen Anne in carrying assistance to the Cevenol Army during the insurrection of 1705, and was connected with the Prophetic movement in England, being a friend of Mazel and Elie Marion. Charles de Portalés and his wife Marguerite Villaret left: (*a*) Charles, who succeeds, II; (*b*) Jacques; (*c*) a daur. who is mentioned in the will of her brother Charles as living in France in 1755 and to whom he leaves 1,000 livres tournois (will proved 21 Ap. 1773).

Jacques de Portalés (*b*) above d. in London 17 Sept. 1765. His will (113 Tyndall) was pr. 3 March 1766: he is described as of Tothill Fields, Westminster, gent., and made his will 27 June 1764. His niece, Frances Belchier, daughter of his brother Charles, was sole executrix. Mary Potter, sp., of the parish of St. Edmund the King, signed as witness, and affirmed personal knowledge of James Portalés; pr. by Frances Belchier, wife of William Belchier, Esq. His wife, Mary Portalés, d. in 1766, and letters of admon. were granted to Frances Belchier, above, 9 June 1766, niece and executrix named in the will of James Portalés. She was living at the time of her death in the parish of St. John the Evangelist, Westr., and was m. at St. Mary Magdalen, Fish St., London, 11 July 1711, née Devaulx.

II. Charles de Portalés was b. 9 Ap. 1676 at Vigan, and d. 30 Nov. 1764. He was Secretary to the Marquis de Miremont, and connected with the Prophetic movement in London. He afterwards lived for many years in Hatton Garden, in the house of Francis Moult, who had adopted the two daughters of Jean Moult his brother (who m. Marguerite Ivens). Charles de Portalés m. Mary Moult, one of these daughters, at St. Mary, Islington (by licence), 1 May 1714. She was born in Aug. 1690, and d. 7 Nov. 1726 at Hatton Garden.(A) By his marriage with Mary Moult he left: (*a*) Margueritte, b. 26 Jan. 1715, d. 26 May 1778, m. firstly in 1728 Mr. Morgan, nephew of the Earl of Lichfield, d. s.p.; secondly, Mr. Wynantz, of Dantzig, who d. in 1774. Their posterity is reported hereafter. (*b*) Mary, b. 4 Sept. 1716, d. 3 Aug. 1717; (*c*) Mary, b. 8 Feb. 1718, d. 22 Feb. 1718; (*d*) Frances, b. 2 Sept. 1719, d. 1812, m. William Belchier, a banker, M.P. for Southwark (1747-1761), d. s.p. in 1772 in Seymour Street; (*e*) a boy, d. at birth 15 Feb. 1721; (*f*) Lucy, b. 7 Feb. 1725, d. 29 July 1725; (*g*) Francis Moult, b. 17 June 1726, d. 12 Nov. 1726; (*h*) Charlotte, b. 25 Sept. 1720, d. 25 Nov. 1725.

The posterity of Mr. Wynantz and Margueritte de Portalés is here given to shew the descent of portraits and heirlooms.

Adelgunda Margueretta Wynantz, daur. of Mr. Wynantz and Margueritte de Portalés was b. 27 Dec. 1738, d. in 1768 at the birth of her son William, at her house at Kensington Gravel Pits. She m. the Rev. Richard Dodd, Rector of Cawley, Bucks, son of the Rev. W. Dodd, of Bourne, Lincs. They had a son, William, d. s.p., and a daur., Frances Margueritta Dodd, b. 1767, d. 1834, who m. William Golightly, of Ham, Surrey, b. 1748, d. 20 May

1810. Their daur., Frances Margaret Golightly, b. 1804, d. Ap. 1845 in India, m. 22 Ap. 1834, Colonel George Templar Graham, Bengal Artillery, of Cossington, Somerset, b. 1 Ap. 1808, d. 1 Aug. 1870; D.L. and J.P. for Somerset. They left a daur., Sarah Helen Margaret Graham, b. 10 Oct. 1835, d. 7 July 1916, m. Tristram Edward Kennedy 4 Sept. 1862 (b. 27 June 1805, d. 20 Nov. 1885), of Henrietta Street, Dublin, M.P. for Co. Louth, son of the Rev. John Pitt Kennedy, Rector of Donagh, co. Donegal, and of Belteagh, co. Derry. They left seven children: (*a*) Horace Graham Kennedy, b. 6 Sept. 1863, who m. Laura Henry, daur. of William Henry, of Dublin; (*b*) George Portalés, d. an infant; (*c*) Tristram Edward Whiteside Kennedy, b. 20 Oct. 1866, m. Bessie . . . .(?); (*d*) Pitt Shadwell Portalés Kennedy, b. 6 May 1868, d. unmarried 11 Feb. 1911; (*e*) Francis Malcolm Evory Kennedy, b. 12 Nov. 1869, m. Lucy Caroline, daur. of the Rev. Thomas Henry Gregory, in whose possession are the portraits and heirlooms of the de Portalés family; (*f*) Theodora, d. an infant; (*g*) Caroline Mary Dorothea Kennedy, b. 3 Ap. 1880, m. Edward Hugh Edward Stack and had: (i) Thomas Lindsay Stack, b. 24 Nov. 1910; (ii) Tristram Bagot Stack, b. 14 Oct. 1912; (iii) Graham Stack, b. 7 Dec. 1915; (iv) Helen La Vie Stack, b. 25 Aug. 1918.

NOTES.

(A) Charles de Portalés mentions in his will, dated 1755, pr. 21 Ap. 1773 (P.C.C., Simpson 263), that his father, Charles de Portalés was alive at that date, but does not state where. He mentions his sons-in-law, William Belchier and Mr. Wynantz, his dear grandson (Peter Charles Wynantz, b. 6 Jan. 1740 at Bell Yard, "vis-à-vis du Monument près du pont de Londres," d. unmarried) and his grand-daughter, Adelgunda Marogueretta Wynantz, to both of whom he leaves £500. To his daur., Frances Belchier, he leaves an annuity for the use of his brother James de Portalés and his wife, and acquits him of all debts (notes of hand and bonds may be returned). He leaves 1,000 livres tournois to his sister, and mentions his niece Mary Potter, and leaves all his books and papers to Frances Belchier. Pr. 1773.

HUGUENOT PEDIGREES

The following is a list of portraits and relics in possession of Major F. M. E. Kennedy, Fellow of the Huguenot Society:

1. Portrait of Charles de Portalés, b. 9 Ap. 1676, about 37 in. by 30 in., supposed to have been painted by a pupil of Sir Peter Lely, and that the latter touched it up; of a distinguished-looking young, man of about twenty-four.

2. Miniature of Charles Portalés, about 4 in. by $3\frac{1}{2}$ in., black and white, at sixty-three years of age.

3. Pastel portrait of Marguerite Wynantz, eldest daur. of Charles de Portalés, by Hoar, of Bath, 24 in. by 18 in. Colours, white and blue; perfect condition.

4. Oval miniature of the Marquis de Miremont, $2\frac{3}{8}$ in. by $1\frac{7}{8}$ in. Inscription on back as follows: " Le Marquis de Miremont, Armand de Bourbon, Lieut.-General, né le 12 . . . . . 1656 au chat^{u} de la Caze en Languedoc. Mort 12 Feb. 1733 à Londres."

5. Miniature of Mr. Francis Moult, uncle and guardian of Marguerite Moult, who m. Charles Portalés. Size, $1\frac{3}{8}$ in. by $1\frac{1}{8}$ in. An elderly man in full-bottomed wig.

6. Battersea enamel watch, belonging to Charles de Portalés, made by P. and J. Debaufre, of Church Street, Soho. Given to him by his great friend, Nicholas Facio, who was closely connected with the Prophetic movement in England and on the Continent. Facio was born in Basle in 1664, d. at Worcester, 1753. He was associated with the Debaufre brothers in the patent obtained by him for watch-jewelling. The watch is contained in a beautiful English lacquer case, $9\frac{1}{2}$ in. in height, which was evidently made to take it.

7. Silver and mother-of-pearl box, round, $1\frac{5}{8}$ in. across, no hall mark, probably French, which belonged to Marguerite Portalés, and inside a bit of paper inscribed—" Cette boitte pour Francoise Portalés née le 2^{d} Sept^{bre} 1719."

8. Dressing gown belonging to Charles de Portalés, of Persian design and workmanship, hand-woven silk, pale green, shot with silver thread; sprigs of small red flowers.

9. His nightcap, of Persian design and workmanship, very fine cotton material, embroidered in coloured silks in minute chain stitch.

10. Manuscripts: (*a*) Bound volume of " Memoires de

la guerre des Cevennes," pages 1 to 40, apparently dictated by Abraham Mazel and taken down by Charles Portalés and witnessed by Elie Marion, D. G. Fage, J. Daudé, dated " à Londres le 25 Aoust 1708." Signed by Abraham Mazel.

Further lengthy memoires dictated to Charles Portalés by Elie Marion; 168 pages of small writing.

(*b*) Several manuscripts dealing with the Prophetic movement in England and Germany.

(*c*) " Recit abregé des persecutions et oppositions, etc., etc.," in the writing of C. Portalés.

(*d*) His notebook, bound in green parchment, 6¼ in. by 4 in., containing, *inter alia*, records of his marriage, and births and deaths of his children and relations, etc.

(*e*) Various memoranda and journals in Mrs. Belchier's writing.

11. " Edict du Roy Sur la Pacification des troubles de ce Royaume." Rouen, 1576.

12. His Bible, containing records of the births and deaths of his children. Mr. William Belchier's bookplate.

The above are in the possession of Major F. M. E. Kennedy C.B., Fellow of the Huguenot Society of London, to whom I am indebted for most of the pedigree. (See also *The Genealogist*, N.S., Vol. XXII, July, 1905.)

DE RAMBOUILLET

Arms: D'azur, à 3 perdrix de sable, 2 and 1.

I. Antoine de Rambouillet, ec. conseiller secretaire du roi in 1584. He is stated to have been the son of Etienne de Rambouillet, prevôt of Provins(A) (MSS. du Chesne). M. after 1576 Marie Maillart, daur. of Guillaume Maillart, of Orleans, and of Nicole de la Vau. Buried 5 Jan. 1626, in the Cemetery of SS. Pères, leaving five children: (*a*) Jean, avocat en Parlement, conseiller du roi, m. Marie Girard, d. 1627, leaving five children; (*b*) François, living in 1587; (*c*) Antoine, secretaire du roi, 1601, in the place of his father, and resigned his office in 1627, 19 March, in favour of Valentin Conrart; (*d*) Nicolas, who succeeds, II; (*e*) Marie, m. Pierre Tallemant, sr. de Boisneau, secretaire du Roi, a quo, Gédéon Tallemant, and Marie, Marquise de Ruvigny (see Ruvigny, Vol. I).

II. Nicolas de Rambouillet, ec. sgr. du Plessis-Franc, de Lancey, de la Sablière, and other places, b. 26 Dec. 1576. Conseiller secretaire du roi (4 July 1648). D. aged 88, and was buried at Charenton, 22 Sept. 1664. His will, dated 17 March 1660, is sealed with his armorial seal. M. firstly, Catherine Bigot, daur. of Jacques Bigot, sr. de Gournay, and of Catherine Bongars, who d. 1644, aged 45; secondly, Anne Gangnot (dec. 1645), daur. of Pierre Gangnot, sr. de Lauzanne, and of Susanne Martin. By his first marriage to Catherine Bigot he left eleven children: (*a*) Nicolas, ec. sr. du Plessis-Franc, de Lancey, du Tertre, conseiller maitre d'hôtel du roi, (1655-79). M. at Basly, near Caen, by Pierre du Bosc, minister of the Protestant church of Caen, 15 May 1572, Dlle. Anne Le Moutonnier, Dame de St. Julien, in the parish of Grentheville, widow of Gilles de Briqueville,(B) chevalier, Marquis de Colombières. Nicolas de Rambouillet abjured, and d. at Tour, near Bayeux, 7 Ap. 1694, buried in the parish church. He had one son, Nicolas, b. 6 Dec. 1673, who d. before his mother, Anne Le Moutonnier: she d. Feb. 1721, at her manor of Tour; (*b*) Catherine, b. in 1621,

m. in 1637 to Jacques de Monceaux, sgr. de l'Estang et de la Rainville.(c) She was a widow in 1651, and d. after 1664. By this marriage she had (i) Nicolas de Monceaux, ec. sgr. de Lestang (1680), (ii) Catherine de Monceaux, wife, in 1637, of Jacques Bigot, tresorier des guerres. (*c*) Antoine, who succeeds, III ; (*d*) Paul, ec. sgr. du Plessis-Rambouillet, bapt. at Charenton, 7 June 1625, conseiller d'etat (30 March 1658), m. by contract dated 13 March 1657 (Le Cat and Le Semelier, notaires, Paris), Dlle. Françoise Le Coq, daur. of Theodore le Coq, sgr. de Forges, near Ruffec, Angoumois, and sister of Pascal Le Coq de St. Germain, whose wife, Elizabeth de Beringhen, was the sister of the Duchesse de La Force, Suzanne de Beringhen who lived at Sunbury-on-Thames. (Will, Isham, 60.)

Françoise Le Coq, wife of Paul Rambouillet above, was imprisoned in the Convent of Bellechasse in 1685, and expelled from France in 1688 as a determined Protestant. She left four children : (i) Nicolas de Rambouillet, d. before 1667 ; (ii) Theodore de Rambouillet, d. before 1667 ; (iii) Marie de Rambouillet, b. 1662, m. 3 Sept. 1685 to John Temple, son of Sir William Temple, English Ambassador in Paris, and of his wife, Dorothy Osborne. John Temple drowned himself in the Thames near London Bridge, 18 Ap. 1689. His widow, Marie de Rambouillet, d. Sept. 1711. Their eldest daur., Elizabeth Temple, d. 1 May 1772, and was buried in the south cloister, Westminster Abbey (Westminster Abbey Reg.). The marriage licence of John Temple (Vic. Gen. 1685) gives : "John Temple, Esq., of Westminster, bach., 35, to Mlle. du Plessis-Rambouillet of Paris. Anywhere in France." (*e*) Anne, bapt. 18 May 1626, was living in 1679 ; (*f*) Jean Henri de Rambouillet, ec. sgr. de Chavanes, bapt. 6 Aug. 1627, a captain in the regiment de Piedmont, killed at Barcelona 23 Ap. 1652, aged 25 ; (*g*) Alexandre, ec. sgr. de Prèvigny, bapt. at Charenton 31 Jan. 1629, a captain in the regiment of Picardy, killed in August 1667 at Lille ; (*h*) Angelique, bapt. 18 May 1630, d. young ; (*i*) Louis, bapt. 20 Sept. 1631, d. 1633 ; (*j*) Pierre, ec. sgr. de Lancey, bapt. in the chapel of the Dutch Embassy, 26 Aug. 1635, m. by contract dated 28 Jan. 1673 (Bouret, notaire, Paris), Dlle. Anne Bourdin, daur. of Pierre Bourdin, ec. sgr. de Pierre-Blanche and de Rongères, secretaire du Roi, and of Madeleine d'Azèmar ; living in 1679. Anne Bourdin abjured, and was living a widow in 1696, when she registered her Arms in the Armorial General : " D'azur, à 3 perdrix d'argent." Pierre and Anne de Rambouillet had four children : (i) Elizabeth, bapt. 23 May 1671 ; (ii) Charles, bapt. at St. Nicolas des Champs, 22 Dec. 1673, and had for godfather, Jacques de Monceaux, ec. sgr. d'Avène, and for godmother Eliz. de Rambouillet, wife of Gédéon Tallemant, ec. sgr. de Réaux ; (iii) Pierre de Rambouillet, bapt. 4 Aug. 1677, d. 1678 ; (iv) Madeleine de Rambouillet, bapt. 15 Jan. 1675 ; (*k*) Elizabeth, b. 6 May 1632, m. at Charenton, 14 Jan. 1646, to Gédéon Tallemant de Réaux, who d. 10 Nov. 1692, buried 12 Nov. in the Cemetery of St. Joseph. She registered her arms in 1696, the same as Anne Bourdin, above.

III. Antoine de Rambouillet, ec. sgr. de la Sablière et du Plessis, b. at Paris 17 June 1624, became conseiller et secretaire du Roi (17 Oct. 1677) in place of his brother Paul. M. at Charenton, 15 March 1654, Marguerite Hessein, daur. of Gilbert Hessein, conseiller, maitre-d'hotel du roi, and of Marguerite Menjot (marr. contract dated 20 Feb. 1654). He made his will 13 Ap. and d. 3 May at Paris, 1679 ; his wife d. 6 Jan. 1693. Their children were : (*a*) Anne, bapt. at Charenton, 14 March 1655, m. in the Temple at Charenton, 11 Dec. 1672, to Jacques Muysson, sgr. du Toillon, conseiller au Parlement de Paris.(E) She refused to abjure and was confined in the Convent of the Miramiones in 1685. She escaped to Holland with her husband and children, and d. at the Hague 11 Ap. 1714 (Will P.C.C., London). (*b*) Nicolas, who succeeds, (IV) ; (*c*) Marguerite, bapt. at Charenton 19 Jan. 1658, m. firstly at Charenton, 10 May 1678, Guillaume Scott, sgr. de la Mesangère, cons. au Parl. at Rouen, son of Guillaume Scott, " Baronet hereditaire d'Angleterre," and of Dame Catherine Fortry (Contrat de mariage, Bouret, notaire, Paris) ; secondly, Charles de Nocé, sgr. de Fontenay-la-Chapelle, premier gent. du Duc d'Orléans. She registered her Arms in 1696 : " D'azur à 3 pigeons d'or," and d. in Paris 30 Nov. 1714 ; her husband, Charles de Nocé, d. at St. Germains-en-Laye, 27 June 1739, aged 75.

IV. Nicolas de Rambouillet, ec. sgr. de la Sablière, du Plessis, du Tertre, de la Touche, baron de Lancey, etc., in the Beauce, was bapt. at Charenton, 10 Feb. 1656. M. at Charenton, 20 July 1679 (Contrat, Bouret, notaire, Paris), Dlle. Louise Madeleine Henry,(F) daur. of Jacques Henry, sgr. des Cheusses, Coudun, la Leu, and la Jarrie, and of his wife Renée de Lauzeré. He was confined in the Bastille, 12 Jan. 1686, but was released and went to Copenhagen with his wife and a daur., Marie-Henriette. Councillor of State to the King of Denmark in 1698. In 1703 he went to England, and was a Director of the French Hospital, 1718-1720. The King granted him a pension of £150. His will is dated 8 May 1717, and was proved, with codicil, by his widow 3 Feb. 1735. In it he mentions his daur., Renée Madeleine, who was in France, to whom his seigneurie of la Sabliere had passed.

The will of Louise Madeleine Henry de Cheusses was made 20 Aug. 1729 and proved in 1735 (Ducie, 37). She mentions her daur., Renée Madeleine, wife of Charles Trudaine, and left by codicil £100 to her godson François de Rambouillet, who d. aged six years, £10 to Mrs. d'Abillon de Portneuf, and by a second codicil a legacy to her cousin de Bellefonds. Jacques Theodore Muysson was a witness.

Nicolas de Rambouillet left five children: (*a*) Renée Madeleine, bapt. at Charenton 8 Dec. 1680. She was confined in the convent of the Filles de la Croix in 1686, but abjured later and m. at St. Eustache, Paris, Charles Trudaine, ec. sgr. de Montigny-Lencoup, in Brie, conseiller d'etat. He d. 21 July 1721, aged 61; his wife d. 20 Dec. 1746, aged 70. By her marriage the estates of the Rambouillet family passed to her husband. Her monumental inscription is in the church of St. Nicolas-des-Champs, Paris. (*b*) Anne Marguerite, bapt. 1683, confined with her sister in 1687, d. after 5 Aug. 1696. (*c*) Marie-Henriette, bapt. at Charenton 8 Dec. 1684; she was put out to nurse in 1686 at a farm near la Sablière, and eventually joined her parents in Copenhagen; m., 21 Dec. 1713, in London, at the French Church of the Savoy, Louis Chevalleau de Boisragon,

Lieut.-Col. in the British Army, aged 47, widower of Louise Royrand de St. George. Her daur., Suzanne Henriette de Boisragon, m. Daniel Pierre de Layard, son of Major Pierre de Layard. (*d*) Antoine, born at Copenhagen. He came to England and was naturalised with his brother Charles William de Rambouillet, 1 Ap. 1708. He became a Director of the French Hospital in 1735 and held a post in the Household of George II. He accompanied the Princess Royal to Holland in 1734, after her marriage to the Prince of Orange. D. a bachelor at the Hague, was buried 15 Dec. 1750. Will pr. 27 Feb. 1751 by his nephew. de Boisragon. (*e*) Francoise du Plessis, buried 12 Sept, 1703, at St. James, Piccadilly, in which parish Nicolas de Rambouillet lived, may have been a daur.; (*f*) Charles William, who succeeds, V.

V. Charles William de Rambouillet du Plessis, sgr. de la Sabliére, bapt. 8 July 1698 at Copenhagen, Colonel of the 1st Foot Guards. Naturalised Ap. 1708. He had a house in the parish of St. James, Piccadilly (1699 Rate Books). M. at Fulham, 18 June 1730, Anne du Prat (bapt. 29 Sept. 1705 at the Fr. Ch. of Le Quarré), daur. of Francois du Prat, sgr. du Charreau, of La Rochelle, and of his wife, Anne Boucher. D. at Willesden in 1747, Nov. 5 (*Gent. Mag.*). In his will (291, Potter) he mentions his wife, Anne du Prat, brother Anthony, and sister Boisragon and desires to be buried near his children in Willesden Church, Neasden. His widow had a house in Poland Street, St. James, in 1754 (Rate Book, " Mrs. Ramboulller "). She re-married, 15 May 1756, at Weston, Bath, the Rev. Arthur Cookson, who d. in 1781. She d. at Weston, aged 84, in 1789.

Charles William de Rambouillet left by his wife, Anne du Prat, seven children: (*a*) Louise, buried at Willesden in the family vault, 8 Feb. 1739; (*b*) Francois, buried at Willesden, 23 May 1739; (*c*) Charles, buried at Willesden 19 Sept. 1741; (*d*) Elizabeth, bapt. at Willesden, circ. 1745, m. at Crayford, Kent, 2 Dec. 1761, to the Rev. John Whitaker, Vicar of Pembury, where he is buried, 27 June 1803.(G) She d. at St. Anne, Westminster, 1 Jan. 1814. (*e*) Charlotte, buried 24 June 1746, at Willesden; (*f*)

Gedeon, d. 14 July 1746; (*g*) Marguerite, who d. at Weston, Bath, buried there 17 Feb. 1806 ("Mrs. Rambouillet, daur. of the late Col. Rambouillet, of the 1st Ft. Gds."—*Gent. Mag*).

NOTES.

(A) The name Rambouillet is a personal one, and the family had no connection with that of d'Angennes de Rambouillet, near Paris, which seigneury was a Marquisat. Nicolas de Rambouillet, however, assumed the Arms and the coronet of a Marquis on his Seal. The fief of Lancey was in the parish of Courville, in the Beauce. La Sablière was near Chartres.

(B) The family of Bricqueville, sgrs. de Bretteville, in the election of Valognes. Gilles de Bricqueville, sgr. de Coulombière, "originaire de Normandie," d. 26 Feb. 1669, aged 58, at Cleusné, Rennes. (Reg. Prot. Cleusné.)

(C) The family of Grange, or Grangues de Monceauxl came from Normandy, near Alençon, and sent severa, members to England. Major-General Isaac de Monceaux de la Mélonière (naturalised in 1699) raised and commanded one of the Refugee infantry regiments which served under William of Orange in Ireland. He had formerly been Colonel of the Regiment of Anjou. M. in 1679, Dlle. Anne Addée du Petit-val, sister of Isaac Addée du Petit-Val, Vicar of Imber, Wilts. He and his wife lived afterwards at Hammersmith (*idem*, Hug. Soc. Proceedings, Vol. IX). The name Addée became Adey. Members of the family of de Grangues in England are variously known as de Granges, de Monceaux, and de l'Etang, the names of different seigneuries.

(D) Le Coq de St. Leger intermarried with several refugee families in England.

(E) The property of Jacques Muysson, husband of Anne de Rambouillet, was claimed by his nearest relatives in France, the sieur and demlle. Conrart (Série T.T., 183). The Conrart family was connected by marriage with the Muysson family and that of Dompierre de Jonquières, and Le Coq de St. Leger. Jacques Muysson d. 27 Sept. 1697, aged 71. His will was made in Holland (Favon, notaire), and proved in London by Anne de Rambouillet. He was son of Henri Muysson and Peronne Conrart. The family originally lived at Valenciennes, and took refuge in France during the persecutions in the Netherlands by the Duke of Alva. (Commission Wallonne, Bulletin, 1894).

The will of Anne de Rambouillet, wife of Jacques Muysson, was made in Holland, 8 Sept. 1714, and proved in London. She described herself as widow of Jacques Muysson, conseiller en Parlement de Paris, sgr. de Toillon, Bailleul, Barre, and Rieux. She mentions her son, de Barre (Muysson de Barre), daur. de Verdun, Monsieur de la Croix a debtor, daur. du Sendat, grand-daughter de la Calmette, Monsieur Philippe Muysson, sr. de Toillon, Bailleul et Rieux and Charlotte Le Coq, his wife, Monsieur Jean Francois Morin, sr du Sendat, and Anne Magdalene Muysson, his wife. Jean Louis Boscq de la Calmette, father and guardian of Mrs. Anne Antoinette and Louise Françoise de la Calmette, his daughter by his deceased wife, Louise Muysson, Monsieur Pierre de l'Isle de Verdun and Marie Anne Muysson his wife, and the children of the aforesaid deceased lady and Monsieur Francois de Morin (*sic*) Baron du Sendat, kinsman of the said deceased lady.

(F) An oil painting of Louise Madeleine Henrie de Cheusses, and of Renée Madeleine de Rambouillet, and of Marie Henriette de Rambouillet who married Louis Chevalleau de Boisragon, are in the possession of Commander Brownlow Villiers Layard, D.S.O., R.N.

(G) Their eldest son, Charles Whitaker, Major 21st Regiment, d. a bachelor in 1815, at New Orleans. Elizabeth and Charlotte Whitaker, daughters, were living in 1826, aged 59 and 50 respectively. George Whitaker, b. 1769, living in 1826.

RAMEZAY DE LUMEAU

Arms: D'argent, à l'aigle de sable, eployé, becqué de gueules.

Alias d'azur, frette d'or.(A)

I. Claude de Ramezay, esc., "gentilhomme escossois vivant 1470, m. Damlle. Lazare de Chartres, daur. of Louis de Chartres, sgr. de Germignonville en Beauce, father of Renaud, II.

II. Renaud de Ramezay, ec. sgr. de Bleuri et d'Orsonville, in the Beauce, known by an Acte of 1547, m. Dlle. Jeanne de Bombel, by contract 16 Jan. 1535 (Quimart, notaire at Gazeray), and had (*a*) Philippe, ec. sgr. d'Orsonville, author of the elder branch, R.C.; (*b*) Marthe; (*c*) Marin de Ramézay, ec. sgr. de Lumeau, author of the second branch, III; (*d*) Louis de Ramezay, ec. co-seigneur de Lumeau, known by a deed of partition with his brothers and sisters; (*e*) Dauphine, wife in 1567 of François de Villeneuve, sgr. d'Amblères; (*f*) Marguerite, wife of François Hebert, ec. sgr. de Ponceaux.

III. Marin de Ramezay, ec. sgr. de Lumeau, did homage for his fief of Lumeau to the Bishop of Orléans. M. Dlle. Barbe de Voré, 1 Sept. 1556 (Contrat, Fort, notaire at Santilly le Moutier),(B) daur. of the late Jean de Voré, sgr. de Fenard, and of Noble Dlle. Anne de Bonpas. They had (*a*) Lazare, who succeeds, IV.; (*b*) Paul de Ramezay, ec. sgr. de Villeprevost, who m. Marguerite de la Motte; his existence is known by a deed of sale (29 May 1598) to Lazare de Ramezay, his brother; father and mother both mentioned.

IV. Lazare de Ramezay, ec. sgr. de Lumeau et de Villeprevost, m. Dlle. Jeanne de Truchon, daur. of the late (24 Sept. 1584) Charles Truchon, ec. sgr. de Chastelliers, parish of Autainville, and of Dlle. Francoise de Villeneuve (Contrat, Boudin, notaire at Santilly le Moutier). They left: (*a*) François de Ramezay, ec. sgr. de Lumeau, who succeeds, V; (*b*) Josué de Ramezay, ec. sgr. de Villéprevost, who m. Dlle. Judith d'Ernoust, daur. of Josias d'Ernoust and of his wife Judith de Beaufilz, and whose children were: (i) Francois de Ramezay, sgr. de Tournoysis, who m. Dlle. Alienor de Bois des Cours; (ii) Anne, wife of David de Cravelle, esc.; (*c*) . . . . de Ramezay, ec. sgr. de Santilly; (*d*) Luc de Ramezay, ec. sgr. de St. Luc, who m. Dlle. Charlotte de Languechin; (*e*) Barbe, wife of Francois de Saumery, ec. sgr. de Villèret.

V. Francois de Ramezay, ec. sgr. de Lumeau, mentioned in deeds of 28 May 1621, 20 March 1625, 27 May 1630 as eldest son of Lazare and husband of Suzanne Brachet. He m. by contract of 25 July 1616 Dlle. Suzanne Brachet, daur. of Michel Brachet, ec. sgr. de Boussay, and left by her: (*a*) Jean de Ramezay, who succeeds, VI; (*b*) Suzanne; (*c*) Marie; (*d*) Louis.

VI. Jean de Ramezay, ec. sgr. de Lumeau, m. by contract dated 27 March 1639 (Regnard, notaire at Châtenay, Bailliage d'Etampes), Dlle. Marthe Stuart, only daur. of Jean Stuart, ec. sgr. de la Grange, and of Dlle. Anne de Brosset. They had (*a*) François de Ramezay, ec. sgr. de Lumeau, m. by contract 26 Feb. 1677 (Gallard, notaire at Jenville), Dlle. Charlotte de la Haie, daur. of the late Jean de la Haie, ec. sgr. de la Poterie, and of his wife Anne de Tuillières. Their daur., Charlotte, was baptised as a Huguenot at Bazoches-en-Dunois, 27 May 1677, by Jérémie Perrot, minister (Preuves de la noblesse de Charlotte Lucrèce de Ramezay, St. Cyr); (*b*) Anne, wife of Eloi de Ramezay, sgr. d'Indreville, son of Nicolas and Anne Marie de l'Epine, his second wife. He was fourth in descent from Philippe de Ramezay, III, above (Sgrs. d'Indreville) (c); (*c*) Louis de Ramezay, VI.

VI. Louis de Ramezay, ec. sgr. de Lumeau, second son of Jean de Ramezay and Marthe Stuart, left France about 1685 and entered the British Army (Commission dated 1689); naturalised in 1689; " born at Lumau, son of John de Ramsay and Martha his wife "; Lt.-Col. of Webb's Regiment in Flanders, killed at Malplaquet. He m., probably in London, Rachel Bernard, to whom admon. was granted in 1710. He is described therein as " late of St. Giles-in-the-Fields." They left a daur., Anne Perside, bapt. 7 Sept. 1697, at the Fr. Ch. of the Tabernacle, Leicester Fields: " Anne Perside, ff. de Louis, et de Rachel Bernard: Par. Jacob de Meauss, Sieur de Sauvancy, mar. Anne de la Valette. Neé 3 Sep. Tém. Anne de la Valette Descury."

There may have been other children, probably in Ireland. A Charlotte Ramzé is godmother to Blandine Charlotte Friboul, 25 Ap. 1731 (Eg. Fr. Unies., Dublin). A Mr. and Madame de Ramsé were present at the marriage in 1699 in Dublin of David Digges La Touche, of Mer in the Vendomois, may well have been Louis and Rachel de Ramézay. The names " Ramsey " in registers of the French churches in London are probably Anglicized spellings of " Ramézay."

NOTES.

(A) The presence of so many Scottish families in France at this date is due to the enlistment by the Kings of France of cadets of Scottish families in the Scottish Archer Guard. On their disbandment in the sixteenth century, owing to the spread of the Reformed doctrine among them, many took service under the English Crown. The 1st Regt. Royal Scots was formed from the descendants of the Scottish Archer Guard. Other families of Ramsay settled in Poitou and the Vendomois, and returned as Huguenot refugees in 1685 and after, among them a cadet branch of the Ramsay of Dalhousie family which had settled in the Vendomois. Jean Baptiste de Ramezay, Governor of Montreal (son of Claude de Ramezay, said to be a descendant of James Ramsay of Dalhousie), after the capitulation of Montreal in 1759 retired to France, and was living at Tours, 5 Sept. 1764, when he signed a document relating to the looting of the house of a Captain Marin de la Malgue at the taking of Quebec (d'Hozier MSS., Art. " Marin," p. 5). The Dalhousie tradition may have some foundation since the family of Ramézay, near Tours, was a cadet branch.

Francois de Ramsay, sgr. de Villeprovost, son of Joseph de Ramsay and of Judith Bernon, Captain in the Regiment of La Fère, abjured at Paris, 21 May 1682. Anne de Ramesay de Lumeau abjured, aged 31 (Haag).

(B) According to the contract of marriage Renaud de Ramezay was dead at this date, as Jeanne de Bombel had married Louis de Voré, sgr. de la Chevallerie. The bridegroom was assisted by his uncle, Jacques de Bombel, sgr. de Villepréau, and by Jacques de Bombel, sgr, de Mongirard; the bride was assisted by Jean de Voré, her brother, and Bernard de Bonpas, her cousin.

(C) Anne Ramézay de Lumeau, in the Beauce, who abjured in 1684, may be the sister of Louis and wife of Eloi de Ramezay. (O. Douen, *Revocation de l'edit de Nantes*, Vol. I, p. 525.)

RAVENEL

(English Branch.)

Arms: De gueulles, à 6 croissants d'or, acc. en chef de 6 étoiles, et en pointe d'une autre étoile, le tout de même (du Boistilleul).(A)

I, II, III, as in Vol. I.

IV. Lucas Ravenel, sr. de la Brouardière, m. 19 Sept. 1550, Dlle. Andrée de Gennes, and left: (*a*) Pierre, bapt. 17 June 1553 (Par. Reg. Vitré); (*b*) Marguerite, bapt. 2 Oct. 1555 (*idem*); (*c*) Catherine, bapt. 31 March 1557: godfather, Jean Ravenel Perray, godmother Catherine de Gennes (*idem*); (*d*) Lucas, who follows, V; (*e*) Jean, sr. de Vassé, m. Jeanne Guillaudeau; (*f*) René, sr. de Mesriais; (*g*) Marguerite, m. 30 June 1591, Guillaume Lemoyne, and d. 30 Aug. 1594.

V. Lucas Ravenel, sr. de Boisguy, m. Marie de Gennes, and had: (*a*) Luc, who m. at Vitré, 15 Aug. 1591, Renée Mauny,(B) daur. of Jean Mauny, sr. des Grands Prés, and of Renée Lemoyne. He d. at Rennes, 15 Sept. 1595, leaving (i) Renée, bapt. 19 July 1592; (ii) Jean, bapt. 20 Feb. 1594; (iii) another Renée, bapt. 6 Feb. 1595; (*b*) Marie, bapt. 29 Aug. 1576; (*c*) Olive, bapt. 2 Jan. 1578; (*d*) André, bapt. 29 March 1579; (*e*) Jean, who follows, VI; (*f*) Pierre, bapt. 22 July 1585.

VI. Jean Ravenel, sr. du Boistilleul, bapt. 20 Ap. 1581, at Vitré, m. 29 Aug. 1604, Jeanne Grislel, daur. of Mathurin Grislel, apothecary, sr. de la Tirelière, and of Marie Seré, and left: (*a*) Luc, a banker at Rennes, who emigrated to Holland, m. Renée de Gennes, by contract dated 26 Aug. 1651, at Terchant, daur. of Jean de Gennes, sr. des Hayers, Procureur-Fiscal at Vitré, and of Renée Jolain his first wife (a daur. of his by his second marriage with Renée Pedron, m. Pierre Nouail, sr. de Cohigné); (*b*) Jean, who succeeds, VII.

VII. Jean Ravenel, sr. du Boistilleul, b. 14 May 1616, elder of the Protestant church at Rennes in 1666, m. firstly, Judith, de Farcy, daur. of Thomas de Farcy, sr. de la Gourtière, and Marie Barbier; secondly, Elizabeth de la

Place, daur. of Josué de la Place, professor at Saumur, and of his wife Elizabeth de la Ferré.(C) By his first marriage he left: (*a*) Benjamin,(D) bapt. at Vitré 1 May 1654, m. 4 Oct. 1685 Dlle. Catherine Françoise de Farcy, daur. of Charles de Farcy,(E) ecuyer, sgr. de la Carterie, and of Marguerite Uzille. He d. at Rennes in 1710, and was buried in the parish of St. Germain; (*b*) Elizabeth, b. 29 May 1670, bapt. at Cleusné 1 June, d. 16 Jan. 1678; (*c*) Paul, bapt. at Cleusné 6 Sept. 1671; (*d*) Samuel, who emigrated to England, VIII. By his second marriage, with Elizabeth de la Place, he had: (*e*) Suzanne, prematurely born, and bapt. 31 Jan. 1672, who joined her brother Samuel in England, and is mentioned as a witness with him to the will of Suzanne de Beringhen, Duchesse de la Force, in 1726, at Sunbury-on-Thames (m. de Boistilleul, Suzanne Ravenel); (*f*) Jeanne, bapt. 10 Feb. 1674, m. in the French Church of the Savoy and Les Grecs, London, 29 Jan. 1706, Bernard Devigneau, of St. Martin in the Fields, London: she was of St. Anne's. Samuel Ravenel was godfather to their child, Samuel, 15 Aug. 1708 (Fr. Ch. Savoy); (*g*) Josué, bapt. 26 March 1676, at Cleusné; (*h*) Marie, whose baptism is not recorded at Cleusné but whose will was proved in London (Isham, 79) in 1731, by Samuel Ravenel and Suzanne, her brother and sister.(F)

VIII. Samuel Ravenel, sr. du Boistilleul, was naturalised in London 25 May 1702, m. at St. Martin's in the Fields, London, Elizabeth Lister (Vic. Gen. Marr. Lic., 20 Oct. 1701), she was 25, he was 35. His admon. of property is dated 4 Aug. 1731 to his son Edward, IX. A child named Sarah Ravenel, buried at St. James, Piccadilly, 10 Sept. 1703, was probably a daughter.

IX. Edward Ravenel, a Director of the French Hospital of La Providence, Hackney, made his will 20 July 1772 (prob. 24 Nov. 1775). He left all his property to " his much valued friend, Mary Johnson." He describes himself of Dean Street, St. Ann's, Westminster. D. unmarried.

NOTES.

(A) The Branch of Boistilleul was maintained in its noblesse in the Reformation of 1677. Originally from Picardy, according to Haag, who states that Jean Ravenel, sr. du Perray, came to Vitré in 1555, m. Marguerite Guesdon, and was father of Luc Ravenel, sr. de la Brouardièrè.

(B) Luc Ravenel and Renée de Gennes fled from Brittany in 1686 (Vaugiraud, Vol. III, p. 146). Renée de Gennes, who may have been wife of Luc Ravenel, was expelled in 1688 as a " huguenote opiniatre " (Haag), in which case she must have been imprisoned in 1685. Their property was given to their three sons, Jacques sr. de Seran, Luc, and Paul, sr. de St. Remy, who remained in France. The wife of Jacques Ravenel, sr. de Seran, went to Jersey, with her daughters Marthe and Anne, whose will was proved in London 8 Ap. 1756 by Marthe Coulon, wife of Charles Coulon, her sister and only next of kin. (Anne Ravenel Seran, *alias* Ravel, late of Jersey. Witnesses, Mrs. Judith Lignard and Mrs. Aubin de Querbouchard).

(C) " Madame de Ravenel, fille de feu Monsieur de la Place professeur en Théologie à Saumur a laissé son mari en France pour le sauver avec les 2 filles : touttes trois ont été quelques semaines en cette ville, et sont partis depuis peu pour alles en Holande " (MSS. Rawll., Bodleian Library, Oxford, C. 984). " Memoire pour presenter à Milord de Londres touchand le nombre et l'etat des protestans que se sont sauvez de Rennes ville capitale de Bretagne, et qui jusques à present ont supporté leur necessité sans implorer le secours de leur frères.")

(D) Benjamin Ravenel left France in 1685, but returned, abjured, and took possession of the family property (Arch. Nat., M. 275, Haag). " Le sr. de la Salle Ravenel vit en huguenot et s'est retiré à Saumur : le sr. Coudières est en Angleterre, ils sont fils dudict sr. des Rochers, et le sr. Kerbouchart jouit de ladite terre par bail, il est aussi huguenot " (Vaugiraud, Vol. III, p. 125, List of Properties left behind in France in 1700). According to Haag, Benjamin Ravenel entered into these properties.

(E) Madame de Farcy, veuve de Monsieur de Farcy, conseiller au Parlement de Rouen a passé avec ses trois enfans, sçavoir une fille de 11 aus, une garçon de 8, et une petite fille de 6. Cette dame a sauvé aussi avec elle une fille de qualité de les amies nommée Mlle. de la Roche-

Guillon à qui. Il est encore venu une sœur depuis peu de jours, cette dame sauva aussi une de ses lagnais qui est demeuré à gerzay : les autres sont tous à Londres comme aussi le sr. de la Place, petit-fils de Mr. de la Place, professeur en Théologie à Saumur, precepteur du fils de lad. Dame de Farcy (*idem*).

Madame de la Ville du Bois femme d'un frère puisné de feu Monsieur de Farcy a passé avec 4 enfantes dont l'Ainé n'a que 6 ans. Elle a laissé Mr. son mari en France d'ont elle sest derobée, et un enfant de 3 mois qu'elle n'a pû sauver, elle a passé avec elle 2 laquais et une servante et ces 8 personnes sont presentemen à Gerzay (*idem*).

"Madame de Mué femme du second frère de feu Mr. de Farcy a passé avec 3 enfans, sçavoir un fils aagé de 13 ans, une fille de 10, et un fils de 8 : elle sest aussi derobée de Mr. son mari. Et a laissé une petite fille de 6 mois qu'elle ne pût sauver : elle a passé aussi un valet, et ces 5 personnes sont presentemt à Gerzay." (*idem*).

(Note to above).—René de Farcy, sgr. de la Villedubois, m. 25 Jan. 1678 at Cleusné, Charlotte de Levesque, daur. of the Protestant minister at Rennes, and left : (*a*) Jacques René, bapt. 26 Dec. 1679 ; (*b*) Gabriel Luc, bapt. 17 Aug. 1681 ; (*c*) Annibal François, bapt. 4 Aug. 1685. He remained in France.

Jean de Farcy, sgr. de Mué, Lieut. in the regiment of Champagne, brother of René, above, m. 20 Ap. 1670, Suzanne Ravenel, and left : (*a*) Jacques Annibal, b. 31 Jan. 1671, bapt. 1 Feb. ; (*b*) Catherine Marie, bapt. 6 Mar. 1674 ; (*c*) Jean Charles Michel, bapt. 16 Oct. 1677.

Madame de Mué is mentioned in the will of the Duchesse de la Force (Suzanne de Beringhen), "with her granddaughter who lives with her at Twickenham."

Monsieur de Ravenel un gentilhomme, ancien de l'église de [Rennes] a passé luÿ cinquieme, sçavoir luy, Madame sa femme, un fille aagé de 13 ans, une fille de 12 ans, et un valet, ces 5 personnes sont à Gerzay. (*Idem*)

(F) Samuel Ravenel is described in the admon. of his property in 1731 as "of Sunbury, Middlesex." He was a witness, 29 Aug. 1726, to the will of the Duchesse de la Force, made at Sunbury. The other witness was René de Saunieres de l'Hermitage. Suzanne Ravenel was witness to a codicil dated 7 Oct. 1726 (Isham, 158, Fox 60). In a later codicil of 1738 (Brodrebb, 98) she leaves a ring of the hair of her late sister Le Coq to Mrs. Gendrault and Mrs. Boistilleul, and to Mrs. Susanne de Ravenel a " small strong coffer, garnished with Brass gilt which is in my bed-chamber at Sunbury." Made at St. James, Westminster.

Susanne Ravenel made her will in 1741, a codicil dated 30 Oct. 1750. Probate, 7 Jan. 1752, at Sunbury (Bettesworth, 21) in French. She made Edward Ravenel, her nephew, universal heir and legatee. Left plate to her god-daughter, Elizabeth Trevigar; to Marthe Ravenel, daur. of M. de Seran (Madame Coulon), a watch and £100, and to his other daur., Anne Ravenel £30. A legacy to Elizabeth Villepierre, and to Elizabeth Railing, daur. of Elizabeth Raling de Ravenel. Jeanne La Salle is mentioned (probably Ravenel de la Salle, daur. of Paul Ravenel, sr. de la Salle, son of Jean Ravenel, sr. des Rochers). Her exors. were Edward Ravenel, nephew, and Luke Trevigar, Rector of Hurstmonceux, Sussex.

Mary Ravenel made her will at Sunbury, 24 Jan. 1717. Prob. 1731, 31 March (Isham, 79) by Samuel Ravenel and her sister Susanne. She mentions her cousin Mr. de Seran, and his daur., and leaves him an annuity of £18 and his daur. after him. To her nephew Edward Ravenel a miniature of her brother Samuel. A legacy to the poor of the French Church at Sunbury; she mentions a cousin, Mr. de Mué.

Numerous members of the de Farcy family settled in England.

The statement of d'Hozier, and since repeated, that Samuel Ravenel married a daughter or niece of the Duke of Marlborough is not substantiated, unless it can be found that Elizabeth Lister was related to the Churchill family.

DES VIGNOLLES

Arms : De sable, à un cep de vigne feuillé et fruité d'argent, soutenu par un echalas de même.

I. Etienne de Vignolles, qualified as noble by a deed dated 15 Dec. 1549. His son,

II. Jean des Vignolles, who m. 18 Sept. 1559, Dlle. Gauside de Parades, or Prades, daur. of Etienne de Prades, ec., and of Jeanne Dautun de Chamclaux, of St. Etienne de Valfrancesque, diocese of Mendes. She made her will 29 Ap. 1595, at which date her husband was dead, and names four sons : (*a*) Pierre, who succeeds, III ; (*b*) Jean, author of the second Branch, R.C. ; (*c*) Paul, author of the third Branch ; (*d*) Jacques, author of the fourth Branch, sgr. de la Valette. They also left a daur., Pierette, m. 16 Nov. 1577, Etienne du Cros.

III. Pierre des Vignolles, ec. sgr. de Prades, conseiller du Roi, Juge Conservateur des Conventions at Nismes, m. by contract passed at Bernis, 30 Oct. 1600, Dlle. Gabrielle de Villages, daur. of Louis de Villages, sgr. de Bernis and de Fontareschy, and of Dlle. Bernardine de Fons. He made his will in 1613, and left : (*a*) Emanuel, b. 29 May 1602, " un peu avant sept heures du matin," bapt. 15 June 1602, d. 29 June 1607 ; (*b*) Bernardine, bapt. 8 Oct., d. Dec. 1603 ; (*c*) Louis, bapt. 25 Dec. 1605, d. before his father, s.p. ; (*d*) François, bapt. Oct. 1607, d. 11 Aug. 1608 ; (*e*) Jacques, who succeeds, IV ; (*f*) Charles, b. 1610, d. after his father, young, s.p. ; (*g*) Gabrielle, b. 1611, d. Ap. 1613.

IV. Jacques des Vignolles, ec. sgr. de Prades, b. 10 June, bapt. 18 June 1609. Maintained his noblesse 2 Jan. 1669. M. at his chateau of Prades, 24 Feb. 1637, Dlle. Louise de Baschi d'Aubais, daur. of Louis de Baschi, sgr. Baron d'Aubais,(A) and of Anne de Rochemaure (who was born 21 March 1618, d. 10 Aug. 1666, near Nismes). They left eleven sons and five daughters : (*a*) Louis, d. an infant ;

(*b*) Louis, bapt. at Aubais, b. 14 Oct. 1640, sgr. de Ste. Croix, Lieut. of Cavalry in 1668, d. at Lauzanne 10 March 1693, having had two sons, d. young, by his wife, Louise Madeleine de Baschi, his cousin germain, whom he m. 19 Aug. 1674 (she was b. Oct. 1653 and d. at Geneva 11 Nov. 1720). They also had nine daurs., most of whom d. young. Marguerite, b. 22 Jan. 1675, m. Monsieur Gaudard, in 1721 and d. at Geneva, 3 Oct. 1733. Anne, b. 10 May 1684, m. Abraham de Crouzas, at Lauzanne. (*c*) Henri, bapt. at Aubais in 1641, 1 Oct., d. s.p.; (*d*) Francoise, b. 2 Nov. 1643, d. at Geneva 14 Jan. 1700; (*e*) Charles, author of the branch in Ireland, who succeeds, V; (*f*) Alphonse, b. 16 Oct. 1645, bapt. at Aubais 2 Dec. following; (*g*) Francois, d. an infant; (*h*) Alphonse, b. 19 Oct. 1649, bapt. at Aubais 11 Jan. 1650, sgr. de St. Geniez, d. a protestant minister at Berlin 24 July 1744, a widower and childless of his seven children by his wife Marguerite Bernard, who d. at the birth of their seventh child, 28 May 1694; (*i*) Henri, b. 30 Nov. 1650, d. 1657; (*j*) Marguerite, b. 16 July 1652, m. in 1683 Pierre Richard, sgr. de Vendargues, d. at Dublin 12 Sept. 1727, aged 75 (will P.C.C., 237 Farrant) (B); (*k*) Louise, b. 15 Oct. 1653, d. at Dublin 22 March 1720; (*l*) Edouard, b. 23 Oct. 1655, at Nismes, sgr. de Masseville, avocat de la chambre de l'Edit., d. 1680, 10 Feb., buried at Nismes (Arch. Consist.); (*m*) Louis, b. 22 Nov. 1656, sgr. de Campes, captain in Auvergne regiment, m. at Amsterdam; (*n*) Françoise, b. 20 Oct. 1657; (*o*) Gaspard, b. 4 May 1659; (*p*) Madeleine, b. 27 Feb. 1661, d. at Berlin 4 March 1727.

Jacques Louis des Vignolles, d. 26 Aug. 1686 at his chateau of Prades.

V. Charles des Vignolles, sgr. de Prades, b. 16 Oct. at Aubais, bapt. 8 Nov. 1645, served as a volunteer in the Gardes (Actes 12 Oct. and 25 Dec. 1664) and in the cavalry regiment of Mellin (6 July 1668). M. firstly, in France, 2 March 1684, Dlle. Marthe du Roure, daur. of Samson de Beauvoir du Roure,(C) sgr. de Bonneaux, and of Gabrielle, daur. of Jean de Restorand and of Louise de Villars, and left by this marriage seven children: (*a*) Louise, b. at Nismes 22 Nov. 1684, d. at Utrecht 10 Jan. 1701; (*b*)

Anne, b. 20 Dec. 1685, d. July 1686; (*c*) Françoise, b. at Nismes 11 Dec. 1686. She m. Captain Pierre Gually, British Army, who d. 17 Jan. 1765. She d. 1708. (*d*) Magdeleine Marie, b. at Nimègue, Aug. 1688, d. Nov. 1689 in London; (*e*) Jacques Louis, b. in London 24 Jan., d. 23 June 1690; (*f* and *g*) two daurs. b. and d. infants in London, 19 June 1691; (*h*) Marguerite, b. in London 18 Oct. 1692, " filleule de M. Restaurand, avocat de Nismes, et de Marguerite des Vignoles, Dame de Vendargues " (MSS. de la Valette). She m. Scipio de Bonneaux du Roure, in Dublin, 6 Ap. 1713 (Fr. Ch. St. Marie), and d. in London 1 July 1721.

Marthe du Roure d. in London 13 Oct. 1692, and Charles des Vignolles m. secondly, 26 Jan. 1694, Dlle. Gabrielle de Sperandieu, daur. of Jacques de Sperandieu, sgr. d'Aiguefonde, and of Dame Madeleine du Faure, b. 15 June 1663 at Castres, d. in Dublin Oct. 1727. By this marriage, nine children: (*a*) Marie, b. in Dublin 25 Oct. 1694, d. at Portarlington 2 July 1781 aged 86, bapt. by Mr. Balaquier, Ministre, 28 Oct. 1694 (m. 27 Nov. 1719, Josué du Fay d'Exoudun, ec., son of Josué du Fay d'Exoudun, a gentleman of Poitou, and of Dlle. Marguerite Marchant, formerly of Niort (Reg. Fr. Ch. Unies., Dublin), captain of dragoons, who d. at Dublin 31 Oct. 1730, aged 58 (Peter St. Fr. Ch.); (*b*) Charlotte, b. at Dublin 11 Ap. 1696, m. 22 June 1715 Charles Nicolas, son of Jean Nicolas, " capitaine refugié," of Jonsac,(D) and Anne Roulin (Nouvelle Eg. St. Marie). She d. a widow, 16 Oct. 1730, in Dublin. (Will, P.C. I, 1734). (*c*) Madeleine, b. at Dublin, 21 June 1697, d. at Berlin 11 Sept. 1757; (*d*) Louise Isabelle, b. at Dublin 5 July 1698, " filleule de M. d'Aulnis " (MSS. de la Valette), d. 12 Aug. 1758 at Dunshaglin, Ireland; (*e*) Henri, b. at Dublin 28 June 1699, bapt. by M. Henri de Rocheblave, d. 21 Ap. 1701; (*f*) Charles, b. at Dublin 12 March 1701, m. 22 Nov. 1746 Dlle. Marie de Gignoux, daur. of Isaac de Gignoux and of Marie Gardies de St. Bres. He d. 11 Oct. 1780: his wife d. 29 Dec. 1782, aged 83. (*g*) Jacques Louis, who succeeds, VI; (*h*) Anne, b. at Dublin 3 July 1703, m. a Mr. Wynne. Her godfather was Charles Boileau de Castelnau and godmother Françoise des Vignolles her sister;

(*i*) Maurice, b. at Dublin 23 Ap. 1705, d. there 9 Dec. 1745, m. Marie Anne Pineault, or Pinneau, 21 Nov. 1728, by whom he left: (i) Charles Guillaume, b. 22 Jan. 1731 at Dublin, d. at Kingston, Jamaica, in 1758; (ii) Benjamin, b. at Dublin 24 Sept. 1732; (iii) Henry, b. at Dublin 27 Aug. 1735, Ensign 31st Foot, d. in Dublin 22 Nov. 1756, aged 19; (iv) Marguerite Anne, b. 10 March 1738. (These four entries, Fr. Ch. Reg., Dublin.)

VI. Jacques Louis des Vignolles, b. at Dublin 6 June 1702, bapt. by M. de Rocheblave; godfather, Jacques Vergès d'Aubussargues, colonel of cavalry; godmother, Dame Marguerite de Villette de Montledier, wife of Mr. d'Avessein, Lieut. of dragoons (MSS. de la Valette). M. firstly, 17 March 1737 at Portarlington, Dlle. Marie Anne de Ligonier, daur. of Antoine de Ligonier de Bonneval (Portarlington Fr. Ch. Reg.). She d. at Portarlington, 14 Jan. 1747.(E) He m. secondly, 28 Nov. 1754, Dlle. Marie Anne d'Aultier de Bonvillette, who d. 13 Oct. 1778 at Dublin, aged 64 (St. Peter's Fr. Ch.) (F). Jacques Louis des Vignolles d. at Portarlington 21 Feb. 1779, aged 76 years and 8 months, Major 31st Regt. (will pr. 11 May 1780). By his first marriage, with Marie Anne de Ligonier, he left one son, John, who succeeds, VII.

VII. John des Vignolles, b. 14 Oct. 1740 at Portarlington, bapt. 3 Nov. in the house of Madame d'Arripe by the Rev. Arthur de Champagné, Vicar of Clonbolough; godfathers, General Lord Ligonier and Charles des Vignolles; godmother, Madame d'Arripe. (Portarlington Fr. Ch. Reg.) He entered the Army and retired as Major 39th Regt.; was ordained, 19 Dec. 1790; Pastor of the French Church at Portarlington (1793-1817). D. at Cornahir, Westmeath, 30 Oct. 1819. M., 13 Jan. 1784, Anna Honoria Low, b. 28 May 1757, daur. of Launcelot Low and Elizabeth Bowen, of Taghmore, co. Westmeath, and d. 6 July 1832 at Cornahir. They had four sons and five daughters: (*a*) Elizabeth Anne, b. 13 Aug. 1785, d. at Clifton, Bristol, 5 Ap. 1854, m. firstly, Colonel Grey, 30th Regt., who was killed at the storming of Badajos in 1812; secondly, in 1815, the Rev. Sir Godfrey Thomas, Bart., Rector of

Bodiam, Sussex. They had two children: (i) Sir Godfrey Thomas, Colonel R.H.A.; (ii) Caroline Margaret Thomas, who m. in 1846 Orme Biddulph. Their daur., Constance Biddulph, Fellow of the Huguenot Society, m. firstly, Lieut. Symons, 14th Regt., secondly, James Orr, co. Cork. (*b*) Letitia, b. 12 July 1786 (Fr. Ch., Portarlington), d. there 20 Dec. 1859, m. 17 March 1809, Philip Brabazon, of Mornington House, co. Meath. They had, among others, Letitia, who m. General John Hawkshaw. (*c*) Charles Augustus, who succeeds, VIII; (*d*) John, b. 18 Oct. 1790, bapt. 8 Jan. 1791 at Portarlington; (*e*) Julie Marguerite, b. 22 Ap. 1792, d. an infant; (*f*) Jaques Francois, b. 9 July 1793, d. at Fragal, West Indies, in 1815, Lieut. R.N.; (*g*) Samuel, b. 23 Ap. 1796, m. Louisa Catherine Ultima Macnamara, daur. of William Nugent Macnamara, of Doolin, co. Clare. He d. at Melbourne, New South Wales, in 1857. They had three sons and three daurs.: (i) Susan Eliza, d. unmarried; (ii) Anna Honoria, d. unmarried; (iii) Cecil Francis, d. unmarried; (iv, v) Arthur Wellesley and Alphonse, d. infants; (vi) Louisa Jane des Vignolles, d. in 1901, m. Henry Guy Carleton, Colonel 10th Lincolnshire Regt. (*h*) Marguerite, b. 19 July 1797 (Portarlington Fr. Ch.), m. . . . Willis, d. s.p.

VIII. Charles Augustus des Vignolles, b. 25 July 1789 at Portarlington, Dean of the Chapel Royal, Dublin, Dean of Ossory, m. 11 July 1811 Elizabeth Durell, daur. of Thomas Durell, of Southampton. They had five sons: (*a*) John, who succeeds, IX; (*b*) Charles Alexander, b. 18 March 1814, Vicar of Clanmacnoise, co. Meath, d. at Hounslow 30 Sept. 1891, aged 76; (*c*) Francis Durell, b. 16 Jan. 1816, Capt. 28th Regt.; (*d*) Thomas Mountjoy, b. 18 March 1819, d. 27 Sept. 1856; (*e*) Samuel Hutchinson, b. 17 Feb. 1824, d. unmarried, 5 July 1853, at Cornahir.

IX. John des Vignolles, m. 18 Aug. 1841, Elinor, eldest daur. of Thomas Fetherstonehaugh, of Bracklyn Castle, co. Westmeath, and of Lady Elinor Howard, daur. of William third Earl of Wicklow. Their son, Charles, X.

X. Charles des Vignolles, b. 12 Nov. 1842 in Dublin Castle, d. unmarried, 17 July 1896, at Cornahir.

DES VIGNOLLES

NOTES.

(A) Baschi d'Aubais. Arms: écartelé 1 and 3, d'argent, à un ours dressé de sable, 2 and 3 d'azur, à la jumelle d'argent: acc. de 3 besans de même en chef, et 3 en pointe, les 3 derniers 2 and 1. Sur la toute de gueules à l' ecu d'arg. en abime fascé de sable.

(B) Pierre Richard, sgr. de Vendarques, d. at Nismes in 1683 (Arch. Com.). (Ped. in Wagner. Vignolles MSS.)

(C) Du Roure is given by M. Wagner, Hug. Soc. Proc., Vol. X, p. 388.

(D) See "Nicolas" Pedigree, in this volume.

(E) Ligonier Pedigree in Hug. Soc. Proc., Vol. VIII, p. 373.

(F) M. de Bonvillette, a merchant of Dublin, m. Marie Anne Madeleine, youngest daur. of Isaac Dumont de Bostaquet. She d. in Dublin, 13 Oct. 1778, aged 64.

The pedigree of Vignolles as given by Burke contains many errors. La Hire de Vignolles was quite a different family, of Béarn.

CORRECTIONS

RAVENEL. (Vol. I.)

The pedigree should begin and continue as follows :—
I. Jean Ravenel, m. Amaurye Lemoyne before 1525, and left Mathurin, b. probably at Vitré circ. 1525, who follows, II.

II. Mathurin Ravenel, sr. des Gesbertieres, m. Françoise Loyleu, circ. 1550, as a Roman Catholic, and had : (*a*) Jacques, bapt. 18 Jan. 1551, godfather, Jacques Loyleu ; (*b*) Renée, bapt. 20 June 1557 ; (*c*) Mathurin, bapt. 13 June 1558, who succeeds, III ; (*d*) André, bapt. 17 Sept. 1559.

The above were bapt. in the parish church at Vitré. Hon. Homme Mathurin Ravenel and his wife Françoise Loyleu became Protestant, and had five children, whose baptisms are recorded in the registers of the Protestant church of Vitré, viz. : (*e*) Marie, bapt. 3 Feb. 1561 ; (*f*) another Marie, bapt. 14 June 1562, m. 8 May 1578 to Guillaume Lemoyne, sr. de la Gasniais, and d. 28 Dec. 1590 ; (*g*) Anne, bapt. 28 Nov. 1563 ; (*h*) Suzanne, bapt. 23 June 1566, m. 28 Jan. 1592 to Pierre de Gennes ; (*i*) Jeanne, m. 22 July 1590 to Daniel Massonnais.

III. Mathurin Ravenel, sr. des Gesbertières, m. 20 Sept. 1579 (Prot. Reg., Vitré) Jacquine Gauvaing, d. 1621, by whom he had : (*a*) Jacquine, bapt. 1 Aug. 1580, m. Daniel Rebondy, 13 Oct. 1617, and d. 3 June 1656 ; (*b*) Anne, bapt. 6 July 1581 ; (*c*) Jacques, bapt. 1 May 1583, sr. des Gesbertières, m. 17 Feb. 1613, Esther Ravenel, d. 13 Nov. 1627 ; (*d*) Pierre, bapt. 29 June 1584 ; (*e*) Marie, bapt. 30 Dec. 1590 ; (*f*) Jeanne, bapt. 26 Ap. 1592, m. 13 Ap. 1625 to Antoine Lefebvre, sr. des Landes ; (*g*) Jean, bapt. 21 Sept. 1593, sr. de la Paignerie ; (*h*) René, bapt. 16 Jan. 1596, sr. de la Paignerie, IV ; (*i*) Anne, bapt. 18 Dec. 1597.

IV. René Ravenel, m. Anne Nouail, as reported in Vol. I (where he is VI).

CORRECTIONS

The error was pointed out to the Editor by a distinguished Breton genealogist, and is due to a mistake in M. Frain's pedigree, which makes René Ravenel son of René, sr. de la Mesriais. The family is divided into so many branches, and is so prolific, both on the Catholic and Protestant sides, that it probably constitutes a record in genealogies.

Note (c). Ravenel Pedigree (Vol. I). Daniel Ravenel is inaccurately spoken of as ancestor of the English branch. He came to England, but left no posterity.

Page 14, lines 20 and 21, *dele* " he had previously . . . . . Henry Boybellaud."

INDEX

Only names of wives, and persons other than those of any particular pedigree, are indexed. Males of a particular pedigree must be looked for under the pedigree itself.

INDEX

INDEX

C

INDEX

INDEX

INDEX

INDEX

INDEX

INDEX

INDEX

INDEX

INDEX

INDEX

INDEX

INDEX

www.ingramcontent.com/pod-product-compliance
Lightning Source LLC
Chambersburg PA
CBHW071852270326
41929CB00013B/2199

* 9 7 8 0 8 0 6 3 0 2 0 7 2 *